RUNNER'S WORLD

Guide to
ROAD
RACING

RUN YOUR FIRST (OR FASTEST) 5-K, 10-K,
HALF-MARATHON OR MARATHON

Katie McDonald Neitz, *Runner's World* Senior Editor

RODALE

This edition first published 2008 by Rodale
an imprint of Pan Macmillan Ltd
Pan Macmillan, 20 New Wharf Road, London N1 9RR
Basingstoke and Oxford
Associated companies throughout the world
www.panmacmillan.com

ISBN 978-1-9057-44-32-9

1 3 5 7 9 8 6 4 2

A CIP catalogue record for this book is available from the British Library.

Printed and bound in Great Britain by Mackays of Chatham plc, Chatham, Kent

The information given in this book is meant to supplement, not replace, proper
exercise training. All forms of exercise pose some inherent risk. The editor and
publisher advise readers to take full responsibility for their safety and know their
limits. Before practising the exercises in this book, ensure that your equipment is
well maintained, and do not take risks beyond your level of experience, aptitude,
training and fitness. The exercise and dietary programmes in this book are not
intended as a substitute for any exercise routine or dietary regime that may have
been prescribed by your doctor. As with all exercises, you should get your
doctor's approval before beginning.

Mention of specific companies, organizations or authorities in this book does not
imply endorsement of the publisher, nor does mention of specific companies,
organizations or authorities in the book imply that they endorse the book.
Addresses, websites and telephone numbers given in this book were correct at the
time of going to press.

Visit **www.panmacmillan.com** to read more about all our books and to buy them.
You will also find features, author interviews and news of any author events, and
you can sign up for e-newsletters so that you're always first to hear about our new
releases.

We inspire and enable people to improve their lives and the world around them

CONTENTS

To Amby Burfoot, David Willey and all the

Runner's World *experts whose support and*

knowledge have fuelled my running and writing

INTRODUCTION

Before I begin this book, I should make a disclaimer. One of the participants of the 1996 Frozen Foot 5-K in Elizabethtown, Pennsylvania, was an out-of-shape, out-of-her-league 20-year-old dressed in layers of bulky sweats and a hefty pair of aerobics sneakers who spent more time than she'd care to admit reaching the finish line. Anyone who witnessed the spectacle (my apologies) or has records of the event (the curse of the Internet) may question that person's ability to put together a book about the sport of road racing. Fair enough. But what that sceptic wouldn't realize is that although this woman's first road race wasn't successful by most people's standards, it was life changing, quite literally. You see, it made her just the type of person who *is* qualified to edit such a book.

I was at university when I decided on a whim to run the 5-K. I'm not sure what made me think I could pull off running 3.1 miles without training, especially being someone with no running experience or real athletic background at all. Unlike most of my friends, I didn't run track or cross-country or play hockey or football at school. Step-aerobics classes and *Buns of Steel* videos were more my speed. Maybe my ill-founded confidence came from the fact that I originally thought the race was a 5-miler (*Oh, if it's only 3.1 miles . . .*). Maybe it was the fact that several of the college's most tenured professors were running it (*If those guys can do it . . .*). Maybe it was the fact that it was held in January, after a Christmas-indulgent break (*Running burns how many calories?*). Whatever the reason – however naive, misguided or silly it was – I was in.

But in for what, exactly?

I don't remember details about the start, or the scenery along the course, or at what point my starting-gun sprint faded to a jog, then to a shuffle, then to a walk. What I do remember is the finish – specifically, the finish line. When I saw it up ahead, a surge of adrenaline kicked in, giving my weakened legs and wounded psyche a much-needed boost of speed and confidence. And when I reached the end of my journey, a feeling of exhilaration (along with a hefty dose of relief) washed over me, erasing the pain and frustration I had felt minutes earlier. I felt incredible – unbelievable, really. Doubts I had about finishing were gone. More important, doubts I had about myself were gone. It was a very *Rocky*-like moment, in more ways than one. See, the exercise-induced feel-good chemicals buzzing around in my brain were already negotiating for a sequel. My muscles were too exhausted to put up a fight.

And so, a month later, I ran another 5-K, then another one the month after that. I had started a modest training programme and set reasonable goals for myself. I ran/walked the February race, and by March, I was able to run the entire distance. Yay! I felt strong, I felt empowered, and – for the first time in my life – I felt athletic. And that felt good.

I started reading *Runner's World* and continued to run in 5-Ks through my university years. I wasn't fast, but I was committed. Running became part of my life, an important daily ritual that helped me find balance and blow off steam in between school, internships and a little thing called trying-to-figure-out-what-to-do-with-my-life.

When you're studying to be a journalist, you're told to write about what you know or, better yet, what you feel passionate about. And so I decided that one day I should write for *Runner's World*. It took me a few years, but I did eventually land my dream job. *Runner's World* is an ideal place to work, and not just because running shoes are acceptable office attire and you don't have to look far for an eager running partner. I'll admit those are great perks. But that's not what really makes *Runner's World* so special.

Runner's World has been a leading authority on the sport since 1966 – providing runners of all backgrounds and abilities valuable information on training, nutrition and racing. The experts who contribute to the magazine are some of the most talented and skilled coaches, athletes, physiotherapists, sports medicine physicians, nutritionists, sports psychologists and gear gurus in the world. Everything you need to know to run and race your best is always an issue – or, in my case, a desk – away. *Runner's World* is also a nurturing, supportive source of inspiration and encouragement. It shows runners that success comes in many forms – that simply making it to the finish line is a victory worth celebrating.

I'm often asked if racing is a job requirement at *Runner's World*. It's not, of course, and time trials aren't part of the interview process, by the way. But most *Runner's World* staff drink the water, so to speak, and end up spending much of their free time either participating in road races or preparing for them. I think it's the same effect of reading the magazine: you become inspired by the stories told. You become excited about the sport. And you become motivated to get out there and toe the line for yourself.

That's what happened to me. Thanks to my experience with *Runner's World*, first as a reader and now as an editor, I've enjoyed many races, from 5-Ks to marathons. And I've learned a lot of things along the way – including the value of a non-chafing sports bra, lightweight running shoes and hill training (my new *Buns of Steel* workout).

My goal for this book is to share the wisdom and support that I've been so lucky to receive. I went straight to the source – *Runner's World* – and compiled the best information the magazine has to offer on preparing for a road race. The training plans, nutritional advice and injury-prevention strategies laid out here will help you run your best race whatever the distance (5-K, 10-K, half-marathon, marathon) or whatever your goal (to run a personal best or simply to finish). The information here is designed to suit runners of all experience levels – beginners starting from scratch, those who've been running for years but are new to the race scene, and people who have racing experience but want to take on a new challenge.

I assure you, you're in good hands. Every tip, every instruction, every recommendation included in this book has been *Runner's World* tested and approved. How's that for a head start?

Katie McDonald Neitz

GETTING STARTED

People become runners for all sorts of reasons. You might have taken up the sport because you wanted to lose weight, lower your blood pressure or reduce stress. Smart move. Scores of research studies have shown that a regular programme not only improves your physical health by reducing your risk of heart disease, diabetes and cancer, but it also enhances your mental well-being, boosting mood, lowering anxiety and depression, and even preventing dementia and Alzheimer's disease. These health benefits are wonderful, and we runners are certainly appreciative of them, especially as we get older. But when you're struggling to wake up for a morning run, reducing your cholesterol a few points may not be motivation enough to get you out of bed. A more immediate goal or reward – a 5-K a few weeks away, for example – may be the incentive you need to fight the urge to sleep in. And because more racing means more running, participating in races increases the odds that you'll fulfil all the goals that got you running in the first place.

REASONS TO RACE

REASON #1: TO MOTIVATE YOURSELF

You might be satisfied with your regular running routine. You get in a 3-miler (or even a 4-, 5-, or 6-miler) a few times a week – until the weather turns nasty or work becomes busy. And then your running becomes anything but regular or routine. Having a race goal – be it a 5-K in 6 weeks or a marathon in 16 weeks – will motivate you to lace up and get out of the door, even on those days when the weather isn't runner-friendly *and* you're up against a deadline.

Signing up for a race gives you more incentive to run – and not only if you have a competitive streak. Striving to race a particular time or be the fastest in your age group is a great way to give your running momentum. But you don't need to take a performance-oriented approach to racing to reap its benefits. Wanting to finish feeling strong and capable is a commendable goal that will motivate you to stick to your training. A 3-mile run might be easy to skip on its own. But when you think of it as a building block that will lead you to your ultimate race-day goal, that 3-miler has greater value. And that makes hitting the roads, not the snooze button, more likely.

Runners tend to approach running differently after signing up for a race; a shift in mind-set makes running more of a priority. Maybe it's the non-refundable registration fee or the peer pressure from signing up with a group of friends. But it seems that for many runners, it's simply the decision to set a goal and put in the time and effort to achieve it that serves as the most powerful motivation. Committing to a race means your runs aren't left up to chance. Running isn't determined by whether you can squeeze it in or if you are in the mood. You've signed up for a race, you're on a training programme and you're going to see it through.

For those who rely on to-do lists and BlackBerrys to get through the day, the structure of a training plan can be especially valuable.

Following a programme – one that tells you when to run and when not to (yes, rest is part of training, too!) – makes it easy to find the time to train. Running becomes a scheduled part of your day, as important as your 10:00 a.m. conference call or 3:00 p.m. meeting.

REASON #2: TO CHALLENGE YOURSELF

When you first started running, simply making it around the block may have been a struggle. But your leg strength, cardiovascular endurance and lung power grew, and one day you were able to cover that ground with little effort. Did you stop there? Probably not. The next time you headed out of the door, you might have extended your run a little further. Or maybe you stuck with the same route but tried to run it faster. This desire to see just how far or fast our bodies can go is what makes us runners. After all, if we weren't willing to push ourselves out of our comfort zones, we'd probably stick with walking.

It's important to remember those early days of your running 'career' and how accomplished you felt when you met milestones – the first time you ran up that killer hill without taking a walk break; the first time you ran 30 minutes without stopping. When running is fresh and new, your motivation is high because almost every run is a challenge – making it around the block, making it up a hill, making it to 30 minutes – waiting to be conquered. But as with any other kind of exercise programme, over time, the routine can become too routine – in other words, boring! To keep the spark alive, it's important to set a goal for yourself, whether it's going further or going faster.

Luckily, runners have lots of opportunities to do this – thanks to organized road races. Races give you options. You can focus on distance and take your running to the next level by advancing from a 5-K (3.1 miles) to a 10-K (6.2 miles) or from a half-marathon (13.1 miles) to a marathon (26.2 miles). Or you can focus on speed by concentrating on a specific race distance and working to improve how fast you can run that event.

People who make running part of their lifestyle know the importance of keeping their running exciting and interesting and often have unique ways of challenging themselves through racing. For example, members of the 100 Marathon Club (www.100marathonclub. org.uk) have achieved the goal of running 100 marathons, while the Marathon Grand Slam Club members have run a marathon on every continent – as well as Antarctica and at the North Pole (www. npmarathon.com).

REASON #3: TO GET FASTER

One of the questions *Runner's World* editors are asked most frequently is: how do I become faster? Lucky for us, it's one of the easiest to answer: to become faster, you've got to run faster. To improve your overall pace, you need to train your body to adapt to the stress of running faster so that eventually that speed feels relaxed and comfortable and you can do it regularly. Some runners accomplish this with formal speedwork sessions (intervals on a track, hill sprints, or 'fartleks' – bursts of speed sprinkled into a run). But races offer another way to achieve this; they're actually speedwork in disguise. The spike in adrenaline, the pull of the pack, the support of the spectators and the lure of a finish line are all things that will quicken your pace, probably without you even realizing it. By racing regularly, your body will learn how it feels to move faster and will adjust and adapt. Your arm drive, leg turnover and overall stamina will improve. These enhancements in your running form and physical conditioning will make you a more efficient runner, which will allow you to sustain a faster pace with less effort. Racing also helps you learn to handle the physical and mental discomforts of pushing your body outside its comfort zone. If your muscles ache or you feel tired on an ordinary run, you can flash back to your last successful race – evidence that you're strong and capable of pushing through to the finish.

REASON #4: TO FEEL GOOD ABOUT YOURSELF

As children, we had gold stars, school assemblies and achievement awards. But as we become older, there aren't many opportunities to feel honoured or celebrated – unless you're a runner, that is. Running a road race makes you feel like a king or queen for a day. Police officers divert traffic out of your way. Marshals offer you bananas and water and, depending on the race, sometimes even jelly babies and beer. Fellow racers alert you of a pothole up ahead, point out if your shoelace has come undone and share support and encouragement. All the while, spectators cheer you on, telling you how good and strong you look. (Even if you look neither good nor strong, they're kind enough to tell you what you need to hear.) Some races even feature brass bands, rock groups, school choirs and DJs along the course – all of which distract you from the miles and make you feel like you're in the middle of a party or parade.

Then there's the finish. It might be the highlight of the entire racing experience, making all those weeks of training worth the effort. After you cross the finish line, you feel like you've gained celebrity-like notoriety. Suddenly, you have an entourage of volunteers handing you post-race refreshments, medical personnel ready to tend to your blisters and spectators – friends, family members and even strangers – congratulating you on your accomplishment. More important is how *you* feel. Any doubts you had about finishing are gone. Any discomfort you felt during the final stretch has faded. The endorphins and other feel-good chemicals buzzing in your brain are a powerful drug, making you feel exhilarated and proud. You feel like you've climbed Mount Everest. You feel like you've won the lottery. The medal around your neck might as well be Olympic gold, because you feel that good. This feels like something you could get used to. That's the idea. Chances are you'll be back for more.

REASON #5: TO SUPPORT A CAUSE

There's another way that racing can make you feel good: you can participate in an event that benefits a charitable cause or organization. You don't have to look hard for one; many local races are organized for this purpose. When you enter these races, a portion of your registration fee goes to a worthy cause, such as a hospice, animal sanctuary, school or even church. And so, when you cross the finish line, you get much more than a sense of personal accomplishment – you get satisfaction from knowing you've made a positive impact on your community. At some races, your contribution extends much further. The first Race for Life events were held in the UK in 1994 to raise funds for pioneering cancer research work. Since then the series of 5-K women-only races has become both an excellent beginner's running programme and the most successful fund-raising event in the UK, with every pound raised in sponsorship funding the charity's research. More than 2.5 million women have run in the races to date, raising more than £200 million for cancer research. In 2007 665,000 took part in 280 races across the country.

Running a 5-K race that donates its proceeds to a non-profit organization is just one type of charity running. Many national charities offer marathon, half-marathon, and triathlon programmes and cover the travel expenses of fund-raising participants. You could run the London Marathon for the British Heart Foundation, or travel further afield and tackle a marathon in Berlin with the Multiple Sclerosis Society. Find out more about charity places at races at www.runnersworld.co.uk/charity. These programmes have been given credit for introducing a whole new generation of runners to the sport of road racing, making it more accessible to people who thought endurance events were out of their reach. And they've made it more appealing to those with a connection to a cause who want to show their support in a dramatic or unique way.

THE EXCUSE (AND HOW TO BEAT IT)

I'M NOT A COMPETITIVE PERSON.

Most runners in most races could use this excuse. In reality, only a handful of participants are actually vying for trophies. The rest are out there for all kinds of reasons, many of which have little to do with seriously competing against others. The most compelling reason to sign up for a race is the boost in motivation you'll receive the minute you pay your registration fee. Having the race date marked on your calendar will motivate you to run on days when you may not otherwise get out the door. And successfully training for and completing a race – regardless of your finishing time – provides an enormous sense of accomplishment and satisfaction. If none of the above reasons entices you to sign up for a race, remember this: runners are positive, energetic people. You're bound to feel better after spending an hour with them at your local 5-K.

I DON'T HAVE TIME TO TRAIN.

For most people, it's a matter of learning how to organize your day to include a run. And once you do that, you'll find you get more done during the rest of the day – thanks to the energy boost you get from running.

1. Use 'dead' times. Set your alarm 30 minutes early. That's enough time to get a run in before the rest of your day begins, but it won't seriously cut into your sleep time. Or run while waiting for the children at football practice or before they get off the school bus. Or sneak in a 20-minute run over your lunch hour. Who needs 60 minutes to eat?

2. Schedule runs in your diary. Once you have your run 'booked', you can relax, knowing you won't have to scramble to find the time later.

3. Run to or from work. This takes a bit more coordination of clothing and transportation. But it can help you gear up for your workday or unwind before you return home.

(continued)

THE EXCUSE (CONTINUED)

4. Beat the rush. Cut down your commute by driving to work before rush hour, then use the time you've saved to run near the office. Or run in the park or on the way home while the traffic dies down.

TRAINING TAKES TIME AWAY FROM MY FAMILY.

Family time and running time need not be mutually exclusive. By including family members in your active pursuits, everyone wins – you spend more time together and they become healthy, too.

1. Join a family-friendly gym with a range of exercise options that meet everyone's needs. Runners need treadmills or a track. Children love a pool.

2. Designate family exercise time once or twice a week. Head out to a park, track or playground, and encourage everyone to play catch, whack around a tennis ball or scramble on the climbing frame. One parent can run while the other plays with the children.

3. Buy a running stroller (load capacities vary, but a child must be at least 6 months old). This gives busy parents a chance to run – and talk – with little ones.

4. Take older children to their sports practices, and run around the field as they play.

5. Select a 5-K race connected with a fun local festival or one known for its quirky prizes that you and your spouse and teenagers can get excited about. Schedule it far enough in advance that everyone can train properly. This could become a new family tradition.

I RUN ONLY IN THE SUMMER BECAUSE ALL THE LOCAL RACES MOTIVATE ME.

The busy summer racing season certainly provides lots of opportunities to test your fitness, which is a great incentive to train hard. But as 5-Ks become sparse with the turn of the season, you can stay motivated by choosing a challenging endurance goal that necessitates training through the winter. If you usually run 5-Ks and 10-Ks during the summer, pick a 10-miler, half-marathon or marathon in late winter or early spring and write it on your calendar. Once you've zeroed in on your new goal, pencil in all the weekend long runs and speed sessions you'll need to prepare for the race. Also, fill in your calendar with the 'maintenance' runs needed between quality workouts. Having a training plan sketched out from the beginning will keep you on track. It's also helpful if you can convince a friend to join you. As you talk about your goal race, you'll keep each other motivated to do the weekly training.

I'M NOT BUILT FOR RACING.

To rid yourself of the notion that runners must look as thin as greyhounds, go to the finish line of any major marathon. You'll be inspired by the thousands of runners of all shapes and sizes. Thanks to our hardy ancestors, humans have inherited the ability to cover long distances. Bigger runners who were once athletes tend to be most prone to injury because it's easy for them to run faster and further than they should when starting to run again. So it's important to ease in. You can find the right programme for you in the next chapter.

I DON'T NEED TO LOSE WEIGHT.

Lucky you. Even so, there's a big difference between being fit and being thin. Running can help you be both. But perhaps the greatest benefits of running are the less mundane ones. Focus on the ways that running energizes the body, mind and spirit.

1. Running regularly improves your physical and mental vitality.

2. After a run, your attitude improves. You can turn a bad day into a good one.

3. The creative side of the brain (the right side) is stimulated more by running than by most other activities. Your best thoughts can come to you on a run.

4. Even an everyday run confers a sense of accomplishment. Frequent runners receive a boost in self-confidence every time they finish a workout.

RACE SELECTION

With thousands of road races occurring every weekend, runners aren't at a loss for options. But with so many to choose from, the selection process can be overwhelming, especially if you are new to the sport. Here's help simplifying the process.

CHOOSE YOUR DISTANCE

5-K (3.1 MILES): If you are brand new to the racing world, this is the perfect place to start. 5-Ks are the easiest races to find – in 2007, there were around 900 registered 5-Ks in the country – especially during the spring and summer months. They also tend to pop up around holidays with fun, festive themes; chances are there's a Christmas Pudding race or Santa Dash somewhere near you. This distance is a good introduction to road racing because the training isn't too demanding or complicated, the time you spend racing is relatively short and bouncing back from a 5-K is easy. (The rule of thumb is that your body needs 1 day of recovery for every mile raced, which means you'll recover from a 5-K within 3 days.) Runners interested in signing up for a 5-K should have about 1 month of running three or four times a week under their belts. To prepare to race this distance, you should be willing to train for about 6 weeks, during which time you'll complete at least one 3-mile run a week or two before the event.

5-MILER, 10-K (6.2 MILES), 10-MILER: Once you've completed a few 5-Ks, you might start thinking about a greater challenge. These race distances aren't as abundant as 5-Ks, so part of the challenge may be finding one close to home. (In 2007, there were 269 5-milers; 787 10-Ks and 154 10-milers in the UK.) But they are good stepping-stones between a 5-K and the very popular half-marathon. Before taking on a 5-miler, 10-K or 10-miler, you should have a running base of 2 to 3 months of running every other day. These races also require more time to train than a 5-K does. A 10-K programme, for instance, involves about 6 weeks of regular training, with a 5- to 7-mile run about 10 to 14 days before race day. Since these distances put a greater strain on your body, they'll take a little longer to recover from, so you'll need to rest or run gently for about a week to 10 days following the race.

HALF-MARATHON (13.1 MILES): Once you've conquered the 10-K, the half-marathon is a great goal. There were 239 races in the UK in 2007. Half-marathons are also popular among aspiring marathon runners. You might have enough of a fitness foundation to go out this weekend and run a 5-K or a 10-K without any special training, but running a half-marathon usually requires more planning, preparation and dedication. Before starting a half-marathon training programme, you should have a running base of about 4 months of running every other day. You should be willing to devote about 12 weeks to a training plan, which will involve doing 'long runs' on weekends, building up to between 10 and 14 miles, depending on your race goal and experience level. Some beginners benefit from a walk/run programme, walking for 1 minute every 10 minutes. Because a half-marathon puts a greater strain on your body, your recovery time will be longer.

MARATHON (26.2 MILES): In 2007, there were 64 marathons in the UK, each one offering a life-changing experience. Runners who are ready for the challenge will find new strength during the 26.2-mile race and enjoy a tremendous sense of achievement. But those who try to do one too early in their running career may end up injured, burned out and put off the sport in general. Most runners become successful marathon runners only after gradually increasing their racing goals – first completing a 5-K, then a 10-K, then a half-marathon. This build-up ensures a gradual adjustment to the training changes and challenges inherent in marathon training. With each shorter race, you add to your running and racing know-how. How do you know when you're ready? Runners who meet the following criteria can probably start planning for a marathon. (1) You've been running for more than

6 months. (2) You run at least three times a week, every week. (3) You can run longer than 60 minutes fairly easily. (4) You are willing to slow down (maybe even take walk breaks) on long runs to help you increase your distances. (5) You are highly motivated and willing to make training a priority. After all, marathon training requires dedication – at least 16 weeks of regular training, with long runs eventually building up to 20 to 22 miles.

QUIZ: WHAT'S THE BEST DISTANCE FOR YOUR PERSONALITY?

Many runners take a Goldilocks approach to choosing races: 5-K? Too short. Marathon? Too long. Half-marathon? Just right. How you come to these decisions isn't based only on how you physically feel. Your brain has just as much say, if not more, over which distance fits you best. If you become bored easily or like to focus on short-term projects, you may struggle through a 16-week marathon-training plan. Switching to a race that better matches your mind-set, such as a 5-K (instant gratification) or triathlon (variety), could improve your outlook on running. 'Picking a race based on what suits your personality can lead to more personal satisfaction and joyfulness with your running,' says Dr Kay Porter, a sports psychologist and author of *The Mental Athlete*. So whether you're new to the racing scene or a seasoned runner wondering if your current regimen is right for you, here's a quiz to help you find your perfect distance.

1. *When it comes to work and goal setting, I:*
    a) Start a lot of projects without finishing them.
    b) Gravitate toward goals I can accomplish with moderate focus.
    c) Seek out long-term projects that can become all-consuming.
    d) Multitask so I don't become bored with one project.

2. *I consider my attention span to be:*
    a) Short but intense; I like instant gratification.
    b) Steady, but I still become restless sometimes.

c) Constant; it's easy for me to stay focused for long periods of time.

d) Sporadic; I become bored easily.

3. *My favourite thing about running is:*
    a) It's efficient: I can fit a great workout in quickly.
    b) It's adaptable: I can train a lot or a little, depending on my schedule.
    c) It's 'me time': long runs help me clear my mind.
    d) It's social: I love being part of a team and/or trying new things.

4. *Regarding distance, I usually:*
    a) Keep my runs short but enjoy speedwork.
    b) Maintain a steady base but like occasional distance runs.
    c) Enjoy weekly long runs and can handle some 40-plus-mile weeks.
    d) Like to do a lot of cross-training in addition to running.

Tally It Up

Mostly As: You like quick results, so 5-Ks and 10-Ks might be best for you. These distances are ideal for energetic 'project starter' types, says running coach Greg McMillan, who operates mcmillanrunning.com. 'Shorter races are ideal for people who have a lot of motivation but have trouble maintaining their focus for a long time.'

Mostly Bs: You strive to attain balance in your life, so half-marathons would suit you well. 'The half is the perfect distance for most runners,' McMillan says. 'It requires a training programme, which provides structure most runners like, without the commitment of a marathon.'

Mostly Cs: You tend to organize your life around long-term goals, so you'd likely do well as a marathon runner. 'Distance

HOW THE PROS PICK THEIR RACES

The Olympian: Mara Yamauchi, first British woman at the 2007 London Marathon

'I start by choosing the top priority race for the year or season then choose other races that fit in with it. My main race is usually a marathon so I'll pick half-marathons and 10-Ks to focus on in the short-term and find out how my training is progressing.'

The Marathon Runner: Huw Lobb, the first solo runner to beat the first horse in the annual Man versus Horse 22-mile cross-country race in mid Wales

'I choose my marathons by looking at the level of competition from previous years and finding a finishing time that is roughly my target time. I also consider the weather conditions. For build-up races, I look at the date relative to the marathon and the travel required to race there.'

The Ultra Runner: Martin Rea, top-30 finisher at the World 100-K Championships 2007

'As an ultra runner I have to plan my races around six months in advance. I tend to sign up for marathons as training runs then target the year's most important championship races – the World Championships and European Championships – and plan my races around them.'

The Extremist: Sharon Gayter, Britain's top female 24-hour runner

'Each year I start with the most important race of the year – the World 24 Hours – then, depending on the time of year I look at a list of races I would love to compete in,' says Gayter. 'I choose races – usually extreme ultras – that won't interfere with my training for the Worlds. I also like to race every weekend in a shorter events building up to marathon distance.'

The All-Rounder: Heidi Wilson, English International ultra runner

'I choose events that give me a mixture of things to focus on. I might select a big race and use the crowds to motivate myself to a personal best, or choose a smaller race to achieve a top-three finish. I generally focus on two or three main races in a year – such as a marathon, an ultra marathon and a triathlon – then tackle shorter races as training runs to gauge my fitness levels.'

runners are stick-to-it people who can focus well on future goals,' McMillan says. If you've done marathons and are craving more, consider an ultramarathon, a race that goes beyond 26.2 miles.

Mostly Ds: You're a multitasker, and events like triathlons, duathlons and relay races can provide the diversity you need. 'Triathlons are perfect for variety seekers,' McMillan says. Plus, events like relays tend to have more of a social, team-oriented component – ideal for runners who seek camaraderie and fun.

PICK YOUR RACE

LOCATION: You need to decide if you want to run a race that's close to home or if you want to travel to a different town, county or even country. There are certain advantages to staying local. Travel time is minimal: you don't have to wake up hours early to drive to the event or stay overnight in a hotel. Course support is optimal: your friends and family are more likely to come out to cheer you on, and it'll be easier to recruit training partners to run the race with you. Preparation is better: you can find out the race route and incorporate it into your training so you're prepared for hills or any other challenging spots.

Running races further from home, on the other hand, can create a memorable experience. For instance, if you have a summer holiday planned, you could find out if the area you're visiting has a summer running festival. Not only is racing while travelling a way to keep up your running and burn off some of those ice-cream cones and cream teas, but it gives you a unique way to explore the area and interact with some friendly, lively locals. Some runners see races as opportunities for adventure, seeking out destination races that double as a holiday. Marathons in such alluring locations as Edinburgh, Paris,

China, South Africa, Egypt, Las Vegas, Argentina and even Antarctica give runners with a travel bug a chance to fulfil their passion.

REPUTATION: You can feel pretty confident entering a race that's celebrating its 25th anniversary. With such a long history and a loyal following of participants, it's likely to be extremely well organized and executed. That's not to say that you should avoid new events, especially those that are put on by experienced race directors or running clubs that have a solid track record of event planning. Experience and reputation are especially important when selecting a half-marathon or marathon. At these races, a poorly marked course, lack of marshals or insufficient water stops can seriously impact your race experience. When in doubt about a race, it's a good idea to do a little research. Ask your running partners, the members of a running club, or the staff at your local running shop if they know anyone who has done the race in the past and what the experience was like. Search online to see if *Runner's World* has recommended it, or check the rate-a-race section on www.runnersworld.co.uk.

ATMOSPHERE: Some runners love the crowds and excitement that comes with big-city races. Others would rather have the more peaceful, meditative experience that smaller events in remote locations offer. Some runners strive for personal bests and want a course that's known to be flat and fast, even if it leads them through boring industrial estates. Others are less concerned about their finish time and don't mind climbing a few hills that lead them to gorgeous views. Take all this into consideration when selecting an event. What do you want to get from the race? What's important to you? Are you out for a fast time or a good time? Luckily, with so many to choose from, there is a race to fit every kind of racer.

WEATHER: One of the best things about road racing is that it's a year-round sport that enables runners to experience and celebrate the seasons. In the depths of December, choose a race with a Christmas theme to celebrate the festive season. At this time of year there are dozens of Christmas Cracker, Xmas Pudding and Santa Dash races to choose from. In spring, races such as the Easter Bunny 10-K in Yeovil usher in the milder weather – and reward you with an Easter egg to refuel afterwards. June's longest day sees runners attempting events like the Malvern Midsummer Marathon and Midsummer Munro Half-Marathon – the equivalent of climbing a Scottish Munro, a mountain over 900 metres high. Autumn is a great time for tackling one of the many European big-city marathons on offer, Berlin leads the way but Venice, Budapest and Amsterdam are all worth considering. Distance runners tend to perform best in cool, crisp conditions and views of the turning leaves will help the training miles pass quickly.

While running in extremes of either heat or cold can earn you bragging rights, it rarely offers a fast finish time – which is fine, of course. Not every event is designed for or should be about setting a record pace. You can run in challenging conditions, so long as you are willing to adjust your pace accordingly (i.e., slow down). Some race officials even declare their events 'fun runs' on days when conditions are too intense for a serious competition. However, if you want to race for time or you want a relaxed, comfortable experience, consider a race where conditions will enhance, not hurt, your performance. Or travel to a location that offers the weather you'd prefer: in the depths of January you could head to Dubai for a marathon in the desert sun.

MAKE IT OFFICIAL

Your local running shop and running club probably have information and recommendations on upcoming races in your area. You can also search online at www.runnersworld.co.uk/events for listings and information on how to enter. Large events usually have their own websites, complete with online registration. Smaller events may require you to print out an entry form to complete and post in or to bring on race day. If in doubt, contact the race director.

The sooner you sign up, the better. First, by registering for a race, you declare your commitment to it. You'll mark it on your calendar, think about it seriously, and be less likely to miss training runs once you are officially entered. Plus, races usually offer discounted rates to those who sign up early. Popular big-city races can sell out months in advance. You don't want to spend time carefully selecting and training for a race, and then go to sign up for it only to discover it's already filled to capacity. Even if you're planning to do a smaller, local event that allows race-day registration, signing up in advance will give you one less thing to worry about on race morning.

GET KITTED OUT

RUNNING SHOES

Part of the beauty of road racing is its simplicity. Although some racers may seem armed for battle with GPS (Global Positioning System) devices, iPods, mobile phones and, yes, even bum bags, the only piece of equipment you really need on race day is a pair of running shoes. Running shoes protect your feet from the impact of running, while helping you perform at your maximum potential. But selecting the right shoes isn't always so simple. There are many brands and models – some offer stability, others offer cushioning; some are for trail running, others are for speed training. It's critical to select a pair that fits you well and provides the correct support for your feet. Wearing the 'wrong' pair (due to improper fit, poor support, too little or too much cushion or simply being worn out) can lead to injury – the last thing you want when you are preparing for a race. Here's everything you need to know to ensure that your shoes will carry you through training – and race day – happily and injury free.

The best, most basic advice for buying running shoes: visit a specialist running shop. Runners need experts who will provide advice on the best shoes and gear and help you find the perfect fit. The staff at running shops aren't simply shoe salespeople – they are specifically trained and very knowledgeable about the sport, the special needs of runners' feet and the construction of running shoes. They will also analyze your specific foot type. To help them fit you successfully, keep these things in mind when you shop.

TAKE YOUR TIME. Sometimes you need to test out multiple pairs before finding the right fit. You don't want to rush this process and then end up with buyer's remorse. Treat a new pair of shoes like a car – you wouldn't purchase it without a test drive. Specialist running shops will either have a treadmill or let you go outside for a short run for this purpose. This is essential. Circling around a shoe display is no substitute for an actual run.

GO PREPARED. Take the shoes you currently wear with you. The sales staff can tell a lot about your foot type and biomechanics from the wear patterns on the soles of your shoes (see 'Everything you need to know about pronation' on page 23). You may have a tried-and-tested shoe that's always worked for you, but there's a chance that model is dated and no longer available. Seeing it will help the staff make an educated recommendation. If you wear inserts or prescription orthotics (for support or to correct biomechanical issues), bring those along as well. And be sure to wear the same type of sock that you plan to train and race in. Additional information that could be helpful to the person fitting your foot: any injuries you've had, what shoes you've liked and which ones you haven't, what kind of race you're training for and the weekly mileage you expect to do.

PUT LOOKS ASIDE. When shopping for a shoe, you need to make fit – not colour or style – a priority. A runner might pick out a shoe because it looks good but then discover after a few runs that it hurts, and by then it's too late to return it. When you buy, think feel and fit, not fashion.

SHOP LATE. Your feet start swelling in the morning and don't stop until about 4:00 p.m. That's as big as they're going to get, so always buy your shoes in the evening. Tight-fitting shoes lead to blisters and black toenails. Women sometimes end up with running shoes that are too small because they are used to wearing close-fitting high heels and can be more self-conscious about the size of their feet. The fit should be roomy enough in the forefoot – about a thumb's width – but not sloppy.

GET MEASURED. People assume that a size is a size – that a 6 in a Nike will be the same as a 6 in a New Balance. But sizes differ because of different lasts (foot forms), shapes of uppers and stitching. Also, as you age, your foot size may gradually change. Women may also experience changes following pregnancy. Have your feet measured every time you buy, and always try shoes on for fit.

KNOW YOUR FOOT TYPE. Most running shop salespeople will be able to take a look at your foot and gauge your foot type – flat, normal or high arches. But knowing this in advance can save you time and make sure you are analyzed correctly. For a simple test to determine your foot type, see 'What's Your Type?' opposite.

TEST THEM OUT. Wear the shoes on a run, noting whether there is adequate room in the toe box and if your feet feel anchored or your heels slip – especially as you run uphill or around corners. If a shoe feels even the slightest bit sloppy on inclines or turns, it'll probably be too wide once you break it in. Women are especially prone to this, as many have narrow heels that don't conform to the shoe industry's conception of foot shape. Many women buy shoes that are too narrow to get a snug fit in the heel, but this can lead to pain and injury in the forefront. Here's how to combat the problem: buy shoes that are wide enough in the forefoot. Lace them up as usual, but when you get to the second eyelet from the top, thread each lace end through the top eyelet on that same side. This forms a small loop. Next, thread the lace ends through the opposite loops, and tie your shoes as you normally would. This will provide a tighter fit at the top and keep your heels more snug.

BREAK THEM IN. Although running shoes should feel good and fit great right out of the box, you don't want to run a race or do an important training run in a brand-new pair. Wear them around the house for a few days so that the sock liner – the thin insert on which your foot rests – can begin conforming to the shape of your foot. Then run some shorter training runs in the shoes so you become used to how they feel. Finally, you can start wearing them for all your runs. Plan to do at least 8 to 10 runs in your new shoes before race day.

TRACK THEM. Running shoes need replacement after 300 to 500 miles. Even if you don't see much cosmetic deterioration, the midsoles will have lost their cushioning and resiliency, which can lead to injuries. Don't wait until you have achy joints or feet to replace

WHAT'S YOUR TYPE?

You can go a long way towards discovering what you need in a running shoe by looking at your feet. There are three basic foot types, each based on the height of your arches. The quickest and easiest way to determine your foot type is by taking the following 'wet footprint test'.

· Pour a thin layer of water into a shallow pan.

· Wet the sole of your foot.

· Step onto a shopping bag or a blank piece of heavy paper.

· Step off and look down.

Observe the shape of your foot, and match it with one of the foot types on the next page. Although other variables (such as your weight, biomechanics, weekly

(continued)

WHAT'S YOUR TYPE? (CONTINUED)

mileage and fit preferences) come into play, knowing your foot type is the first step toward finding the right shoe for you.

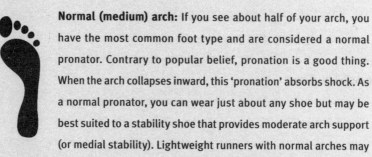

Normal (medium) arch: If you see about half of your arch, you have the most common foot type and are considered a normal pronator. Contrary to popular belief, pronation is a good thing. When the arch collapses inward, this 'pronation' absorbs shock. As a normal pronator, you can wear just about any shoe but may be best suited to a stability shoe that provides moderate arch support (or medial stability). Lightweight runners with normal arches may prefer neutral-cushioned shoes without added support or even a performance-training shoe that offers some support but less weight for a faster feel.

Flat (low) arch: If you see almost your entire footprint, you have a flatfoot, which means you're probably an overpronator. That is, a microsecond after footstrike, your arch collapses inward too much, resulting in excessive foot motion and increasing your risk of injuries. You need either stability shoes, which employ devices such as dual-density midsoles and supportive 'posts' to reduce pronation and are best for mild to moderate overpronators, or motion-control shoes, which have firmer support devices and are best for severe overpronators, as well as tall, heavy (over 75kg), or bowlegged runners.

High arch: If you see just your heel, the ball of your foot, and a thin line on the outside of your foot, you have a high arch, the least common foot type. This means you're likely an underpronator, or supinator, which can result in too much shock travelling up your legs, since your arches don't collapse enough to absorb it. Underpronators are best suited to neutral-cushioned shoes because they need a softer midsole to encourage pronation. It's vital that an underpronator's shoes have no added stability devices to reduce or control pronation, the way a stability or motion-control shoe would.

EVERYTHING YOU NEED TO KNOW ABOUT PRONATION

Pronation is simply a normal foot in motion, from foot-strike on the outside of the heel through the inward roll of the foot. Everyone pronates – it occurs as the foot rolls from the outer edge to the inner edge, and it's critical to shock absorption. If the foot pronates too much or too little and does so frequently, several biomechanical problems may result, decreasing performance and increasing the possibility of injury.

Normal pronation: The outside part of the heel makes initial contact with the ground. The foot 'rolls' inwards about 5 per cent, comes into complete contact with the ground, and can support your body weight without any problem. The rolling in optimally distributes the forces of impact, and at the end of the gait cycle, you push off evenly from the front of the foot.

Overpronation: As with the normal pronation sequence, the outside of the heel makes the initial contact with the ground. However, the foot rolls inwards more than the ideal 5 per cent, which is called overpronation. This means the foot and ankle have problems stabilizing the body, and shock isn't absorbed as efficiently. At the end of the gait cycle, the front of the foot pushes off the ground using mainly the big toe and second toe, which then must do all the work.

Underpronation: Again, the outside of the heel makes initial contact with the ground, but the foot's inward movement occurs at less than 4 per cent (there's less rolling in than for those with normal feet or flatfeet). Consequently, forces of impact are concentrated on a smaller area of the foot – the outside part – and are not distributed as efficiently. In the push-off phase, most of the work is done by the smaller toes on the outside of the foot.

Which one? One way you can tell what kind of running gait you have is by looking at a pair of your used running shoes. Place them side by side on a table, toes pointing away from you. Look at the shoes at eye level. If you have a neutral gait, the shoes will lie flat. If you are an overpronator, they'll have an inward tilt. If you are an underpronator, they'll have an outward tilt.

EVERYTHING YOU NEED TO KNOW ABOUT PRONATION (CONTINUED)

The Anatomy of a Shoe

Collar: the inside back portion that provides comfort around the ankle

Dual-density midsole: a mechanism, most often a firmer wedge of foam on the medial (inner) side, used to correct excessive pronation

Eyelets: the holes the laces run through

Heel counter: an internal support feature in the rear that conforms to the shape of your heel

Heel tab: the part that surrounds the Achilles tendon and helps lock the shoe around the heel; also called Achilles tendon protector or Achilles tendon notch

Midsole: the material (usually EVA or polyurethane foam) that sits below the upper and above the outsole, providing protection from impact forces and often encasing non-foam technologies, such as gel or air, to increase durability and protection

Outsole: the durable part that makes contact with the ground, providing traction

Overlays: reinforcing strips at key stress points that help give the shoe structure

Quarter panel: the material that makes up the sides

Sockliner: a removable insert that sits just below the foot and helps the shoe fit the foot better

Tongue: the soft elongated flap that fits over the top of the foot to protect the tendons and blood vessels from pressure caused by the laces

Upper: the part that encases the foot

your shoes. Since it's easy to lose track of how long you've had a particular pair, it's a good idea to write down the date that you bought them in a training diary, calendar or even directly on your shoe.

RUNNING WEAR

While it's true that your main concern as a runner should be what goes on your feet, how you dress the rest of your body can also have an impact on your race performance and experience. High-tech running gear may seem extravagant, but as many runners have found, once you go technical, you don't go back. Technical apparel is made from fabrics that offer performance features and benefits that a cotton T-shirt and tracksuit trousers don't. Technical apparel that's worn next to your skin – whether it's a top, sports bra, tights or underwear – is designed to pull, or wick, moisture (that is, sweat) away from your body. Cotton clothing, by contrast, holds sweat, which can make you cold and miserable, even on a warm day. Technical clothing also dries quickly, a bonus regardless of the temperature. For beginning racers on a run/walk programme, high-tech fabric can be particularly useful, as it moves sweat off you during run portions so that you're not cold during the walk sections.

Technical clothing is comfortable for another reason, too: many items are made of lightweight, stretchy fabrics, making them less bulky. On cold days, instead of piling on thick layers, a couple of thin but insulating pieces of technical wear will keep you feeling toasty without looking like the Michelin Man.

Another advantage of technical running clothing is that it's designed for athletes. Just about every runner I know has a story about the 'wow' he or she felt during the first run in a technical top. Often runners don't realize how uncomfortable their other clothes are until they make the switch. This is especially true for women who try technical sports bras, which are made with flat seams to reduce chafing. This kind of attention to detail increases the cost, but because most of these garments are well made, they last a long time, and you'll get your money's worth. Buying winter clothes at the beginning of spring, or buying summer clothes at the beginning of winter, is a good way to find stuff on sale, as specialist running retailers make room for the next season's items. Start with basics – a technical top and a pair of shorts. Wear your new gear on training runs, not for the first time on race day. Training runs can serve as dress rehearsals, confirming that what you plan to race in fits well and feels comfortable.

Dressing for training runs and races can be tricky and takes a bit of practice, especially during autumn and spring, when temperatures tend to be unpredictable. Here's something worth noting: once you start running and your body warms up, it will feel considerably warmer. So if your race-day forecast is for 10°C, you should dress as if it's going to be 20°C. That means you'll start your runs feeling slightly chilly, and that's okay. If you feel 100 per cent comfortable – or warm – to start, you'll probably feel overheated 10 minutes into your run. This is when dressing in layers can be helpful. You could strip off a top layer – a long-sleeved top or jacket – and tie it around your waist. Or you could do what many experienced racers do, and dress in 'throwaway' layers. Many runners wear old clothes over their racing attire to help them stay warm before the race begins. Then, minutes before the starting gun fires or a mile or two into the race, they shed the extra layers, leaving them behind on the side of the road. At big city races the clothes are collected and given to charity.

If you do decide to gear up, here are the basics, head to toe.

WINTER HAT: A warm hat that covers your ears is a must on cold days, especially windy ones, and can be one of the best steps you take to keep warm. CoolMax or other technical-fibre hats are available at specialist running shops.

HAT WITH VISOR: A hat with a visor not only keeps the sun out of your eyes but also shields them from blowing snow and rain. A light-coloured hat helps keep your head cool on warm days.

SUNGLASSES: By keeping the sun out of your eyes, a good pair of sunglasses can save you energy by allowing you to relax your face (no squinting). Though their uses are obvious on sunny summer days, shades are also helpful on bright winter days or any time glare is likely to be an issue.

JACKET: A jacket, usually a polyester blend, keeps you warm; protects you from wind, rain and snow; and manages your perspiration. It's an essential piece of equipment on cold, windy and/or rainy days.

LONG-SLEEVED TOP: A long-sleeved top made of high-tech polyester will pull moisture away from your skin, keeping you from becoming clammy and cold on a cooler day.

SHORT-SLEEVED TOP: Short sleeves, a sleeveless singlet, or (for women) as little as a sports bra provides the minimum upper-body coverage. While it may look like a classic T-shirt, a short-sleeved top in a technical fabric like CoolMax will pull sweat away from the skin instead of absorbing it like cotton does. This added comfort, combined with sun protection, can make a technical tee a better choice than no shirt at all.

GLOVES: Gloves keep your hands warm on a cold day, although mittens work better when temperatures drop below freezing. When in doubt, better to take your gloves with you. They're easy to tuck into your shorts or tights if you don't need them.

TIGHTS: The first level of insulation for your legs, classic tights are generally a polyester and Lycra blend. Looser running bottoms (also stretchy but not as formfitting) are another option. In extreme cold, wearing tights under bottoms is a good layering strategy.

SHORTS: The basic element of any runner's wardrobe, shorts are usually made of nylon or technical fibre. Some runners prefer short shorts – perhaps they make them feel faster. Other runners feel more comfortable with more coverage. But no matter what length they are, performance features abound. Longer shorts now feature lighter-weight materials and smarter designs to keep you from looking like you're going to the beach. And new short shorts have extra features like pockets and cuts that don't necessarily bare all.

SOCKS: Form-fitting knits and advanced fibres make it possible to match different socks with where and when you run. Do you want a wool blend that adds warmth for a cool day? A heavily cushioned sock for long road runs? Something sleek and nimble for a speed workout or a race? Or a dark sock to hide the dirt you pick up running cross-country? No matter which you choose, virtually every new running sock is made with a blend of breathable materials – including nylon, polyester, wool, CoolMax, Lycra or Spandex – that help keep your feet dry and comfortable.

ELECTRONICS

Some runners enjoy knowing exactly what pace, distance and time they run. Others would rather run in blissful ignorance. It all depends on your personality and your approach to training and racing. If you are after a top performance, then souped-up sports watches that track your mileage and measure your effort can be great training partners.

Heart-Rate Monitors

There is a simple, compelling reason to use a heart-rate monitor: to train and to race at the best pace for you. Once considered the gadget du jour for hard-core professional athletes, heart-rate monitors have gone mainstream. Everyone from fitness runners to veteran marathon runners is wearing them for the same reason: your heart rate provides an objective gauge of exertion, one that's usually more exact than your own perception of how hard you're working. No matter what type of runner you are – beginner, intermediate or advanced – a heart-rate monitor will help you train more effectively.

Newcomers to running are some of the biggest fans of these gadgets for two main reasons: tracking heart rate ensures you're working hard enough to reap fitness benefits; on the flip side, setting a maximum heart rate can keep overzealous novices from overdoing it. Beginners should choose a target heart-rate zone – generally between 65 and 75 per cent of maximum heart rate (the highest rate that a person should achieve during maximal physical exertion: you can find yours at www.runnersworld.co.uk/heartrate) – and stay within it for most of their workouts. Runners who haven't yet developed a sense of their speed and effort can learn pacing from a monitor.

If you've run for a year or more and have a solid mileage base, you'll find the monitor a great help as you start doing more challenging workouts. Intermediate and advanced runners are renowned for running too hard on recovery days, and a monitor can remedy this. Many advanced runners also use a monitor to track recovery during interval workouts. Instead of waiting a pre-determined number of minutes or jogging a certain distance between repeats, you can check for your heart rate to drop before beginning the next repeat.

GPS

The standard way of plotting a running route used to be to drive it and measure it with your car's odometer. Today, runners who want to know exactly where and how far they are running can save time – and petrol – by using a GPS unit. Pedometers measure distance based on stride length, which decreases as you tire, so their readings aren't necessarily accurate. A GPS unit can pinpoint your exact location, plot out routes, calculate the distance you've run and give altitude readings and current, maximum and average speed readings.

MP3 Players

Tiny, lightweight, portable music players are ubiquitous, including on running roads and trails. Yes, listening to music can inspire and motivate you, which can improve your running. But it can also be unsafe. When you run wearing headphones, you're less aware of what's going on around you, so you're more prone to injuries and accidents and more vulnerable to attacks. If you choose to tune in, keep the following safety tips in mind.

- Limit yourself to listening to music only while on a treadmill or during races (although some don't allow it).
- Listen to music that will pump you up before the start of a race.
- If you're outdoors, run in safe, familiar, public areas with minimal (better still, non-existent) traffic.
- Whenever possible, run with a partner. Running friends who don't listen to music may feel a bit snubbed, but there's safety in numbers, and it's always good to have at least one pair of unencumbered ears.
- Run with a dog. Man's best friend loves exercise even more than we do. Dogs offer great security, and they don't mind being tuned out.
- Consider open-air, or supra-aural, headphones, which do not seal off your ear canal, allowing more ambient noise (like car horns and cycling pelotons) to remain audible.
- Set the volume just loud enough to hear the music but low enough that you can hear the sounds around you. It's a fine balance – but it's worth locating.
- Don't assume that the one-ear-only method is any safer. Research shows that using headphones in just one ear can confuse your brain – perhaps more dangerous than listening with both sides of your head.

WHAT MOVES YOU?

Four elite runners reveal their 21st-century versions of 'Chariots of Fire' – the music that motivates and inspires them

'I sometimes listen to music when I am running easy – but not usually during hard sessions as I need to concentrate. I like to listen to music before I warm up for an important event as it is both relaxing and motivating. At the moment I'm listening to anything by U2 and the Killers.'
Jo Pavey, fourth in the 10,000m at the 2007 World Championships

'I listen to music when I'm training in the morning. I go for dance music that is mainly strong beats and baselines backed up by light vocals with a feel-good theme. If I'm in a bad mood, I occasionally switch to My Chemical Romance or something more rocky.'
Huw Lobb, the first man ever to beat the horse at the annual Man versus Horse 22-mile cross-country race in Wales

'Other than when I'm racing, I always listen to music when I run. I love the slower songs, as they are the ones where you can run twice to the beat and really power along. My favourite running songs are "Chasing Cars" by Snow Patrol, "Stop and Stare" by One Republic, "Caribbean Blue" by Enya, "Beautiful Day" by U2 and "Denial" by Sugarbabes.'
Heidi Wilson, English international ultra runner

'If I'm running in the UK I listen to Talk Sport Radio. I tend to train in the mornings at around 6 a.m., which coincides with the fantastic Alan Brazil Show. When I do listen to music, I go for Queen as it has a certain beat to it!'
Martin Rea, ultra runner and top-30 finisher at the World 100-K Championships 2007

TRAINING

It's time for the fun to begin. That's right, fun. Training for a race takes dedication, commitment and, yes, a lot of hard work. But most runners revel in the process. I know I do. That's because there are so many positives that come out of training. As your mileage grows, you'll feel strong, fit and energized. A distance or pace that seemed out of reach a few weeks ago is no longer just doable but actually comfortable. Training can be very social, introducing you to new friends or deepening friendships that you already have – you learn a lot about someone during long runs. Training for a race also gives you the opportunity to do something for yourself. We often define ourselves by what we do (teacher, lawyer, writer) or who we are to others (wife, mother, husband, father). The time you spend out on the roads is all about you. And in the end, when you become healthier and feel better about yourself, those around you will benefit, too.

This chapter provides training plans for the four most popular race distances: 5-K, 10-K, half-marathon and marathon. Each plan offers three levels – beginner, intermediate and advanced – which means there is something for everyone, from the newbie racer to the experienced veteran looking to improve on past performances. The schedules that follow have the weekly long run scheduled for Sundays, but you can rearrange this to fit your own needs. I prefer to run long Saturday mornings (gets it out of the way), so I simply shift my workouts over 1 day. You could make your long-run day Wednesday if you wanted. It really makes no difference, as long as you pay attention to the order of your runs. You wouldn't want to rearrange the schedule and have back-to-back hard workouts, like a speed workout the day before a long run.

Naturally, the further you want to race, the longer it will take you to prepare. So if you are looking to do a race in 6 weeks, a 5-K is your best bet. If you want to do a longer race, such as a marathon, advanced planning is necessary. The marathon training plans here are 16 weeks long, so if 26.2 is what you want to do, you'll need to pick a race that's at least 4 months away.

After the training plans, you'll find information on extra workouts that you can swap in. If this is your first time racing or you are an experienced runner but don't want to experiment, just stick with the base plans. They will prepare you well.

THE ULTIMATE 5-K PLAN

The 5-K is a great distance for every level of runner. It's fail-safe short for first-timers. There's one nearly every weekend for personal-best-chasing intermediates. And it's the ideal fast time trial, tough tempo run or tune-up for veteran competitors. On the following pages, you'll find 6-week schedules for each of the three groups. Look at each level to determine which describes you best and, therefore, what schedule you should follow. These are not one-size-fits-all plans, so if you can't complete a given workout, don't. If you want to rearrange training days to fit your schedule, go for it.

5-K TRAINING UNIVERSALS:
THINGS TO KNOW BEFORE YOU START

REST: This means no running at all. Walk, bike or swim if you want to – just not very hard. You don't have to regard rest days as 'nothing' days but, rather, a different kind of training that allows your body to recover while it absorbs and consolidates the strength gains your hard runs produce.

EASY RUN: This is a totally comfortable pace. You breathe hard enough to know that you're running but are still able to hold up your end of an on-the-run conversation. If you can't, your pace is too hard; on the other hand, if a walker passes you, it's too easy.

LONG RUN: This is anything longer than race distance for the purpose of building endurance – specifically, the ability to run comfortably for longer and longer periods of time.

SPEED: These shorter-than-race-distance repetitions at or below goal race pace can be hard to very hard to nearly flat-out. These runs produce leg speed, elevated lactic threshold, stamina, biomechanical efficiency and the ability to tolerate the discomfort that's essential to racing fitness.

Beginner

You're running recreationally two or three times a week for a total of 6 to 8-plus miles. But now you want to enter a real race – and finish. Join the order of road racers. Score that first race T-shirt. Earn some bragging rights at the office. At this stage, you just run – a little more this week than the week before; a tad more the week to follow. No interval training, no flirting with injuries, no serious discomfort. Just run. 'For runners without a competitive past, the first training goal is to raise mileage by adding easy volume,' says former Olympian and online coach Jon Sinclair of Anaerobic Management (www.anaerobic. net). 'First of all, it develops increased aerobic conditioning, which by itself yields faster times. Second, it produces the physical strength on which later, harder training can be built.'

What about interval training (alternating bursts of speed with recovery jogs) at this level? 'Not a good idea,' says Sinclair. 'Adding any intensity to a person's programme can be dangerous and counterproductive. At this stage in a runner's development, the first rule should be: do no harm. If they just run more, they will, in a few months, run faster.'

Remember: every run in this 6-week schedule should be a steady one, done at an effort that has you breathing 'comfortably hard' but well short of squinty-eyed wheezing. Enjoy each run, feel yourself becoming stronger and leaner and be proud of what you're doing.

THE PLAN

Week	Mon	Tues	Wed	Thurs	Fri	Sat	Sun	TOTAL
1	Rest	2 mi	Rest	2 mi	Rest	2 mi	Rest	6 mi
2	Rest	2.5 mi	Rest	2.5 mi	Rest	2.5 mi	Rest	7.5 mi
3	Rest	3 mi	Rest	3 mi	Rest	2.5 mi	2 mi	10.5 mi
4	Rest	3.5 mi	Rest	3.5 mi	Rest	3 mi	2 mi	12 mi
5	Rest	4 mi	2 mi	3.5 mi	Rest	3.5 mi	2 mi	15 mi
Taper	Rest	4 mi	2 mi	Rest	2 mi	Rest	5-K race	

RACE DAY: 'For a beginner, expending energy in a race can be scary and looked upon as a big barrier,' says coach Bob Williams (www.pacethyself.com), a contributor to *How to Train* by Hal Higdon. 'But if you've run at least that long in training many times and run negative splits (first half slower than the second) in the race, you'll enjoy the experience and finish feeling good.' Have a light breakfast with some fluids, then arrive early so you can pick up your race number and avoid the drain of queues. Do a little warm-up walking and jogging, sip some water, stretch a bit and generally chill out and stay stress-free until the start. Remind yourself that your goal is to run the whole way and finish feeling tired – but not exhausted.

Intermediate

You've been running consistently for at least a year and have run in a few races but mainly for the experience. You've dabbled in some modest interval training. Now you want to think seriously about your finishing time and how to lower it: to race, not just participate. To segue from finisher to racer, you'll need to add more weekly miles, yes, but more important, increase intensity in the form of timed intervals both at (pace intervals) and below (speed intervals) your 5-K goal pace, along with a crucial weekly hill-training session.

'Running hills once a week – a five- to six-grade is optimal – at a fairly hard effort for up to 3 minutes at a time is an ideal way to get stronger,' says Sinclair. Hill training greatly improves leg and gluteal strength while increasing aerobic capacity and stride length, along with ankle flexion that enables you to 'pop' off the ground more quickly.

How hard is 'fairly hard'? A classic study from years ago found that running up even a slight hill at a steady pace raises your heart rate up to 26 beats higher than the same effort on flat ground. So doing hill training at 5-K effort (not pace) is what to aim for.

Again, regarding intensity as opposed to mileage, a study in the online journal *Peak Performance* found that you'll run your best races from 5-K up not when you've run the most miles but when you hit a reasonable mileage level, and then crank up your intensity.

PACE INTERVALS (PI): If your 5-K goal is 10:00 (10-minute mile) pace (31:02 finishing time), run pace intervals at 1:15 (for 200 metres), 2:30 (400 metres), 5:00 (800 metres). For 9:00 pace (27:56), run 1:07 (200 metres), 2:15 (400 metres), 4:30 (800 metres). For 8:00 pace (24:50), run 1:00 (200 metres), 2:00 (400 metres), 4:00 (800 metres). For 7:00 pace (21:44), run 0:53 (200 metres), 1:45 (400 metres), 3:30 (800 metres). Recovery time for pace intervals: slowly jog half the distance of the repetition (i.e., 200-metre jog after 400-metre repetitions).

THE PLAN

Week	Mon	Tues	Wed	Thurs	Fri	Sat	Sun	Total
1	Rest	6 × 400 m PI	2–5 mi easy	Hills, 5–8 min	Rest	2–5 mi easy	4–6 mi easy	19–30 mi
2	Rest	2 × 800 m PI, 2 × 400 m PI, 2 × 200 m PI	2–5 mi easy	Hills, 5–8 min	Rest	2–5 mi easy	4–6 mi easy	19–30 mi
3	Rest	2 × 800 m PI, 2 × 400 m SI, 4 × 200 m SI	2–5 mi easy	Hills, 6–9 min	Rest	2–5 mi easy	5–7 mi easy	22–33 mi
4	Rest	2 × 800 m PI, 1 × 800 m SI, 2 × 400 m SI, 2 × 200 m SI	2–5 mi easy	Hills, 6–9 min	Rest	2–5 mi easy	5–8 mi easy	23–35 mi
5	Rest	2 × 800 m SI, 4 × 400 m SI, 4 × 200 m SI	2–5 mi easy	Hills, 7–10 min	Rest	2–5 mi easy	6–9 mi easy	26–38 mi
Taper	Rest	4 × 400 m SI, 4 × 200 m SI	2–5 mi easy	Rest	3 × 200 m SI, 3 × 150 m SI, 6 × 100 m SI	Rest	5-K race	

SPEED INTERVALS (SI): For 10:00 (10-minute mile) pace, run 1:11 (for 200 metres), 2:22 (400 metres), 4:44 (800 metres). For 9:00 pace, run 1:04 (200 metres), 2:08 (400 metres), 4:15 (800 metres). For 8:00 pace, run 0:56 (200 metres), 1:53 (400 metres), 3:45 (800 metres). For 7:00 pace, run 0:49 (200 metres), 1:38 (400 metres), 3:15 (800 metres). Recovery time for speed intervals: jog equal distance (i.e., 400-metre jog after 400-metre repetitions).

HILLS AND EASY RUNS: For 9-minute-mile pace, use the lower number; 7-minute-mile runners, move towards the higher.

INTERVAL AND HILL DAYS: Jog 2 miles to warm up, then run 4 × 100-metre strides to prime yourself for the workout. Jog 2 miles to cool down, then stretch.

RACE DAY: 'It's all about negative splits,' says Williams. 'Always.' That means you run the first half of the race slower than the second half. Hold back in the first mile, Williams advises, then 'seek out other runners to pass in the second mile, but don't push beyond a comfortably hard effort.' Increase gradually to discomfort in the last mile, and over the final 400 metres, try to pick it up.

Advanced

You have at least several years of serious running behind you, follow a year-round schedule, have run in many races at various distances, have done regular interval training, want to discover your personal performance ceiling, and are willing to push hard in training.

Two words define the training goal at this stage of your running life: *race feel*. To reach your 5-K ceiling, you must replicate in training how it feels to run that far that fast. That means timed repetitions both at (pace) and faster than (speed) your 5-K goal pace but with short recovery – uncomfortably short – because in a race, of course, there is no recovery. So the more intimate you become with the sensations of the race itself on a twice-weekly basis, the more you'll be able to handle the 5-K's physical and mental combination punches on race day.

We have legendary British coach Frank Horwill to thank for this. He found that when athletes were stuck at a certain 5-K time – sometimes for years – and could not break through, they were almost always running lots of repetitions significantly faster than 5-K race pace (sometimes as fast as 56 seconds) with 400-metre jogs. When Horwill pointed out that they would not have

400-metre recovery periods in a race, the usual reply was, 'But I'm running so much faster than race pace.' Sorry, Horwill said, it doesn't work that way. Invariably, when he had his runners do the repeats slightly faster than projected 5-K pace, with recovery jogs as short as 50 metres (about 20 seconds), their times dropped. 'They needed to get the feel of what it was like to run a tough 5-K race,' Horwill explains. 'The recovery time after repetitions at 5-K pace is a crucial factor. Aim to jog a quarter to half of the distance of the repetition.

PACE INTERVALS (PI): For 8:00 (8-minute mile) goal pace (24:50 finishing time), run 1:00 (for 200 metres), 1:30 (300 metres), 2:00 (400 metres), 4:00 (800 metres), 6:00 (1,200 metres). For 6:00 pace (18:38), run 0:45 (200 metres), 1:07 (300 metres), 1:30 (400 metres), 3:00 (800 metres), 4:30 (1,200 metres). To recover between pace intervals, jog a quarter the distance of the repetition (i.e., 100-metre jog after 400-metre repetitions).

SPEED INTERVALS (SI): For 8:00 minute-mile pace, run 0:56 (200 metres), 1:19 (300 metres), 1:52 (400 metres), 3:44 (800 metres), 5:38 (1,200 metres). For 6:00 pace, run 0:41 (200 metres), 1:01 (300 metres), 1:22 (400 metres), 2:44 (800 metres), 4:08 (1,200 metres). To recover between speed intervals, jog half the distance.

STRIDES (S): Gradually pick up speed to 90 per cent effort, hold that for 20 metres, and then decelerate. Do four to six repetitions of 80 to 100 metres after Wednesday and/or Saturday runs.

INTERVAL AND HILL DAYS: Jog 2 miles to warm up, then do 4 × 100-metre strides to prime yourself for the workout. Jog 2 miles to cool down, then stretch.

RACE DAY: Know the course. 'If you know how the hills and turns go,' says Sinclair, 'you can more easily match your efforts to the course. Also, study the last mile. In fact, run it as a warm-up. Look for markers a certain distance from the finish so you can expend your final energy at the right time.'

THE PLAN

Week	Mon	Tues	Wed	Thurs	Fri	Sat	Sun	Total
1	Rest	2 × 1,200 m PI, 2 × 800 m PI, 4 × 100 m S	4–6 mi easy	2 × 800 m SI, 2 × 400 m SI, 4 × 200 m SI	Rest	7–9 mi easy	4–6 mi easy	31–37 mi
2	Rest	10 × 300 m PI, 4 × 100 m S	4–6 mi easy	2 × 1,200 m SI, 1 × 800 m SI, 2 × 400 m SI, 4 × 200 m SI	Rest	7–9 mi easy	4–6 mi easy	31–37 mi
3	Rest	2 × 1,200 m PI, 2 × 800 m PI, 2 × 400 m PI, 4 × 400 m S	4–6 mi easy	2 × 800 m SI, 4 × 400 m SI, 4 × 200 m SI	Rest	8–10 mi easy	4–6 mi easy	32–38 mi
4	Rest	3 × 800 m SI, 4 × 100 m S	4–6 mi easy	3 × 800 m SI, 3 × 400 m SI, 3 × 200 m SI, 2 × 100 m S	Rest	8–10 mi easy	4–6 mi easy	32–38 mi
5	Rest	2 × 1,200 m PI, 2 × 800 m PI, 2 × 400 m PI, 2 × 200 m PI	4–6 mi easy	4 × 400 m SI, 4 × 300 m SI, 4 × 200 m SI, 4 × 100 m S	Rest	8–10 mi easy	4–6 mi easy	33–39 mi
Taper	Rest	2 × 400 m SI, 2 × 300 m SI, 2 × 200 m SI, full recovery, 6 × 100 m S	3 mi easy	4 × 200 m SI, 4 × 100 m S	Rest	5-K race	2 mi easy	

THE ULTIMATE 10-K PLAN

You'll be glad to hear that 10-K training forms the foundation of all-round fitness because it includes ample amounts of the three core components of distance running – strength, stamina and speed. You can use it to train for your goal 6.2-miler, yet with certain adjustments, you can also use it to prepare for everything from the 5-K to the marathon.

10-K TRAINING UNIVERSALS:
THINGS TO KNOW BEFORE YOU START

REST: Rest means no running – none. Give your muscles and synapses some serious rest so all systems are primed for the next workout. Better 2 quality days and 2 of total rest than 4 days of mediocrity resulting from lingering fatigue. Rest days give you a mental break as well, so you'll come back feeling refreshed.

EASY RUN: *Easy* means totally comfortable and controlled. If you're running with someone else, you should be able to converse easily. You'll likely feel as if you could go faster. Don't. Here's some incentive to take it easy: you'll still be burning 100 calories every mile you run, no matter how slow you go.

LONG RUN: This is any steady run at or longer than race distance designed to enhance endurance, which enables you to run longer and longer and feel strong doing it. A great long-run tip: find a weekly training partner for company. You'll have plenty of time to talk about anything that comes up.

SPEEDWORK: This means running in bursts at a distance shorter than the race – some at your race goal pace, some faster – which increases cardiac strength, biomechanical efficiency that translates into more miles per gallon and the psychological toughness racing demands. Remember, though, that you're not trying to kill yourself. Keep it fun.

Beginner

You're a notch above novice. You've been running at least 6 months and maybe have done a 5-K or two. You run 3 to 5 miles 3 or 4 days a week, have done a little fast running when you felt like it, and now you want to enter – and finish – what you consider a real 'distance race'. If you're a beginner, your 10-K goal is less a PB (personal best) than an LDF (longest distance finished). You want to run the whole 6.2 miles, so you're going for endurance. 'Basic aerobic strength is every runner's first need,' says coach Jon Sinclair of Anaerobic Management (www.anaerobic.net). So you'll do most of your running at a steady, moderate pace. But we're also going to add a dash of pseudo-speedwork into your endurance stew for flavour. This will put some added spring into your step, give you a brief taste of what it feels like to run a little faster and hasten your segue to the intermediate level. Every week, in addition to steady running, you're going to do two extra things: aerobic intervals and gentle pick-ups.

THE PLAN

Week	Mon	Tues	Wed	Thurs	Fri	Sat	Sun	Total
1	Rest	2 mi, 4 × 1:00 AI, 2 mi	3 mi or rest	4 mi + 3 GP	Rest	5 mi	Rest	13–20 mi
2	Rest	2 mi	3 mi or rest	4 mi + 3 GP	Rest	5.5 mi	3.5 mi	15–21 mi
3	Rest	2 mi, 4 × 1:30 AI, 2 mi	3 mi or rest	4.5 mi + 3 GP	Rest	6 mi	4 mi	18.5–22 mi
4	Rest	2 mi, 6 × 1:30 AI, 2 mi	3 mi or rest	4.5 mi + 6 GP	Rest	6.5 mi	4.5 mi	20–24 mi
5	Rest	2 mi, 4 × 2:00 AI, 2 mi	2 mi	Rest	2 mi + 2GP	Rest	10-K race	

AEROBIC INTERVALS (AI): Push the pace just a bit and breathe a little harder. Follow by slowly jogging until you feel rested enough to resume your regular tempo. And you always, always stay well short of going anaerobic (simply stated: squinty-eyed and gasping for breath). Treat these runs like play. When you do them, try to re-create that feeling you had as a child when you ran to the park and couldn't wait to get there.

GENTLE PICK-UPS (GP): Gradually increase your pace over 100 metres to about 90 per cent of all-out, hold it there for 10 to 20 metres, then gradually decelerate. Walk to full recovery before you start the next one. Nothing big, nothing really stressful – just enough to let your body say, 'Ah, so this is what it feels like to go fast.' Note: after a few AI/GP weeks, your normal pace will begin to feel more comfortable. And you'll become race-fit more quickly this way.

RACE DAY: Have some fluids and a light breakfast about 2 hours before the start, and arrive early enough to collect your number without the stress of long queues (if you haven't received it in advance). Walk around about 10 minutes before the start; maybe even do a few minutes of slow jogging. Start off slower than you think you should and work gradually into a comfortable and controlled pace. Let the race come to you. If there is a drinks station, stop to drink and relax for 10 seconds.

Intermediate

You've been running a year or more, done some 5-Ks, maybe even a 10-K. But you always finish feeling like you could have or should have gone faster. You consider yourself mainly a recreational runner, but you still want to make a commitment to see how fast you can go. Here's the two-pronged approach that will move you to the cusp of competitive athlete.

First, you'll add miles to your endurance-building long run until it makes up 30 per cent of your weekly mileage. Second, you'll now do a substantial amount of tempo running aimed at elevating your anaerobic threshold, the speed above which blood lactate levels skyrocket – a gulping-and-gasping prelude to your engine shutting down for the day. How to avoid this unpleasantness? With regular sessions at a little slower than 10-K pace – that is, tempo-run pace. This will significantly improve your endurance and running efficiency in just 6 weeks. So your tempo work will include weekly '10-10s', along with a mix of intervals and uphill running, all of which strengthen your running muscles, heart and related aerobic systems.

Oh, one more thing: running fast requires effort – and some discomfort. Still, be conservative. If you can't maintain the same pace throughout a given workout or your body shrieks '*No more!*' then call it a day. And maybe adjust your pace next time.

PACE INTERVALS (PI): Run at 10-K goal pace to improve efficiency and stamina and to give you the feel of your race pace. With pace and speed intervals (below), jog half the interval distance to recover. For 10:00 (10-minute mile) goal pace (a 1:02:06 10-K), run 2:30 (for 400 metres), 5:00 (800 metres), 7:30 (1,200 metres). For 9:00 pace (55:53), run 2:15 (400 metres), 4:30 (800 metres), 6:45 (1,200 metres). For 8:00 pace (49:40), run 2:00 (400 metres), 4:00 (800 metres), 6:00 (1,200 metres).

SPEED INTERVALS (SI): Run these at 30 seconds per mile faster than goal pace. For 10:00 minute mile pace, run 2:22 (400 metres), 4:44 (800 metres), 7:06 (1,200 metres). For 9:00 pace, run 2:08 (400 metres), 4:16 (800 metres), 6:24 (1,200 metres). For 8:00 pace, run 1:53 (400 metres), 3:45 (800 metres), 5:38 (1,200 metres).

10-10S: Run 10-minute tempo repeats at 30 seconds per mile slower than 10-K goal pace; follow each with a 3- to 5-minute slow jog.

TOTAL UPHILL TIME (TUT): Run repetitions up the same hill, or work the uphill sections of a road or trail course.

STRIDES (S): Over 100 metres, gradually accelerate to about 90 per cent of all-out, hold it there for 5 seconds, and then smoothly decelerate. Walk to full recovery after each.

RACE DAY: 'Many intermediate runners run too fast in the first 5-K,' says Sinclair. 'That's the surest way to run a mediocre time. Even pace is best, which means the first half of the race should feel really easy.' Sinclair's wife and co-coach, Kim Jones, also a former Olympian, adds this: 'Divide the race into three 2-mile sections: doable pace for the first 2, push a bit the middle 2, then go hard the last 2.'

THE PLAN

Week	Mon	Tues	Wed	Thurs	Fri	Sat	Sun	Total
1	Rest	2 mi, 1 or 2 × 10-10, 2 mi	4 mi	1 × 400 m PI, 1 × 800 m PI, 1 × 1,200 m PI, 1 × 800 m PI, 1 × 400 m PI	Rest	4 mi, 4 × 100 m S	6–7 mi	23–24 mi
2	Rest	6 mi, incl 6:00 TUT	4 mi	1 × 1,200 m PI, 2 × 800 m PI, 4 × 200 m PI, 4 × 200 m SI, 4 × 100 m S	Rest	4.5 mi, 5 × 100 m S	7–8 mi	29–30 mi
3	Rest	2 mi, 2 or 3 × 10-10, 2 mi	4 mi	1 × 800 m PI, 1 × 1,200 m PI, 1 × 800 m PI, 2 × 400 m SI, 4 × 200 m SI	Rest	5 mi, 6 × 100 m S	7–8 mi	29–30 mi

Week	Mon	Tues	Wed	Thurs	Fri	Sat	Sun	Total
4	Rest	6–7 mi, incl 8:00 TUT	4 mi	1 × 1,200 m SI, 1 × 800 m SI, 2 × 400 m SI, 2 × 200 m SI, 4 × 100 m S	Rest	5 mi, 6 × 100 m S	8–9 mi	30–32 mi
5	Rest	2 mi, 3 or 4 × 10-10, 2 mi	4 mi	1 × 800 m SI, 4 × 400 m SI, 4 × 200 m SI, 1 × 800 m SI, 4 × 100 m S	Rest	6 mi, 6 × 100 m S	8–9 mi	31–32 mi
Taper	Rest	800 m SI, 2 × 200 m SI, 400 m SI, 2 × 200 m SI, 6 × 100 m S	4 mi, 4 × 200 m SI, 4 × 100 m S	Rest	3 mi easy, 3 × 100 m S	10-K race		

Advanced

You've been a serious runner for several years and have run many races – perhaps even a marathon. You're familiar with fartleks and intervals and can run comfortably for an hour-plus. Now you want a breakthrough time – and you're willing to put in a rigorous 6 weeks to achieve it.

The cornerstone of 10-K training has long been the tempo run – great for stamina-seeking intermediates working their way up the racing-fitness food chain, but not for you. Why not? A study found that short intervals at – not below – 5-K and 10-K race pace (roughly, our speed and pace intervals below) produced huge improvements, compared with tempo runs. (Note: tempo running produced improvements, but faster running did better still.) The study, reported in the journal *Peak Performance*, found that 'those doing intervals trained faster than the tempo runners and therefore developed better economy, coordination and comfort while running fast,' which translated into faster 10-K running. Moreover, the interval group spent just 31 minutes during two sessions per week running their reps, while the tempo runners required 58 minutes for their two sessions. So there you go. That's why we're going to put you on a 6-week diet of quick stuff – medium long on Tuesdays, short and swift on Thursdays. And we're going to make sure you maintain your vital aerobic base, as you'll be doing solid mileage as well.

PACE INTERVALS (PI): For both pace and speed intervals, run 2 miles easy, plus four 100-metre strides before each session and 2 miles easy afterward. For 8:00 (8-minute mile) goal pace (49:40 finishing time), run 2:00 (for 400 metres), 4:00 (800 metres), 6:00 (1,200 metres). For 7:00 pace (43:28), run 0:53 (200 metres), 1:45 (400 metres), 3:30 (800 metres), 5:15 (1,200 metres). For 6:00 pace (37:15), run 0:45 (200 metres), 1:30 (400 metres), 4:30 (1,200 metres). Recovery is a 1-minute jog (after 400-metre reps), 2:00 (800 metres), and 3:00 (1,200 metres).

SPEED INTERVALS (SI): For 8:00 minute mile pace, run 1:53 (400 metres), 3:45 (800 metres) 5:38 (1,200 metres). For 7:00 pace, run 0:49 (200 metres), 1:38 (400 metres), 4:53 (1,200 metres). For 6:00 pace, run 0:41 (200 metres), 1:22 (400 metres), 2:44 (800 metres), 4:08 (1,200 metres).

LACTATE SESSIONS (LS): LS training involves running about as fast as you can for 1 minute, followed by 3 to 4 minutes of slow jogging.

THE PLAN

Week	Mon	Tues	Wed	Thurs	Fri	Sat	Sun	Total
1	Rest	2 × 1,200 PI, 2 × 800 PI, 4 × 400 PI, 6 × 100 S	4–6 mi	2 × 800 SI, 4 × 400 SI, 4 × 200 SI, 4 × 100 S	Rest or 3–4 mi easy	4–6 mi, 6 × 100 S	8–10 mi	32–42 mi
2	Rest	2 × 1,200 SI, 1 × 800 SI, 1 × 400 SI, 1 × 200 SI, 6 × 100 S	4–6 mi	4 × 200 SI, 4 LS, 4 × 100 S	Rest or 3–4 mi easy	5–7 mi, 6 × 100 S	8–10 mi	32–42 mi
3	Rest	2 × 1 mi PI, 1 × 1,200 SI, 1 × 800 SI, 1 × 400 SI, 6 × 100 S	4–6 mi	4 × 200 SI, 4 LS, 4 × 200 SI, 4 × 100 S	Rest or 3–4 mi easy	5–7 mi	9–11 mi	33–43 mi
4	Rest	2 × 1,200 SI, 1 × 800 SI, 1 × 400 SI, 1 × 200 SI, 6 × 100 S	4–6 mi	5–7 LS, 6 × 100 S	Rest or 3–4 mi easy	5–7 mi, 6 × 100 S	9–11 mi	33–44 mi
5	Rest	2 × 400 SI, 1 × 800 SI, 1 × 200 SI, 1 × 800 SI, 6 × 100 S	4–6 mi	6–8 mi	Rest or 3–4 mi easy	5–7 mi, 6 × 100 S	10–12 mi	34–46 mi
Taper	Rest	1 × 1,200 SI, 1 × 800 S, 2 × 400 SI, 4 × 100 S	Rest	4 × 200 SI, 4 × 100 S, 4 × 200 SI, 4 × 100 S	Rest	3 mi easy, 3 × 100 S	10-K race	

STRIDES (S): Over 100 metres, gradually accelerate to about 90 per cent of all-out, hold it there for 5 seconds, and then smoothly decelerate. Walk to full recovery after each. Strides aren't meant to tire you out – just the opposite. They'll add zip to your legs.

RACE DAY: Know the course. 'If you know how the hills and turns go,' says Sinclair, 'you can more easily match your efforts to the course. Also, study the last mile. In fact, run it as a warm-up. Look for markers a certain distance from the finish so you can expend your final energy at the right time.'

THE ULTIMATE HALF-MARATHON TRAINING PLAN

Half-marathons are becoming as enticing as their big brother the marathon. The popularity of the world's biggest half, the Great North Run, shows no signs of waning and other halfs keep growing too. Here's why: for newer racers who've maybe finished a couple of 5- or 10-Ks, the half offers a worthy-yet-doable challenge without the training and racing commitment of the marathon. For more experienced athletes, training for a half bolsters stamina for shorter, faster races, plus it boosts endurance for a full 26.2-mile challenge down the road. In fact, the half is the ideal dress rehearsal for its twice-as-long kin. And unlike a marathon, which can leave your tank drained for a month or more, you can bounce back from a hard half in as little as 2 weeks. So find a flat, friendly half a few months away. To get you there primed and ready, here are three can't-fail schedules.

HALF-MARATHON TRAINING UNIVERSALS: THINGS TO KNOW BEFORE YOU START

REST: This means no running. Give your muscles and synapses some serious rest so all systems are primed for the next workout.

Better 2 quality days and 2 of total rest than 4 days of mediocrity resulting from lingering fatigue. Rest days give you a mental break as well, so you come back refreshed.

EASY RUN: This is totally comfortable and controlled. If you're running with someone else, you should be able to converse easily. You'll likely feel as if you could go faster. Don't.

LONG RUN: This is any steady run at or longer than race distance designed to enhance endurance, which enables you to run longer and longer and feel strong doing it.

SPEEDWORK: This means running in bursts at a distance shorter than the race – some at your race goal pace, some faster – which increases cardiac strength, biomechanical efficiency, better running economy and the psychological toughness that racing demands. Still, you want to keep it fun.

Beginner

You've run for at least a year, but you're still a racing neophyte. You can run 5 miles at a time without distress, average 15 to 20 miles a week and have finished a 5-K, perhaps even a 10-K. Now you want to go longer, though not yet to a full marathon, and your race time is less important to you than finishing.

As a beginner, you're going to do two things: first, incrementally increase your weekly mileage and long run, which translates into more endurance. You'll need this in order to run for more than 2 hours. Second, you'll do some gradually longer bits of running at faster than your normal pace to build up your stamina and keep you strong over the last third of the race.

'Even for a beginner, 2 of your training days a week should be challenging,' says coach Bob Williams. 'The goal here is to boost the endurance needed to run 13.1 miles.' To this end, if you can handle it, make uphill running a part of your Thursday routine.

Note that in week 7 or 8, you'll log 10 miles – your first-ever double-digit run and a worthy achievement in its own right: a run you won't forget in a hurry.

THE PLAN

Week	Mon	Tues	Wed	Thurs	Fri	Sat	Sun	Total
1	Rest	2 mi, 5–7 × 1:00 AI, 2 mi	Rest	4 mi + 4 GP	Rest	3–4 mi	6–7 mi	19–21 mi
2	Rest	2 mi, 5–7 × 1:00 AI, 2 mi	Rest	4 mi + 4 GP	Rest	3–4 mi	6–7 mi	19–21 mi
3	Rest	2 mi, 2 × [1:00, 1:30, or 2:00] AI, 2 mi	Rest	4 mi, incl 4 × 1:00 AI + 5–6 GP	Rest	5-K race	4–5 mi	16–17 mi
4	Rest	3 mi, 3 × [2:00 or 2:30] AI, 2 mi	Rest	5–6 mi, incl 4 × 1:30 AI + 6 GP	Rest	3–4 mi	7–8 mi	21–24 mi
5	Rest	3 mi, 3 × [2:00 or 2:30] AI, 2 mi	Rest	5–6 mi, incl 4 × 1:30 AI + 6 GP	Rest	3–4 mi	7–8 mi	21–24 mi
6	Rest	3 mi, 2 × 2:00 AI, 2 × 2:30 AI, 1 × 3:00 AI + 6 GP, 2 mi	Rest	5–6 mi + 4 GP	Rest	10-K race	4 mi	22–30 mi
7	Rest	3 mi, 2 × [2:00, 3:00, or 4:00] AI, 2 mi	Rest	6 mi, incl 4 × 2:00 AI + 6 GP	Rest	5–6 mi	9–10 mi	26–28 mi
8	Rest	3 mi, 2 × [2:00, 3:00, or 4:00] AI, 2 mi	Rest	6 mi, incl. 4 × 2:00 AI + 6 GP	Rest	5–6 mi	9–10 mi	26–28 mi
Taper	Rest	2 mi, 4 × 1:00 AI	Rest	2 mi easy, 4 × GP	Rest	2 mi	Half-mara-thon race	

AEROBIC INTERVALS (AI): You push the pace but just a little. Find a tempo that feels somewhere between comfortable and 'I'm stretching myself a little.' Don't run this too hard. Trying to add too much intensity while you're also increasing mileage spells I-N-J-U-R-Y. When you finish the timed AI, jog very slowly until your breathing returns to normal, then work back into your regular pace. On all other days, just run your assigned miles as you feel.

GENTLE PICK-UPS (GP): At the end of your run, walk for several minutes, then slowly increase your leg turnover on a flat stretch for 100 metres – the straight away on a track – up to the point where you start to breathe hard. Hold it there for 10 to 20 metres, then gradually slow down. Walk to full recovery before you start the next one. The purpose of both AI and GP is to improve your stamina, leg speed and running efficiency and to make your normal pace feel more comfortable. What's more, this kind of up-tempo running adds variety to your training – always a good thing.

RACE DAY: Start at the back of the pack and run more slowly than you think you should for the first few miles. Keep it reined in. Stay completely comfortable. Work your way into a controlled rhythm as the race proceeds, and stop at drinks stations as you need to. Slow down to a walk, drink, stretch your legs, and rest a bit if you'd like. Then get going again. With a well-rested body from your taper week, and thanks to race-day adrenaline and the energy of the field, you'll get through the last 3 miles with no trouble.

Intermediate

You have a solid aerobic base. You have been running consistently for several years, tried various kinds of speed training, average 25 to 30 miles a week and may even have finished a half-marathon. But now you want to race a half. That is, you have a specific finishing time in mind, and you're willing to train hard to achieve it.

'Intermediate runners have enough experience and strength to support some faster running – but within the context of increased weekly mileage and an adequate long run, which remains the key to improvement at this level,' says coach Jon Sinclair of Anaerobic Management (www.anaerobic.net). 'So be careful when you add speed, because what we're after here is greater endurance, the ability to run longer at race pace.' That's the crux of the intermediate plan. Sinclair also suggests 'adding some tempo to at least some of the long runs when you're maybe going just a bit faster over the final 10 to 15 minutes.' That's *a bit* faster, okay? No eye-popping straining.

'I would also include some interval miles at faster-than-projected race pace,' Sinclair adds. 'Interval tempo here should be challenging but not too crazy. And the recovery should be enough to support the effort – down to a 120 heart rate, 400-metre jog, whatever it takes. If the rest isn't long enough, you can't maintain the quality.'

PACE INTERVALS (PI): These relatively lengthy repetitions at your goal half-marathon per-mile pace build endurance and develop pace judgment. Note: all numbers in parentheses in the plan denote distance of recovery jog.

CRUISE INTERVALS (CI): Run these at 10-K race pace to promote stamina and the ability to run strong when tired. For 10:00 (10-minute mile) goal pace (2:11:06), run 7:07 (for 1,200 metres), 4:45 (800 metres). For 9:00 pace (1:57:59), run 6:24 (1,200 metres), 4:16 (800 metres). For 8:00 pace (1:44:52), run 5:42 (1,200 metres), 3:48 (800 metres).

SPEED INTERVALS (SI): Run these at 5-K race pace to promote relaxed speed and a sense of comfort at your considerably slower half-marathon pace. For 10:00 minute mile pace, run 4:30 (800 metres), 2:15 (400 metres), 1:07 (200 metres). For 9:00 pace, run 4:04 (800 metres), 2:02 (400 metres), 1:01 (200 metres). For 8:00 pace, run 3:37 (800 metres), 1:48 (400 metres), 0:54 (200 metres).

THE PLAN

Week	Mon	Tues	Wed	Thurs	Fri	Sat	Sun	Total
1	Rest	1 × 1,200 PI (400), 2 × 800 CI (200), 4 × 200 SI (200)	3–4 mi or rest	2 × 2 mi PI (800) + 4 × 100 S	Rest	4 mi + 4 × 100 S	8–9 mi	25–30 mi
2	Rest	1 × 1,200 PI (400), 2 × 800 CI (200), 4 × 200 SI (200)	3–4 mi or rest	2 × 2 mi PI (800) + 4 × 100S	Rest	4 mi + 4 × 100 S	8–9 mi (incl 4:00 TUT)	25–30 mi
3	Rest	2 × [1,200 CI (600), 800 CI (400), 400 SI (200)]	2 mi	3 mi + 4 × 100 S	Rest	5-K race	6 mi	24 mi
4	Rest	2 × 1-mi CI (800), 6 × 200 SI (200)	3–4 mi or rest	4 mi PI (800), 1 mi CI + 6 × 100 S	Rest	5 mi + 6 × 100 S	10 mi, incl 6:00 TUT	28–32 mi
5	Rest	2 × 1 mi CI (800), 6 × 200 SI (200)	3–4 mi or rest	4 mi PI (800), 1 mi CI + 6 × 100 S	Rest	5 mi + 6 × 100 S	11 mi	28–32 mi
6	Rest	2 × [800 SI (400), 400 SI (200), 200 SI (200), 1,200 PI]	3–4 mi or rest	4 mi (incl 6 × 1:00 SI) + 4 × 100 S	Rest	10-K race	8 mi	30 mi
7	Rest	2 × 1,200 CI (600), 4 × 400 SI (200), 4 × 200 SI (100)	3–4 mi or rest	4 mi PI (800), 1 × 800 CI (400), 2 mi PI	Rest	6 mi + 6 × 100 S	11–12 mi, incl 8:00 TUT	32–37 mi
8	Rest	2 × 1,200 CI (600), 4 × 400 SI (200), 4 × 200 SI (100)	3–4 mi or rest	4 mi PI (800), 1 × 800 CI (400), 2 mi PI	Rest	6 mi + 6 × 100 S	6 mi	32–36 mi
Taper	Rest	4 × 400 CI (200), 2 × 200 SI (100)	2 mi PI + 4 × 100 S	2 × 400 CI (200), 1 × 200 SI	Rest	3 mi easy	Half-mara-thon race	

STRIDES (S): Over 100 metres, gradually accelerate to 90 per cent of all-out, hold it for 5 seconds, and then decelerate. Walk to full recovery after each.

TOTAL UPHILL TIME (TUT): Work the uphill sections during your run at something near a strong 10-K effort in the total time called for.

RACE DAY: To warm up, jog just 800 metres, then do a few fast strides. That's it. Keep your glycogen tanks topped off and your legs fresh. Divide your half like this: 10-mile run, 5-K race. Run the first mile just slower than goal pace, then work into a rhythm and run just below your lactate threshold level so you don't implode an hour into it. And draft off other runners to conserve energy. Do all that, and you'll be fine.

Advanced

You've run and raced for many years. You've finished just about every distance – half-marathon and perhaps full marathon included – and have averaged 35-plus miles a week for at least the last 6 months. You've run some PBs at shorter distances, and now you want to push yourself without putting in the major mileage a marathon demands. And you're willing, even eager, to increase the intensity of your speedwork.

'A primary goal at the advanced level is increased weekly mileage, and make sure it includes an adequate long run,' advises Sinclair. 'Everyone understands the need to do a long run for a marathon, but too many fail to see the need for it in training for a half. Don't do loads of them, but doing one or two really helps.'

And there's another thing: at this point in your running life, 'long run' doesn't mean just more time on your feet. It means sticking some intensity in there. Focusing less on adding length and more on adding quality is vital to a good racing effort over a long distance like the half. This plan has a few patterns for you to play with, such as LRS (long run stamina) and LRFF (long run fast finish). It also has you doing increasingly longer runs at your half-marathon pace to teach your body what it feels like.

Last, to run a PB half, you must be able – and willing – to maintain a fast-for-you pace in the face of increasing fatigue. So you need to train to run goal pace after having already done enough running to tire yourself. This is the purpose of our fatigue-fighter sessions – short, sub-race-pace reps followed by an extended run at your half-marathon goal speed to simulate the demands of the race itself.

PACE INTERVALS (PI): These relatively lengthy repetitions at your goal half-marathon per-mile pace build endurance and develop pace judgment. Note: all numbers in parentheses in the plan denote distance of recovery jog.

CRUISE INTERVALS (CI): Run these at 10-K race pace to promote stamina and the ability to run strong when tired. For 8:00 (8-minute mile) goal pace (1:44:52 finishing time), run 5:42 (for 1,200 metres), 3:48 (800 metres). For 7:00 pace (1:31:46), run 6:40 (1 mile), 5:00 (1,200 metres), 3:20 (800 metres). For 6:00 pace (1:18:39), run 5:34 (1mile), 4:10 (1,200 metres), 2:47 (800 metres).

SPEED INTERVALS (SI): Run these at 5-K race pace to promote relaxed speed and a sense of comfort at your considerably slower half-marathon pace. For 8:00 minute mile goal pace (1:44:52), run 3:37 (800 metres), 1:48 (400 metres), 0:54 (200 metres). For 7:00 pace, run 3:09 (800 metres), 1:35 (400 metres), 0:48 (200 metres). For 6:00 pace, run 2:42 (800 metres), 1:22 (400 metres), 0:41 (200 metres).

STRIDES (S): Over 100 metres, gradually accelerate to 90 per cent of all-out, hold it for 5 seconds and then decelerate. Walk to full recovery after each.

FATIGUE-FIGHTER INTERVALS (FFI): These combine speed and pace intervals nearly back-to-back-to-back (very short recoveries) to work on maintaining pace and staying relaxed as you gradually tire. Yes, they're challenging. Jog 5 to 7 minutes easy between sets.

THE PLAN

Week	Mon	Tues	Wed	Thurs	Fri	Sat	Sun	Total
1	Rest	4 × 1 mi PI (400), 6 × 200 SI (100)	4 mi or rest	3 mi PI, 2 × 800 CI (200) + 4 × 100 S	4 mi or rest	6 mi + 4 × 100 S	13 mi LR	31–39 mi
2	Rest	4 × 1 mi PI (400), 6 × 200 SI (100)	4 mi or rest	3 mi PI, 2 × 800 CI (200) + 4 × 100 S	4 mi or rest	6 mi + 4 × 100 S	14 mi LRFF	33–41 mi
3	Rest	FFI 2 × [400 SI (100), 1,200 CI (200), 2,000 PI]	4 mi + 6 × 100 fast S	4 mi PI	Rest	5-K race	10 mi LR	28 mi
4	Rest	3 × 1.5 mi CI (400)	4 mi or rest	6 mi alternating 2:00–3:00 CI w/1:00 jogs	3 mi easy or rest	6 mi + 6 × 100 S	15 mi LRS	32–39 mi
5	Rest	FFI 2 × [400 SI (100), 1,200 CI (200), 2,400 PI]	4 mi or rest	6 mi alternating 2:00–3:00 CI w/1:00 jogs	3 mi easy or rest	6 mi + 6 × 100 S	16 mi LRF	34–41 mi
6	Rest	4 × 1,200 CI (200), 6 × 200 SI (100)	4 mi or rest	2 × [400 SI (100), 800 SI (200), 400 SI]	Rest	10-K race	12 mi LR	30–34 mi
7	Rest	FFI 2 × [400 SI (100), 1,200 CI (200), 3,200 PI]	3 mi PI	5–6 mi PI	Rest	6 mi + 6 × 100 S	17 mi LRS	39–40 mi
8	Rest	2 × 1,200 SI (400), 6 × 200 SI (55), 2 × 1,200 SI (400)	3 mi PI	6–7 mi PI	Rest	6 mi + 6 × 100 fast S	10 mi LR	33–34 mi
Taper	Rest	6 × 400 CI (100)	3 mi PI	2 × 400 CI (200), 2 × 200 SI (100)	Rest	3 mi easy	Half-marathon race	

LONG RUN (LR): This means a moderate pace (roughly 60 to 75 seconds slower than your half-marathon goal pace). Long run stamina (LRS) means to run 3 to 6 miles at half-marathon goal pace in the middle third of the run, long run fartlek (LRF) means to alternate 1 minute at 10-K pace with 1-minute jogs in the middle third of the run, and long run fast finish (LRFF) means to run the final 15 minutes at 10-K pace.

THE ULTIMATE MARATHON TRAINING PLAN

The 5-K is friendly; the 10-K, classic; and the half-marathon, a self-esteem pumping long-distance race. But none of these has the cachet that is the marathon's alone. From the time you finish your first shorter race, the spectre of the 26.2-miler hovers in your mind, something that one day you want to do. Have to do. Will do. Why? Because, like Everest, the marathon is there. It gives the ordinary person an opportunity to do something extraordinary. And for those who have finished a marathon and now want to race one, well, there's a plan here for you, too. So, ready to commit to your first finish or your fastest time? Good. Then read through our three runner profiles, work out which of our plans fits you best, go to the matching 16-week schedule – and get going.

MARATHON TRAINING UNIVERSALS:
THINGS TO KNOW BEFORE YOU START

REST: This doesn't merely mean no running; it means no cross-training as well. It's a day off, full stop. Try to relax as much as possible. Your body and mind will need this weekly reprieve, especially when you hit your mega-mile weeks.

REPEAT: All of your non-race training weeks will be repeated; that is, weeks 1 and 2, 6 and 7, and so on will be the same. This lets you make adaptations in pace and recovery based on your experience the first time around – an opportunity to master one cycle before moving on to the next, more rigorous one.

GO SOFT: In training, run on even grass, trails or hard-packed ground whenever possible to reduce impact.

HYDRATE WISELY: Drink the same sports drinks or fluids in training that you will use in the marathon. No need to add stomach problems to the stress of race day.

BECOME RACE FIT: Shorter races are terrific fitness boosters that let you run much faster than your marathon goal pace – an effort that you just cannot replicate in training, no matter how motivated you are. So all three schedules feature two races.

Beginner

You've run 15 to 20 miles a week for at least 6 months, completed a 5-K or 10-K – perhaps even something longer. You can run 5 or 6 miles without collapsing afterwards and want to gradually become a stronger runner able to finish your first marathon – in the words of coach Bob Williams – 'feeling good and excited to run another one.'

You're going to train just 3 to 4 days a week and gradually increase your weekly mileage for a total of around 17 to 35-plus miles a week. The biggest key of all will be your weekend long run. 'The beginner needs to focus almost entirely on the long run,' says coach Jon Sinclair of Anaerobic Management (www.anaerobic.net), 'but it's also good to throw in a little hill work and some aerobic intervals on alternate weeks to bolster your stamina and to liven up your training.' Last, you'll run two low-key races to get the feel of competition before the big day.

AEROBIC INTERVALS (AI): These timed repetitions (of 2 to 3 minutes) are slightly faster than your normal training pace – enough to make you breathe harder but still not go anaerobic (panting, gasping, on the verge of out of breath). Jog slowly after each repetition until you are refreshed enough to run the next.

THE PLAN

Week	Mon	Tues	Wed	Thurs	Fri	Sat	Sun	Total
1	Rest	4 mi, incl 4:00 TUT	Rest	1-hr run	Rest	4 mi	6 mi	19–20 mi
2	Rest	4 mi, incl 4:00 TUT	Rest	1-hr run	Rest	4 mi	7 mi	20–21 mi
3	Rest	4 mi, incl 5:00 TUT	Rest	6 mi	Rest	Rest	8 mi	18 mi
4	Rest	4 mi, incl 5:00 TUT	Rest	6 mi	Rest	Rest	9 mi	19 mi
5	Rest	4 mi, incl 3 × 2:00 AI	Rest	4 mi	Rest	5-K race	6–8 mi	17–19 mi
6	Rest	5 mi, incl 6:00 TUT	Rest	7 mi	Rest	Rest	10 mi	22 mi
7	Rest	5 mi, incl 6:00 TUT	Rest	7 mi	Rest	Rest	12 mi	24 mi
8	Rest	5 mi, incl 7:00 TUT	Rest	8 mi	Rest	Rest	12 mi	25 mi
9	Rest	5 mi, incl 7:00 TUT	Rest	8 mi	Rest	Rest	14 mi	27 mi
10	Rest	5 mi, incl 3 × 3:00 AI	Rest	4 mi	Rest	10-K race	5 mi	20 mi
11	Rest	5 mi, incl 8:00 TUT	Rest	9 mi	Rest	Rest	16 mi	30 mi
12	Rest	5 mi, incl 8:00 TUT	Rest	9 mi	Rest	Rest	18 mi	32 mi
13	Rest	5 mi, incl 9:00 TUT	Rest	10 mi	Rest	4 mi	20 mi	39 mi
14	Rest	5 mi, incl 9:00 TUT	Rest	10 mi	Rest	4 mi	10 mi	29 mi
15	Rest	3 mi, incl 3 × 3:00 AI	Rest	5 mi	Rest	3 mi, incl 3 × 2:00 AI	5 mi	16 mi
16	Rest	3 mi, incl 3 × 2:00 AI	Rest	3 mi jog	Rest	2 mi jog	Marathon	

TOTAL UPHILL TIME (TUT): This is the total number of minutes you spend running semivigorously up inclines – could be repeats up the same hill or over a hilly loop.

EASY RUN: This should be totally comfortable and controlled. If you're running with someone else, you should be able to chat easily. You'll likely feel as if you could go faster, but don't.

LONG RUN: This is any steady run up to 22 miles. It will enhance endurance, which enables you to run longer and longer and feel strong doing it.

SPEEDWORK: This means running in bursts at a distance shorter than the race – some at your race goal pace, some faster – which improves cardiac strength, biomechanical efficiency, running economy and the psychological toughness that racing demands.

RACE DAY: Run slower than you feel like you should over the first 12 to 13 miles. Look around and chat a bit with fellow runners. Walk through the aid stations, drink fluids, take a little break then slowly resume your running.

Intermediate

You regularly run 20 to 30 miles a week and have done so for a year or more. You do a weekly long run of 8 to 10 miles and have some experience with tempo runs or intervals. You've run 10-K races and probably finished a half-marathon, maybe even a full marathon. But now you have a specific marathon goal time in mind, and you want to do the training to make it a reality.

THE PLAN

Week	Mon	Tues	Wed	Thurs	Fri	Sat	Sun	Total
1	Rest	2 mi GP, 2 mi T, 2 mi GP	3 mi 4 × 100 S	1-hr run, incl 4:00–5:00 TUT	Rest	4 mi	8 mi	27–31 mi
2	Rest	2 mi GP, 2 mi T, 2 mi GP	3 mi 4 × 100 S	1-hr run, incl 4:00–5:00 TUT	Rest	4 mi	10 mi	29–33 mi
3	Rest	2 mi GP, 4 × 1 mi T (1:00), 2 mi GP	3 mi 5 × 100 S	70-min run, incl 5:00–6:00 TUT	Rest	5 mi	12 mi	35–39 mi
4	Rest	2 mi GP, 4 × 1 mi T (1:00), 2 mi GP	3 mi 5 × 100 S	70-min run, incl 5:00–6:00 TUT	Rest	5 mi	14 mi	32–33 mi

Week	Mon	Tues	Wed	Thurs	Fri	Sat	Sun	Total
5	Rest	4 × 1,200 C	3 mi 4 × 100 S	4 × 800 SI	Rest	5-K race	10 mi	28–30 mi
6	Rest	2 mi GP, 2 × 2 mi T, 3 mi GP	3 mi, 6 × 100 S	80-min run, incl 6:00–8:00 TUT	Rest	5 mi	15 mi	39–43 mi
7	Rest	2 mi GP, 2 × 2 mi T, 3 mi GP	3 mi, 6 × 100 S	80-min run, incl 6:00–8:00 TUT	Rest	5 mi	16 mi	40–44 mi
8	Rest	2 mi GP, 3 × 2 mi T (2:00), 3 mi GP	3 mi, 6 × 100 S	4 × 1 mi	Rest	5 mi	16 mi	44–47 mi
9	Rest	2 mi GP, 3 × 2 mi T (2:00), 3 mi GP	3 mi, 6 × 100 S	4 × 1 mi	Rest	5 mi	17 mi	45–48 mi
10	Rest	1-hr run, incl 2 × 1,200 C, 2 × 400 SI	4 mi	4 × 800 S, 6 × 100 S	Rest	10-K race	6–8 mi	32–34 mi
11	Rest	2 mi GP, 4 × 2 mi T (2:00), 3 mi GP	3 mi, 6 × 100 S	90-min run, incl 8:00–10:00 TUT	Rest	4 mi	18 mi	45–51 mi
12	Rest	2 mi GP, 4 × 2 mi T (2:00), 3 mi GP	3 mi, 6 × 100 S	90-min run, incl 8:00–10:00 TUT	Rest	4 mi	19 mi	46–52 mi
13	Rest	3 × 1 mi C, 3 × 800 SI	3 mi, 6 × 100 S	75-min run, incl 6:00–8:00 TUT	Rest	4 mi	20 mi	46 mi
14	Rest	3 × 1 mi C, 3 × 800 SI	3 mi, 6 × 100 S	75-min run, incl 6:00–8:00 TUT	Rest	4 mi	13 mi	45 mi
15	Rest	2 mi GP, 4 mi T	3 mi, 6 × 100 S	1-hr run, incl 6 × 400 SI	Rest	Rest	1-hr run	27–29 mi
16	Rest	4 × 400 SI	Rest	3 mi, 6 × 100 S	Rest	2 mi jog	Marathon	

'Long runs are the basis of marathon training, but at this level it's important to add some intensity to the programme,' says Sinclair. You'll gradually increase the length of the weekly long run to adapt your mind and body to the rigours of running non-stop for several hours. But running 18 to 20 miles at a time isn't all you need, so you'll supplement these runs with some higher-effort running twice a week, including sustained-tempo runs at your half-marathon race pace. These promote aerobic strength and efficiency and help you find that groove you'd like to be in during a longer race, according to Sinclair. You'll also do a smattering of speedwork.

GOAL PACE (GP): This is your per-mile goal marathon pace.

TEMPO RUN (T): For 11:00 (11-minute mile) marathon goal pace (MGP) (4:48:25 finishing time), run 10:28 (1 mile). For 10:00 MGP (4:22:12), run 9:31. For 9:00 MGP (3:55:58), run 8:34. Recovery is slow jogging for the number of minutes in parentheses.

CRUISE INTERVALS (C): For 11:00 MGP, run 9:56 (1 mile), 7:49 (1,200 metres). For 10:00 MGP, run 9:02 and 6:47. For 9:00 MGP, run 8:07 and 6:06. Recovery is half the distance of the repetition.

SPEED INTERVALS (SI): For 11:00 MGP, run 4:52 (800 metres), 2:26 (400 metres). For 10:00 MGP, run 4:17, 2:08. For 9:00 MGP, run 3:50, 1:55. Recovery is equal distance (e.g., 400-metre jog for 400-metre repeats).

TOTAL UPHILL TIME (TUT): This is the total number of minutes you spend running semivigorously up inclines – repeats up the same hill or over a hilly loop.

WARM-UP/COOLDOWN: Run 15 minutes easy followed by 4 × 100-metre strides before each Tuesday/Thursday session and 15 minutes easy at the end.

STRIDES (S): These are gradual, smooth accelerations over 100 metres (straights on a track), running fast and controlled over the middle third – but never sprinting – then just as gradually decelerating. Walk to full recovery after each.

RACE DAY: 'Go 10 to even 15 seconds per mile slower than your goal pace for the first 5 to 8 miles,' says Williams. You will see a big payoff later. When things start to become interesting – say, at 18 to 20 miles – you'll have something left in the tank.

Advanced

You're a running veteran, someone who's been at it for at least 3 or 4 years and logs 35 to 40 miles a week. You've regularly, if cyclically, included serious interval training in your regimen. You've raced them all, from 5-K to full marathon, and now want to score that most prized runner's achievement: the PB, the absolute fastest 26.2 miles you're capable of. 'You'll have to be willing to hit 50 miles a week,' Sinclair says. 'For an advanced marathon effort, inadequate miles just won't cut it.' At this level, your goal is to learn how to maintain a strong, solid pace for several hours. So, along with the standard long runs, you'll spend 2 days a week developing stamina at half-marathon, 10-K and 5-K race pace. On Thursdays, you'll be served a marathon goal pace/tempo/cruise combination – an extended effort that develops focus, strength, and the capacity to hold a strong pace as fatigue sets in. 'Long runs and mileage get you to the finish line,' says Sinclair. 'Intensity in your training will get you to the finish line faster.'

GOAL PACE (GP): This is your per-mile marathon goal pace.

TEMPO RUN (T): For 8:00 (8-minute mile) marathon goal pace (MGP) (3:29:45 finishing time), run 7:38 (1 mile). For 7:00 MGP (3:03:32), run 6:39. For 6:00 MGP (2:37:19), run 5:43. Recovery is slow jogging for the number of minutes in parentheses.

CRUISE INTERVALS (C): For 8:00 MGP, run 7:14 (1 mile), 3:37 (800 metres). For 7:00 MGP, run 6:19 and 3:09. For 6:00 MGP, run 5:25 and 2:43. Recovery is 2 to 3 minutes for mile repeats, 1 to 2 minutes for 800 metres.

SPEED INTERVALS (SI): For 8:00 MGP, run 3:27 (800 metres),

1:42 (400 metres). For 7:00 MGP, run 2:59 and 1:30. For 6:00 MGP, do 2:36, 1:18. Recovery is 2 to 3 minutes for 800-metre repeats, 1 to 1½ minutes for 400 metres.

THE PLAN

Week	Mon	Tues	Wed	Thurs	Fri	Sat	Sun	Total
1	Rest	4 × 1 mile C	4 mi, 4 × 100 S	2 mi GP, 2–3 mi T, 2 mi GP	Rest	45–60 min easy	10 mi WH	33–35 mi
2	Rest	4 × 1 mile C	4 mi, 4 × 100 S	2 mi GP, 2–3 mi T, 2 mi GP	Rest	45–60 min easy	11 mi FF	34–36 mi
3	Rest	8–10 mi, incl 6:00 TUT	4 mi, 6 × 100 S	2 mi GP, 4 mi T, 2 mi GP	Rest	45–60 min easy	12 mi	38–44 mi
4	Rest	8–10 mi, incl 6:00 TUT	4 mi, 6 × 100 S	2 mi GP, 4 mi T, 2 mi GP	Rest	45–60 min easy	13 mi FF	39–45 mi
5	Rest	2 × 3 mi T	4 mi, 6 × 100 S	4 × 800 SI, 4 × 400 SI	Rest	5-K race	12 mi	34–36 mi
6	Rest	10 mi, incl 8:00 TUT	4 mi, 6 × 100 S	3 mi GP, 3–4 × 800 C, 3 mi T	Rest	45–60 min easy	14 mi	40–50 mi
7	Rest	10 mi, incl 8:00 TUT	4 mi, 6 × 100 S	3 mi GP, 3–4 × 800 C, 3 mi T	Rest	45–60 min easy	16 mi FF	42–52 mi
8	Rest	2 × 1 mi C, 4 × 800 SI, 2 × 1 mi C	4 mi, 6 × 100 S	3 mi GP, 4–6 × 800 C, 3 mi T	Rest	45–60 min easy	18 mi	47–53 mi
9	Rest	2 × 1 mi C, 4 × 800 SI, 2 × 1 mi C	4 mi, 6 × 100 S	3 mi GP, 4–6 × 800 C, 3 mi T	Rest	45–60 min easy	20 mi	49–55 mi
10	Rest	2 × 4 mi T	4 mi, 6 × 100 S	4 × 800 SI, 4 × 400 SI	Rest	10-K race	10 mi	34–36 mi

Week	Mon	Tues	Wed	Thurs	Fri	Sat	Sun	Total
11	Rest	10–12 mi, incl 10:00 TUT	4 mi, 6 × 100 S	3 mi GP, 6–8 × 800 C, 3 mi T	Rest	45–60 min easy	20 mi FF	51–55 mi
12	Rest	10–12 mi, incl 10:00 TUT	4 mi, 6 × 100 S	3 mi GP, 6–8 × 800 C, 3 mi T	Rest	45–60 min easy	22 mi	53–57 mi
13	Rest	8–10 mi, incl 6:00 TUT	4 mi, 6 × 100 S	4 × 1 mile C, 2 × 800 SI	Rest	45–60 min easy	20 mi WH	43–47 mi
14	Rest	8–10 mi, incl 6:00 TUT	4 mi, 6 × 100 S	4 × 1 mile C, 2 × 800 SI	Rest	45–60 min easy	13 mi FF	36–40 mi
15	Rest	4 × 400 SI, 2 × 800 C, 4 × 400 SI	4 mi, 6 × 100 S	2 mi, 2 × 800 C, 2 × 400 SI	Rest	5 mi	60- to 75-min run	34–37 mi
16	Rest	2 mi T, 2 × 800 C, 2 × 400 SI	3 mi (easy), 4 × 100 S	4 × 400 SI	Rest	3-mi jog	Marathon	

WARM-UP/COOLDOWN: Run 15 minutes easy followed by 4 × 100-metre strides before each Tuesday/Thursday session and 15 minutes easy at the end. Sunday long-run adaptations: 'FF' means 'fast finish' (do tempo pace for the final 15 minutes of the run); 'WH' means 'with hills' (do part of your run over a hilly or undulating course).

TOTAL UPHILL TIME (TUT): See intermediate schedule.

STRIDES (S): These are gradual, smooth accelerations over 100 metres, running fast and controlled over the middle third – but never sprinting – then just as gradually decelerating. Walk to full recovery after each.

RACE DAY: Start slowly, forcing yourself to hold back – run the first mile 15 to 20 seconds slower than goal pace. You know the drill. Moreover, 'have a goal time for each 5-mile split and hit it,' says Williams. 'This will ensure that you reach your finish goal time.'

RECOVERY AID

Long runs are the centrepiece of a training programme. But the key isn't just how you run them – it's also how you recover from them. Muscles regenerate and become stronger during the rest period after hard bouts of exercise. So to run well and stay injury free, you should follow this recovery routine. Work it into your schedule after every long run, especially those of 15 miles or more.

Hydrate: Drink 240ml to 480ml of sports drink, which replenishes electrolytes and minerals lost through sweat.

Change: Your body needs to cool down; put on dry clothes (even just a fresh top) immediately to help your body regulate its temperature.

Reload: Consume a mix of carbs and protein within 15 minutes after a run to jump-start muscle recovery. Chocolate milk is a great choice.

Shower: Warm water relaxes the nervous system and helps your body readjust its temperature.

Stretch: Doing flexibility training within an hour of ending a run boosts circulation, which aids recovery.

Refuel again: Once your stomach has settled, eat a meal with a balance of carbs and protein to replace your glycogen (energy) stores and rebuild damaged muscle.

Get horizontal: Naps are ideal, but you'll benefit from even a 15- to 30-minute break with your feet up (it promotes circulation and relaxes heart rate).

Cool down: In the evening, soak in a cool or cold bath for 10 minutes to aid muscle recovery and prevent soreness the next day.

Self-massage: A sports massage can be too intense post-long run; kneading your own muscles helps you regulate your comfort level.

THE MARATHON TAPER

The final 3 weeks are the most important in any marathon-training programme. Every good plan should 'taper' during those final 21 days. That means you run less and rest more. For some people, the idea of backing off on training just before the big race seems counter-intuitive. 'So many runners train hard right up to the day of the marathon because they're desperately afraid of losing fitness if they don't,' explains coach and 1983 London Marathon winner Mike Gratton. 'What they don't realize is that in those last few weeks, it's the rest more than the work that makes you strong. And you don't lose fitness in 3 weeks of tapering. In fact, studies show that your aerobic capacity, the best gauge of fitness, doesn't change at all.'

Research reveals a lot more than that. A review of 50 studies on tapering published in the journal *Medicine & Science in Sports & Exercise* shows that levels of muscle glycogen, enzymes, anti-oxidants and hormones – all depleted by high mileage – return to optimal ranges during a taper. The muscle damage that occurs during sustained training is also repaired. And if that isn't enough, immune function and muscle strength also improve, reducing the odds you'll catch a cold or become injured just before the race. And get this: the average performance improvement by the subjects who tapered in these studies was 3 per cent. That works out to 5 to 10 minutes in a marathon. The review's main conclusion: 'The primary aim of the taper should be to minimize accumulated fatigue, rather than to attain additional physiological adaptations or fitness gains.' In other words, it's time to take it easier. The following plan shows you exactly how to modify your running, thinking and eating in those 3 crucial weeks before you reach the start line.

3 WEEKS TO GO

Week 1 of the taper begins the day after your last long run of about 20 miles, 3 weeks before the marathon. The taper starts gradually because this training still counts, and a dramatic drop in workload isn't necessary yet. This week, you need to run a bit less, eat a bit more protein, troubleshoot your race plan and consider buying shoes for race day if your trainers have exceeded their mileage.

Training Checklist

- Last week should have been your highest-mileage week. This week, stick with the same basic schedule you've been following, but decrease your total mileage from last week by at least 20 per cent.
- Your shorter weekday runs shouldn't be much different than last week's, but shave a mile or 2 off your longer midweek runs.
- Generally, weekday training should consist of one medium-long run of 8 to 10 miles, one marathon-goal-pace run of 4 to 6 miles, one nonrunning day and two runs of 3 to 5 miles.
- Your weekend long run (2 weeks before the marathon) should be a 12- to 14-miler at the same pace – not faster – as the previous week's 20-miler.
- Except for the goal-pace run, all running this week should be at a relaxed pace of $1\frac{1}{2}$ to 2 minutes slower per mile than marathon goal pace.
- Avoid running extremely hilly courses, hill repetitions or speed workouts. This kind of training leads to muscle-tissue damage, which you need to minimize throughout your taper.

Mental Preparation

'Think of all the problems that could arise and work through how you'll handle them,' says Dr Kate Hays, a sports psychologist, and author of *Working it Out: Using Exercise in Psychotherapy.* 'Doing this will provide solutions so that you won't panic in case one of the scenarios does occur, and it reduces your anxiety because you'll know you're ready for any situation.' Mentally rehearse the following scenarios.

- It's hot, freezing or blustery. Less-than-ideal conditions mean you have to adjust your time goals. Headwinds can slow your finish time by several minutes, and heat or cold by even more. A survey of marathon finish times suggests that 17.8°C is the ideal temperature, a temperature of 1.6° or 23.8°C adds 7 per cent to your time, and a 29.4°C day adds 10 per cent.

- You start out ahead of goal pace. Slow down to goal pace as soon as you work this out (hopefully, no later than when you hit the first-mile marker) because running at an even pace is crucial.

- You start out slower than goal pace. Speed up, but only to goal pace, because trying to make up for lost time is a fool's game. You can still achieve your goal time by speeding up slightly during the second half of the race.

- You slip off goal pace mid-race. This is the time to become your own coach. Coax yourself back into the groove by thinking about all the training you put in and how badly you want to achieve your goal.

- Your old knee/shin/foot problem acts up mid-race. Decide in advance how bad it has to become before you'll drop out. A good guideline: if the pain forces you to alter your stride, drop out so you don't develop a long-term injury.

- A side stitch strikes. As excruciating as these can be, plan to hang in there; most stitches vanish within a couple of miles – especially if you slow down and apply pressure to the area where you feel the stitch. Rehydrating can also help.

Nutritional Needs

- 'Take in a lot of protein this week to aid in the repair and recovery of muscle tissue damaged during the high-mileage phase of marathon training,' says nutritionist Anita Bean, author of *The Complete Guide to Sports Nutrition*. Aim for 75 to 100 grams of protein per day. If you don't eat meat, fill up on protein from eggs, beans, dairy, nuts and soya products.

- To rebuild your literally run-down immune defences and possibly prevent a cold or flu, load up on vitamin C. Kiwi, orange juice, red peppers, broccoli and strawberries are the most potent food sources. Stock up on lysine, an amino acid found mostly in meat and fish that will further help your immune function. Wheat germ or a 500-milligramme supplement are the best vegetarian options.

And Don't Forget

This week, buy the shoes you plan to wear in the marathon, and wear them on most of your runs until race day. Stick with a make or model that's worked well for you in the past. If you already have a pair in mind, be sure they're adequately broken in but not worn down. Most running shoes lose their cushioning and resiliency at 300 to 500 miles.

2 WEEKS TO GO

Week 2 is a transitional period. You're halfway between the agony of your last 20-miler and the ecstasy of the marathon. Rest truly replaces training as the most important element of your race preparations, and race strategizing takes on increasing importance.

Training Checklist

- Your mileage this week should be about half to two-thirds the amount you ran during your highest mileage week.
- Almost all running should be slow (1½ to 2 minutes slower than marathon goal pace), except for 2 miles run in the middle of a midweek 4-miler at marathon goal pace. 'Even this small amount of goal-pace running is important because it physically and mentally reinforces the pace you want to run on race day,' says coach Nick Anderson of www.fullpotential.co.uk. 'This follows the rule of specificity – simulating as closely as possible what you hope to do in competition.' It's also fine to throw in a few 100-metre strides after one or two workouts just to help you stay smooth and loose.
- Weekday short runs should not exceed 4 miles.
- Your longest weekday run should be 6 to 10 miles.
- Your weekend long run (1 week before the race) should be 8 to 10 miles. Any longer and your muscles may not be able to fully rebound before the race.

Mental Preparation

- 'Set multiple goals so you won't come away from the race empty-handed,' says Hays. 'Set three time goals – "fantastic", "really good" and "I can live with that" finish times.' These can each be separated by 5 to 15 minutes.
- Set general goals, such as not walking, finishing strong or simply enjoying yourself.
- Check the race website for race-morning particulars such as start time, and work out the details of how you'll get to the start. Logistics you'll want to consider: where you'll park; how early you want to arrive (at least an hour before start time is ideal); where you'll leave your gear during the race.

Nutritional Needs

- Keep those calories coming in as usual, even though your mileage may be dwindling. Your body still needs to repair tissue damaged during your mileage build up. 'This is no time to diet,' says Bean.

- Resist the temptation to cut back on fat because you're running less. A reasonable proportion of dietary fat (30 per cent of your daily calories) is beneficial because it can be accessed as a back-up energy source when stored carbs are used up. Fat reserves can therefore postpone or prevent a race-day collision with the notorious 'wall'.

- Eat foods high in unsaturated fat, such as nuts or fish cooked in olive oil. Limit foods that are high in saturated fat and trans fats, such as pizza and ice cream.

And Don't Forget

If you've been lifting weights as part of your training programme, stop. Weight training at this stage of the game can't help your race, but it can sap your strength or cause an injury.

1 WEEK TO GO

During week 3 of your taper, you might start to feel frustrated. Two weeks ago, you ran 20 miles in a single run, but now you may not run this amount all week. You might feel irritable and tired as your body adjusts to your reduced activity level. And as your mileage plummets, your worries can skyrocket. But take comfort in knowing that thousands of other marathon runners preparing to race this coming weekend are going through the same thing. And take refuge in your final mission: to ensure that your body is sufficiently fuelled, hydrated, refreshed and recovered for the task.

Training Checklist

- Starting Monday, do no runs longer than 4 miles. When you do head out, remember that these jaunts are more for your head than your body; training has little effect this week.
- Almost all running should be at 1½ to 2 minutes per mile slower than marathon goal pace – except a Tuesday 2-miler at marathon goal pace, sandwiched by 1-mile jogs. Again, if you want, throw in some quick 100-metre strides after one or two of your workouts. This helps fight off the sluggish feeling that can occur during your taper.
- Three days before the race, run just 2 to 3 miles easy.
- Two days before the race, don't run at all.
- On the day before the race, jog 2 miles to take the edge off your pent-up energy so you'll sleep better that night.

Mental Preparation

- 'Confidence should be the focus of the final week,' says Hays, 'but you may still experience anxiety. If so, remind yourself that you're physically prepared because you did the necessary training, and you're mentally prepared because you did the necessary trouble-shooting and goal-setting.'
- Try to minimize job, relationship and travel stresses all week.
- If you're nervous about the race, relax with breathing exercises. Breathe in and out as slowly and deeply as possible, letting your belly expand as you inhale. Focus your attention on the breathing and any positive, calming image.
- If you're too supercharged to sleep, try this relaxation exercise. First tense, then relax your muscles, one at a time, starting with the muscles in your face and working down to your toes.

Nutritional Needs

• 'Emphasize carbohydrates more than usual in the last 3 days before the race,' says Bean. About 60 to 70 per cent of your calories should come from carbohydrate sources. Pasta, potatoes, rice, cereals and fruit are healthy choices that turn into muscle glycogen.

• Wash all those carbs down with fluids so your energy and water levels are high on race morning. Alcoholic beverages don't count towards your fluid totals, however, and you'll need to make up for their diuretic effect by drinking extra fluids. You know you're adequately hydrated if your urine is clear or pale yellow.

• Don't restrict the salt in your diet. Low salt intake combined with excessive hydration can lead to hyponatraemia, a rare but dangerous condition that can afflict marathon runners. Drinking sports drinks and snacking on salted popcorn will help keep your sodium levels up.

• Don't look at the scales. Because of your fully stocked fluid and fuel stores, you're likely to gain a little weight this week. But it's worth it. Having your body's energy reserves at full capacity will do more for your race than weighing a little less – and you'll lose it by the finish line anyway.

And Don't Forget

• Don't do anything tiring. Let the grass grow. Let the children do the housework. Let the dog walk itself.

• Don't try anything new – no new foods, drinks or sports. Don't cross-train, walk or cycle. Don't have a sports massage unless it's part of your routine. You may feel bruised a couple of days afterwards if you're not accustomed to it.

• Stay off your feet and catch up on films, books and sleep. If you go to the pre-race expo, don't stay long. Remember: During this final week, you can't underdo. You can only overdo.

TAPER TIPS FOR SHORTER RACES

The taper is nearly as important for a short race as for a marathon; it just doesn't need to last as long.

• For half-marathons, limit your long run on the weekend before to 8 or 10 miles, and cut your usual run distances in half the rest of the week.

• For 5-Ks to 10-milers, cut your mileage in half for 3 to 5 days before the race.

• If you do any speedwork in the last 3 to 6 days before a sub-marathon-distance race, make it only a third of a normal speed session.

• Carbo-load in the last 3 days before a half-marathon if you wish, though it's less crucial than it is for a marathon.

• Don't carbo-load before races shorter than 10 miles. It doesn't help, and the extra weight you may gain will slow you down.

• If you're nervous in the days before a sub-marathon race, remind yourself that you can run another one in a few weeks if it doesn't go well.

EXTRA CREDIT

The plans and advice provided so far will prepare any runner to race well. But since no single training plan suits every single runner, there's always room for improvement. Here are some additional strategies that could lead you to a breakthrough performance. Experiment with them to develop the optimal plan for you.

TEMPO TRAINING

There are lots of workouts runners can – and should – do regularly. Training variety improves your fitness, staves off injuries and keeps motivation high. But if pressed to name the one workout that has the greatest impact on racing performance at any distance, many experts would say the tempo run. Tempo runs will make you a stronger miler,

PREDICT YOUR PERFORMANCE

You can estimate an appropriate race pace by taking your times from previous hard efforts and looking them up on pace-predictor tables, like the one below. For instance, a previous mile time can be used to predict a future 5-K race pace. (If you haven't raced before or lately, time yourself running a mile on a local track.) While you can make race-pace predictions for longer races than the 5-K based on your mile time, the further away you get from the distance you've actually run, the less accurate your prediction is likely to be. So a better predictor for your 10-K race pace is a previous 5-K race pace. And to predict your race pace for a marathon, a half-marathon time will be more accurate. The following table is based on the race times of thousands of average runners.

1-MILE	5-K	10-K	HALF-MARATHON	MARATHON
4:20	15:00	31:08	1:08:40	2:23:47
4:38	16:00	33:12	1:13:19	2:33:25
4:56	17:00	35:17	1:17:58	2:43:01
5:14	18:00	37:21	1:22:38	2:52:34
5:33	19:00	39:26	1:27:19	3:02:06
5:51	20:00	41:31	1:31:59	3:11:35
6:09	21:00	43:36	1:36:36	3:21:00
6:28	22:00	45:41	1:41:18	3:30:23
6:46	23:00	47:46	1:45:57	3:39:42
7:05	24:00	49:51	1:50:34	3:48:57
7:24	25:00	51:56	1:55:11	3:58:08
7:42	26:00	54:00	1:59:46	4:07:16
8:01	27:00	56:04	2:04:20	4:16:19
8:19	28:00	58:08	2:08:53	4:25:19
8:37	29:00	1:00:12	2:13:24	4:34:14
8:56	30:00	1:02:15	2:17:53	4:43:06

a faster 5-K runner and a less-fatigued marathon runner. How can one workout benefit such a wide range of race distances? Simply put: tempo runs teach your body to run faster before fatiguing.

Studies indicate that the best predictor of distance-running performance is your lactate threshold, which is the speed you are able to run before lactic acid begins to accumulate in the blood. By regularly including tempo runs in your training schedule, you will increase the speed that you can run before lactic acid begins to slow you down. To use a car analogy, tempo runs allow your engine to rev faster without blowing up. Before tempo training, you may have blown up at an 8-minute-per-mile pace. After a few months of tempo runs, your legs won't turn to jelly until you reach a 7:30-per-mile pace.

Once you determine your tempo-run pace (see 'What's My Tempo?' on page 81), you can run it in a variety of workouts. Here are three of the best options designated for beginning, intermediate, and advanced runners, although runners of all levels can adapt any of these workouts and alternate them for training variety.

TRADITIONAL TEMPO RUN

Nothing fancy here. After a 2-mile warm-up and some strides to loosen up your legs, just get out there and roll at tempo pace. Avoid the temptation to check your watch too soon. Be patient and get into your rhythm before you assess your pace. If you're fatiguing so much that you're slowing down towards the end, you started too fast. A traditional tempo run lasts at least 20 minutes and maxes out at about 35 minutes. But remember: your tempo pace is one that you could maintain for up to an hour if it were a race. Start with tempo runs that are about 2 miles and add half a mile every 2 weeks until you hit 4 miles. Faster runners (those who can cover more than 4 miles in 35 minutes) can extend tempo runs beyond 4 miles with a mini-break at the halfway mark. By taking a 30- to 45-second breather (jog very slowly), you can extend tempo runs to 5 or 6 miles without the enormity of the distance fazing you. So, instead of a 5-mile tempo run, think of it as two × 2.5-mile tempo runs with a 45-second recovery break – enough rest to give a psychological break without letting your heart rate or blood lactate levels totally recover. As the weeks progress, you can continue to diminish the mini-break until it no longer exists and you're running 6 miles of pure tempo. When you finish your tempo run, cool down with an easy 2 miles.

DOUBLE TEMPO RUN

In this workout, you give yourself a substantial recovery period of 5 to 7 minutes sandwiched between two tempo-paced runs. Once again, warm up by running 2 miles and doing some strides. Then do a 15-minute tempo run. While this initial tempo run is hard enough to fall in the tempo-run effort zone, it should feel like it's more on the comfortable side of the comfortable-hard effort scale. After a recovery jog of 5 to 7 minutes, run a second tempo run of about the same length. This pace should be slightly more aggressive and more on the hard side. This perception will be partly from the fatigue induced by the previous tempo run and partly because you're actually running a little faster. As you become stronger, you can extend the length of each run until your total time at tempo pace reaches 45 minutes. The advantage of this type of tempo workout is that with the lengthy recovery period between the two runs, you're able to run more overall volume at tempo-run pace. This means you'll spend more time working at your lactate threshold.

TEMPO RUN 1,000s

As the name indicates, this workout consists of 1,000-metre repeats done at tempo-run pace with 60 seconds of recovery in between. Start with six 1,000-metre repeats, and add one per week until you can run 8 to 10 comfortably. Don't be put off by the fact that this workout is done on the track. Because of the pace, it's still more of a controlled tempo run than a speedy interval session. This is a good workout for inexperienced runners who might have a hard time running evenly for a 5- or 6-mile traditional tempo run. Or run tempo 1,000s every 2 to 3 weeks in place of a standard tempo run to add variety to your tempo training.

SPEED-FORM TRAINING

The purpose of speed-form training is to improve your leg turnover (or stride frequency, as some call it), power, running economy and relaxation while running. The best way to achieve all this is through a variety of speed drills that you run faster than other workouts, like tempo runs or mile repeats. You should run these repeats (200 metres

'WHAT'S MY TEMPO?'

You can use any of the following four ways to determine your lactate threshold and, consequently, your tempo-run pace.

1. Perceived effort. In general, your perceived effort is how hard you feel you're working when you're running. For a tempo run, your perceived effort should be 'comfortably hard'. How can something be comfortable and hard at the same time? You're running fast enough so that you know you're working hard, but if you had to, you could keep up the pace for up to an hour. If you're on a tempo run with a training partner, you're able to say a few words here and there, but you can't deliver a lengthy diatribe.

2. Heart rate. Although heart rate at lactate threshold varies from person to person, it usually falls between 85 and 95 per cent of your maximum (women are often on the higher end). Experts in the field of exercise science have come up with an equation to help you calculate percentages of maximum heart rate. Plug in your own numbers below to calculate 85 per cent of your maximum heart rate:

205 minus half your age minus resting heart rate × 0.85 + resting heart rate = 85 per cent of your max heart rate.

So, if a 40-year-old runner had a resting heart rate of 50 (measured first thing

(continued)

'WHAT'S MY TEMPO?' (CONTINUED)

in the morning before getting out of bed), he'd be crunching these numbers: 205 minus 20 minus 50 = 135 x 0.85 = 115 +50, which equals roughly 165 beats per minute.

Once you know your tempo heart rate range, strap on a heart-rate monitor as you head out of the door, and it'll tell you if you're hitting your range. If you don't run with a monitor, you'll need to keep track of your heart rate yourself. Halfway through your tempo run, slow down for a brief walk and find your pulse. Count the beats for 10 seconds, and multiply that number by 6 to see if you're in your tempo range. Then continue with your workout.

3. Respiration rate. When you hit your lactate threshold, your breathing intensity also increases. Most runners breathe in a rhythm that coincides with their stride rate. The breathing patterns of three to three (taking three strides while you breathe in and three strides while you breathe out) and two to two are most common for easy running. But when you hit two to one (two strides while you breathe in and one while you breathe out), you've achieved tempo pace.

4. Racing pace. You can base your tempo pace on either your 10-K or 5-K race pace. Aim for about 20 seconds per mile slower than 10-K pace or 30 seconds per mile slower than 5-K pace.

is a good length) at about the same pace you could run in a 1-mile race. Since the 200-metre repeats represent only an eighth of the mile distance, you should be able to run these hard and fast but without straining. Another way to work out your pace is to run your 5-K race pace minus 30 to 40 seconds per mile (for faster runners) or 40 to 60 seconds per mile (for slower runners). Either way, you should be able to complete six to eight repeats of 200 metres at this pace. Take a 2- to 4-minute recovery jog after each repeat before beginning the next one. While running, concentrate on feeling smooth, powerful, relaxed and controlled. Don't overstride or pump your arms excessively.

Strides offer another way to work on your speed and form. While the previous workout is essentially an interval workout, with its mix of faster and slower running on a track or other good surface, strides are less structured. You can do them almost anytime, anywhere. They take only a few minutes at the end of a workout.

Basically, strides are gradual accelerations over 60 to 80 metres. By running four to six strides several times a week, you help your legs and the rest of your body remember what it's like to run fast. Without strides or some type of speed-form drill, it's easy to get sloppy and do only slow running with bad form. You can find yourself slipping into a pattern where you're training to run slowly and inefficiently rather than faster and more economically.

Here's how to do strides. Finish your workout, stretch for 5 to 10 minutes, and then find a smooth, level place to run (a grassy field is excellent). Lean into your first stride as you would the beginning of a race, and continue accelerating for 60 to 80 metres. Concentrate on your form, staying smooth and strong (but not straining) as you accelerate. As you reach about 90 per cent of your top speed, relax and allow your body to decelerate. Jog for a minute or two, and then repeat another four or five times.

YASSO 800s

One of the most popular speed workouts for marathon runners is Yasso 800s, named for a workout developed by Bart Yasso, who has worked at *Runner's World* for more than 2 decades and has run more than 150 marathons. One of the reasons it's so popular is that it's not only simple but it works. Bart's goal during his marathon training was to build up to ten 800s in the same time as his marathon goal time: 'If I can get my 800s down to 2 minutes 50 seconds, I'm in 2:50 marathon shape. If I can get down to 2:40, I can run a 2:40 marathon.' It turns out that the formula works right down the line – 4-hour marathons, 5-hour marathons, etc. Want to run a 3:30 marathon? Then train to run a set of 800s in 3:30 each. Between the 800s, jog for the same number of minutes it took you to run your repeats. Bart begins running his Yasso 800s a couple of months before his goal marathon. The first week he does four in one workout. Every other week, he adds one more until he reaches 10. The last workout of Yasso 800s should be completed at least 10 days (preferably, 14 to 17) before your marathon. The rest of the time, just do your normal marathon training.

COURSE TRAINING

You might have a mix of speed, tempo and hills already in your programme. But training specifically for the course you are going to race is the extra ingredient that helps ensure success on race day. 'Specificity is critical,' says Pete Rea, elite coach and founder of www.zapfitness.com. 'It helps you build the strength you need to tackle the demands of the course.'

FLAT AND FAST

Flat courses seem like an obvious choice for runners chasing personal bests. But surprisingly, races that have no significant hills can wreak havoc on your legs. In fact, the repetitiveness of running on a level surface fatigues leg muscles faster than running on rolling terrain. The solution, says Rea, is getting used to pushing the pace for longer periods of time on a flat course and building leg power with hill workouts.

THE WORKOUT: Run 2 × 10 to 20 minutes at 10 seconds slower than 10-K. Do the first half of this tempo run on slightly rolling terrain, the rest on level ground. In the same week, do the hill repeats in the next section with an easy day in between.

ALL DOWNHILL FROM HERE

Likewise, a downhill race is harder than you'd think. Courses with a significant net drop can trash your quads. According to a small 2005 study in the Journal of Biomechanics, the impact on a runner's legs can be as much as 54 per cent greater downhill than on a level

WHAT'S THAT? RUNNING JARGON, TRANSLATED

Negative splits: running the second half of a race or workout faster than the first half.

Hitting the wall: to be overcome by fatigue mid-run. This also occurs when a runner's muscle-glycogen (energy) reserves become seriously depleted.

Maximum heart rate: the highest heart rate achieved during high-intensity exercise. Sixty to 80 per cent of your maximum heart rate is considered your training heart rate.

Target heart rate: a range to be reached during training to enable an athlete to gain maximum cardiovascular benefits. Aerobic conditioning occurs at about 70 per cent of maximum heart rate.

Chip time: a finishing time recorded by a small electronic chip attached to a runner's shoelaces. The chip sends a signal to a device when it crosses both the starting and finish lines, giving an exact race time.

Fartlek: means 'speed play' in Swedish. Fartlek training involves varying your pace by integrating intense sprints into your workout, followed by a recovery run or slow jog slightly below your normal running pace.

Pick-ups: accelerations performed during a run. Pick-ups are generally shorter in duration than fartleks and usually added to easy runs for extra training benefit.

Runner's high: a feeling of exhilaration during a run thought to be brought on by endorphins (feel-good chemicals released in the brain) or endocannabinoids (substances in the brain that have a marijuana-like effect).

surface, potentially leading to muscle-fibre damage, upper-leg fatigue and knee pain. This is less likely to happen in a 5-K or 10-K simply because it's shorter, but any downhill course can wear out your legs. To reduce your suffering and the chance of knee pain, strengthen your quads by training on descents.

THE WORKOUT: Do 2 to 7 miles sustained downhill running at 5 to 10 seconds faster per mile than goal race pace. If you don't live in an area with long downhills, do this tempo run on a treadmill, varying the grade from –1 to –5 (newer treadmills have this option).

HILLS, AND THEN SOME

A course profile resembling the spikes and drops of an EKG might be tough, but climbing and descending gives your legs a much-needed break from the pounding they take on flats. In the above-mentioned study, researchers found that running up moderate hills results in a softer impact because the foot has less distance to fall and there's less of a weight load on strides. The challenge, then, is getting up those hills as close to race-pace as you can. That requires running varied hill workouts throughout your programme. The consistency will build the leg and lung power that hills require. Start by doing easy miles on rolling terrain. As you progress, add a weekly fartlek workout: surge for 30 seconds on every hill on your route.

THE WORKOUT: Do 6 to 8 × 1- to 3-minute uphill repeats hard but not all-out; downhill jog; 2 to 6 minutes recovery. Find a moderately sloped hill and one slightly steeper, and alternate your workout each week between them; varying grades boosts leg strength better.

TREADMILL TRAINING

Some runners find treadmill running boring and tedious. They argue that there's nothing to look at, indoor air is stale and real runners do it outdoors. Perhaps, but treadmill running has its converts and its benefits. The predictability of treadmill running may also be its greatest virtue. The reliable roll of the belt, comfortable indoor temperature and safety and security of a well-lit surface certainly beat running outdoors when it's dark or cold or you're travelling in an unfamiliar area. Plus, 'predictable' doesn't have to mean 'boring'. With a little imagination, you can design treadmill workouts more variable and precise than on a road or track. Finally, a modern, motorized treadmill lets you control pace and hills, so you can create workouts specifically targeted to improving your running.

Below are four treadmill workouts that will make you a stronger, faster runner. Each takes less than an hour, so they're easy to fit into your schedule. But keep these two points in mind: don't do more than two of these workouts per week (the rest of the time, just run easily), and set the treadmill's elevation at 1 degree. This compensates for the lack of air resistance in treadmill running and makes your speeds roughly equivalent to similar speeds outdoors. By regularly running treadmill workouts, you can develop a better sense of pace, increase your running economy and learn to deal with hills more efficiently. Best of all, you'll be ready to set some new PBs.

SPEED DEMON: Run easily for 10 minutes, then set the treadmill speed about 20 seconds per mile faster than your best recent 5-K pace. Run three 3-minute repeats at this speed, alternating with 3 minutes of very slow jogging. After completing a set of three repeats and recovery jogs, rest for 5 minutes by jogging. Then run a second set of three repeats and recovery jogs. When finished, run easily for 5 minutes to cool down.

PROGRESSION: Begin with a 10-minute warm-up, and then set the speed about 15 seconds per mile faster than your best recent 5-K pace (this new pace becomes your 5-K goal pace). For your first treadmill workout at this pace, run continuously for 5 minutes. Finish the workout with 10 to 20 minutes of easy cooldown running. For each of the next 10 weeks, run the same workout, but increase the time you spend at your goal pace by 1 minute per week. At the end of 10 weeks, you should be able to run a 5-K race at your goal pace.

INDOOR HILLS: Warm up for 10 minutes, then set the treadmill at your approximate marathon pace. (If you've never run a marathon, estimate your time using the 'Predict Your Performance' chart on page 78.) With the treadmill elevated 1 degree, run for 2 minutes at marathon pace, then elevate the incline to 2 degrees and run for 2 minutes. Next, return to 1 degree for 2 minutes, but then climb to 3 degrees for 2 minutes. Continue in this manner, raising the grade on every other 2-minute repeat, until you've reached 7 degrees (the inclination pattern is 1-2-1-3-1-4-1-5-1-6-1-7). If you feel exhausted before you reach 7 degrees, stop, and don't let it worry you. Try the workout several more times, and you'll develop the ability to handle the hills. Finish the workout by running an easy 8- to 10-minute cooldown.

THE 10-4: Warm up for 10 minutes, then run for 10 minutes at your current 10-K race pace. Jog very easily for 4 minutes to recover, then surge again for 10 minutes at 10-K tempo. Recover for 4 minutes, and complete the workout with 10 minutes of easy cooldown running.

ASK RUNNER'S WORLD

Q: How far apart should I space my races?

A: Full recovery between races is important not only to ensure that you don't overload your muscles, joints and bones – leaving them vulnerable to injury – but also to keep you physically and mentally fresh. For each mile raced, allow an equal number of days to recover before returning to full training, and double the number of miles you raced before racing again. So after a half-marathon, build your training volume and intensity back up over 13 days, but don't race again for 25 days. Add 10 to 20 per cent more recovery time to the formula if you train fewer than 20 miles a week and for each decade over 40. First-year runners and those who often become injured should double the formula. These are minimum recovery periods and shouldn't be followed year-round. No one should repeatedly race half-marathons every month, marathons every 2 months, or 5-Ks every week.

Q: *I know that the rule of thumb for increasing mileage is no more than 10 per cent per week. Is there a rule for safely increasing pace over time?*

A: Coaches and physiotherapists often suggest the 10 per cent rule to beginners and runners coming back from an injury as a general guideline for increasing mileage. But a 10 per cent weekly increase may be too aggressive or too conservative, depending on your goals, years of training, current mileage, age and fitness level. The same is true for increasing pace. You can increase the speed of your mid-distance runs (6- to 9-milers) by 1 to 3 per cent per week – about 5 seconds per mile – without increasing injury risk. And you can continue with those increases until your pace for these runs is just 20 seconds slower than your 10-K race pace. When you're trying to become faster, however, the quality of your mileage is more important than the quantity. So limit your training to 4 or 5 days a week, but include a tempo run, a speed-oriented workout, a long run and one or two medium runs per week. The medium-distance runs should not be 'recovery' runs but runs at a solid training pace (70 to 80 per cent of your maximum heart rate) that can be increased by 1 to 3 per cent a week. The days you don't run will provide recovery. This incremental approach to increasing pace will improve your fitness without requiring extra mileage.

Q: *I have a physical job. Can I get away with less training than someone with a desk job?*

A: That depends on your job and your goals. If you stand all day behind a counter, you expend only slightly more energy than someone who sits. If you're a postman who walks several miles on your round, however, you'll accrue many health and cardiorespiratory benefits. And if you're a builder who does heavy lifting, you'll expend substantial energy and build strength. If your main goal is to improve your times as a competitive runner, you can't 'cheat' your training schedule just because you have a physical job – unless, of course, you run on the job. Your active job might help you burn calories and develop fitness, but to prepare for a race, you still have to put in the miles.

Q: *I'd like to do two marathons, and they're 4 weeks apart. Is that too close?*

A: You *can* do two marathons, but it's almost impossible to run your best in both, so prioritize one over the other. The best choice for an all-out effort is the first of the two marathons. That's because your training leading into it can be optimal, with a progressive mileage buildup and a taper of 3 weeks before race day. Plan to do the second for fun, with a goal of just finishing and enjoying yourself. If the second marathon is the one you're determined to 'race', run the first at a very easy pace, at least 30 to 60 seconds per mile slower than your marathon pace. That way your muscles should fully recover in time for the second marathon. Whether you run the first one easy or hard, recovery is key. You can't take off the whole month between, but do take a few days off, and minimize speedwork and long runs.

Q: *I've heard of runners dropping dead of heart attacks in marathons. Is this something I should worry about?*

A: Although deaths during marathons generate a lot of press when they occur, they are very rare. There is only one death for every 50,000 marathon runners. When heart-related deaths do happen, it's usually due to inherited heart disease in people younger than 30 and heart attacks caused by clogged arteries in older runners. Because exercise helps prevent cholesterol buildup in the first place, runners are at less risk for heart disease than sedentary people are. Nevertheless, being a runner doesn't automatically shield you from heart trouble. It's important for runners to keep their cholesterol and blood pressure under control. Also, runners shouldn't ignore heart attack symptoms (shortness of breath, chest pains, etc.), especially those that appear with exertion and disappear with rest.

Q: I don't race longer than 10-K, so do my training runs need to exceed that distance?

A: Yes, if you want to improve on your time. Longer runs are beneficial even for 5-K and 10-K runners because there is a relationship between endurance and speed. Legendary running coach Arthur Lydiard advocated building a base of long, steady runs to develop cardiovascular and muscle capacity and lay the foundation for distance-running performance. Adding aerobic miles (those done at about 70 to 80 per cent of your maximum heart rate) serves to increase your aerobic threshold – your top aerobic speed – so you can run a faster pace with the same effort. This translates to faster race times. As your body becomes more aerobically efficient through endurance training, your ability to take in oxygen and recruit muscle fibres improves, which has a direct impact on 5-K and 10-K racing speed. Your connective tissue is also strengthened. Most of these adaptations occur in the later stages of a longer run, when you're pushing into new territory, which is why long runs are so important. Some coaches recommend a weekly run of 90 minutes for runners racing these shorter distances. Gradually build up to the distance, and run them at a speed that feels comfortable.

Q: If I follow a training plan, can I shift workouts around to fit my schedule?

A: You're the boss. But when you rearrange a training programme, you need to follow a few guidelines to maximize the benefits while avoiding fatigue, or worse, injury.

- Track changes using a running log, calendar, notebook or spreadsheet.

- Identify the key workouts within each week, such as long runs and speed days, and make them a priority.

- Take a day off or run short and easy before and after each of your challenging workouts.

- Run one long run every weekend. If you miss one, make up for it another day that week.

- If you take a week or more off, ease back into your programme by running slower and taking more walk breaks for at least 1 week. Take twice the amount of time you took off to slowly rebuild your mileage.

Q: Can I race during pregnancy?

A: It's fine, as long as you don't push the pace. (Save the pushing for labour.) The baby usually receives about 20 per cent of your bloodflow, but during hard efforts, that drops to about 5 per cent, which is not good for the foetus. Strenuous running can also lead to overheating, so play it safe and keep your pace conversational. Many expectant women put racing on hold and just enjoy casual events until delivery. If you experience any leaking fluid, bleeding or pain or notice decreased foetal movement, stop running and see your doctor before resuming. And, of course, keep your obstetrician advised about your running throughout your pregnancy.

Q: Is there any advantage to doing a short, easy run the day before a race?

A: An ideal pre-race taper concludes with either complete rest or a light workout 1 or 2 days before the event. What you do depends on your fitness level and the race distance. Well-trained runners might want to skip running 2 days before a long race (a half-marathon or marathon) and then do a light workout – a 10- to 20-minute jog followed by a few race-pace pick-ups – the day before the race. This final run should energize and loosen your muscles and calm pre-race jitters. For shorter races, well-trained runners needn't take any days off, but the last 2 days should be limited to short, easy runs. Novice and low-mileage runners should take 2 rest days before a long race and 1 rest day before a 5-K or 10-K. No single strategy works for everyone. What's most important to keep in mind is that any running you do in the last 2 days before a race won't help but can certainly hurt your performance if it's too much. Arriving at the starting line with fresh legs should be your main goal.

Q: When's the best time to train?

A: The absolute best time to train is when it's most convenient for you. Fitting in your runs is what's most important – it doesn't matter when you get them done. However, there are some advantages and disadvantages to running at different times of the day.

- Morning: many runners run first thing. Running can both waken and refresh you, and if you have a busy day ahead, it's one less thing to squeeze in later. If you run in the dark (particularly in winter), wear a reflective vest so cars can see you. The one downside of training at this hour is that morning runners seem to become injured more often than afternoon runners, probably because they're still stiff. To combat this problem, start your morning run by walking or running very slowly, and make time to stretch afterwards.

- Afternoon: if you have an hour or more for lunch, you may be able to squeeze in a workout. Some offices have gyms with showers and encourage workers to exercise during their lunch break. Learn to manage your time. Plan your lunch in advance so you can grab something quickly before returning to work. Noon is a good time to run during winter because temperatures can be warmer, but it's bad for that same reason during the hot days of summer.

- Evening: stop for a workout on your way home from work, or go for a quick run before dinner. If you're the one who puts food on the table or there are children waiting to be fed, negotiate days when you and your partner can alternate training and cooking. Late evening is another option, but unless you can jump on a treadmill, this probably means running in the dark. You should always run in a safe area, wear reflective gear and, if possible, run with a friend.

- Weekends: you may want to plan your workout week to do most of your mileage on Saturdays and Sundays, when most runners (particularly those training for marathons) have more time for training.

- Anytime: there's no rule that says you need to run at the same time every day. There's a virtue in regularity, but you can also become stuck in a rut. Feel free to experiment with different training patterns to see what suits you best.

Q: I start races too slow and have too much left at the end. How can I learn to judge pace?
A: It's definitely helpful to know how to push the pace in the mid to later stages of races. To learn pace judgment, try this drill once a week on a track or measured course that's about 400m.

- After 10 minutes of easy running, time yourself as you run one lap very easy. Then walk/jog for 2 minutes.
- Time a second lap, and try to run it 2 to 5 seconds faster than the first. Walk/jog for 3 minutes.
- On the third lap, try again to shave off 2 to 5 seconds.
- Cool down for 10 minutes.

- Next week, try again and add a fourth lap. Walk/jog for 3 minutes between the third and fourth laps.

  Continue to do this drill once a week, adding one more lap until you work up to six laps. At that point, your goal becomes running all of the laps at the fastest pace you achieved. By slowly building your pace over the weeks and then striving to maintain it, you'll learn how to pace yourself.

Q: *For my first marathon, what should my goal be?*

A: Above all, your goal should be to finish. Beyond that, many things can surprise you on race day – the weather, the course, your body – so having several goal options will give you more control over your marathon experience. Try these.

GOAL 1: To enjoy the whole race, from start to finish. Take in the scenery, talk to the runners around you, thank the crowd and take part in the post-marathon party. If you accomplish only this goal, your experience will be positive.

GOAL 2: To finish strong, wanting to run another marathon. This requires restraint during the first half of the race. For the first 15 miles or so, the pace should feel easy. If you start to breathe heavily early on, slow down immediately. It may seem overly cautious, but if you make the correction quickly, you'll avoid a greater slowdown later in the race.

GOAL 3: To run a realistic time. Use the 'Predict Your Performance' table on page 78. First-timers running just 'to finish' should have a very good experience if they run 1 to 2 minutes per mile slower than the prediction table states. Veterans should still run at least 20 seconds per mile slower than goal pace for the first 5 to 8 miles. If you had a time goal but your body isn't cooperating, stick with goals 1 and 2.

MIND + BODY

No one understands the mind/body connection better than a runner. We feel our best after a long, fast or hard training run and our worst when we can't run at all.

Many research studies have been done on exercise-induced neuro-chemicals, which have been proven to produce feelings of elation, inner harmony and peacefulness. The runner's high, once believed to be caused by endorphins, has more recently been attributed to endocannabinoids – substances released with exercise that produce an effect similar to a marijuana high. Also contributing to this state of euphoria is epinephrine (adrenaline) – the surge that comes with becoming excited for a race, which also has the power to boost confidence and kill pain. Add to that serotonin and dopamine, two other feel-good brain chemicals, and you've got a physiological cocktail that can transform a workout into happy hour – and make it almost as addictive. Our cravings for these feel-good chemicals make us want to lace up every day. But becoming greedy can backfire. Increasing the mileage and intensity of your workouts can set you up for injury, and you know what that means: bye-bye runner's high. To keep reaping all the positive physical and psychological effects of running, you need to do everything in your power to stay strong and healthy. This chapter will show you how.

INJURY PREVENTION

Training for a race is one of the healthiest things you can do – it'll help you manage your weight, lower your cholesterol and blood pressure levels, reduce stress and feel happier and better about yourself. But to keep reaping those benefits – and get to the starting line healthy and strong – it's important to stay injury free.

Runners don't have to worry about being tackled, tripped or booed by rowdy spectators, but our sport still delivers its share of damage. The average distance runner lands on each leg 750 times per mile, which has quite an impact (three to six times your weight) on your body. Avoiding overuse injuries isn't impossible, however. The key is to listen to your body. The following 10 rules of injury prevention will help you do just that. And while no one can guarantee that you'll always run injury free for a lifetime, following these rules will increase your odds of having a long and healthy running and racing career.

RULE 1: INCREASE MILEAGE GRADUALLY

WHY: Bumping up your weekly total with a few miles here and there may not seem like a major burden on your body – until you think about all those steps that make up each of those miles. That's why sudden jumps in mileage are a leading cause of injury. Your body needs adequate rest to recover, and that requires a gradual approach.

HOW: Increase mileage by no more than 10 to 20 per cent a week. So if you're running 3 miles a day, three times a week, the next week you'd run about 3.5 miles on those 3 days. Also, build plateaus into your training. After increasing mileage for 3 weeks, hold steady for a week or two before increasing again. If you aim to run 4 days a week, you'd still want to increase your overall time running by only 10 to 20 per cent. If you're a veteran coming back from a break, don't try to pick up where you left off. Determine a comfortable base volume from which to start – no more than 50 per cent of your previous weekly mileage. If you've been off for only a few weeks, you might start from a base of 3 miles a day and then increase, following the same 10 to 20 per cent principle.

RULE 2: INCREASE INTENSITY GRADUALLY

WHY: Not every workout should leave you gasping for air. If you train hard every day, you're more susceptible to injury. Faster running places greater strain on the body, which means muscles work harder and suffer more damage, joints absorb greater impact and your body expends more overall energy.

HOW: Intense workouts – hills, intervals, tempo runs (you read about these in Chapter 2) – should make up no more than 20 per cent of your training. Never add more than one of these elements to your training at a time. If you're doing hill workouts once a week, wait 2 or 3 weeks before adding track or tempo workouts to your weekly mix. Likewise, increase the intensity of each type of workout gradually. If you usually do a 2-mile tempo run but now you want to train for a marathon, don't bump up the length of the tempo to 5 miles right away. Increase it to 3 for a few weeks, and then to 4 for a few weeks after that.

RULE 3: INCREASE MILEAGE BEFORE SPEED

WHY: As you gain fitness, you'll naturally want to run longer – and faster. That's great. Just don't do both at the same time. Increased mileage and speed place more stress on your body, and each requires greater recovery.

HOW: By building a base of solid mileage at a slower, steady speed, you prepare your body to handle the stresses of faster workouts to come. For beginners gearing up for a 5-K, a good goal is to be able to run 4 or 5 days a week, with one of those runs lasting 45 minutes or more. Once you can do this for several weeks, you can introduce some intensity. Experienced runners should follow the same principle. After a half-marathon or marathon training season, take a break of a month at lower mileage. Then focus on building a base for a month or two before adding some light speedwork (fartleks). A month later, you'll be ready to do some more intense speedwork (intervals or tempo runs).

RULE 4: ALTERNATE HARD EFFORTS WITH REST

WHY: Intense running produces more inflammation and microtears in the muscles than easy jogging does, so recovery afterwards is essential. Some studies have shown that the number of consecutive training days directly correlates to the incidence of injury, which is why it's key to build at least 1 day of complete rest into your weekly schedule.

HOW: For beginners, every run is hard because the body is adapting to all the new stresses of running. So the best programme is one that alternates training and rest or cross-training days. Veteran runners still need rest between hard efforts, but because their bodies are better conditioned, they can recover with a slower, easier run. When training hard, monitor your body and be flexible. Sometimes a single rest day isn't enough. Also, allow your body at least a full week of rest each year. Plan your break for after a marathon or another goal race, or schedule it around a holiday or a business trip, when training can be more of a burden than a pleasure.

RULE 5: PAY ATTENTION TO EARLY WARNING SIGNS

WHY: In most cases, your body will send you signals before an injury manifests itself fully: pain in a joint; soreness in the heel; something not quite right that doesn't go away after a day or two but instead grows worse. Don't dismiss it. After all, it's much easier to apply ice and rest for a couple of days than to recover from a torn muscle.

HOW: You can expect a certain amount of achiness when you begin running or increase the intensity of your training. Non-localized soreness that diminishes in a few days isn't cause for concern, but sharp pain or joint discomfort during a run is a red flag. If pain is sudden or becomes worse, slow down. If the pain doesn't stop, walk back, taking the shortest route possible. You can try running the next day, but if the pain returns, see your GP or a physiotherapist.

RULE 6: WEAR THE RIGHT RUNNING SHOES

WHY: Just because all running shoes cushion and protect your feet doesn't mean any old shoe will do. Each is designed with a particular type of body and stride in mind. The right shoe will minimize your biomechanical abnormalities; the wrong one can easily exacerbate such problems.

HOW: Visit a specialist running shop to determine if you need a motion-control shoe (to control excess pronation), a neutral-cushioned shoe (for maximum shock absorption) or a stability shoe (which provides a moderate degree of stability and cushioning). It's important to replace your shoes every 300 to 500 miles. Also, get a new pair after an injury to ensure maximum support as you heal, as well as whenever your training changes dramatically, such as when you increase your mileage to prepare for a race or you end a cycle of high mileage.

RULE 7: VARY YOUR WORKOUTS AND TERRAIN

WHY: Too much of any one thing isn't a wise running plan. For example, running hills every day could overstress your quadriceps and Achilles tendons. Be careful, too, of always running the same route. Many roads have a slant, or camber, that raises one leg higher than the other and places both feet on a pronounced tilt, an invitation for injury. Soft surfaces generate less impact and are therefore more forgiving for runners. Trails and dirt paths are also beneficial because the uneven nature of the terrain means your feet won't land in exactly the same manner with every footstep. This variety is less likely to cause overuse injuries, and it develops balance and strength in the foot and ankle.

HOW: Avoid running the same route every day, especially if you usually run on roads or hills. Make an effort to get out on dirt trails, a canal tow path or even a football pitch at least once a week. Treadmills offer a cushioned surface that also reduces impact.

RULE 8: FUEL PROPERLY

WHY: What you eat and drink can affect your injury risk. Protein, for example, is a must for muscle repair. Calcium helps protect bones from fractures. Dehydrated muscles are more susceptible to strains and tears. Even if you're trying to lose weight, you need enough calories to fuel your running. Adding workouts and subtracting too many calories can put you in an energy deficit, making you feel fatigued and off-kilter, which could trip you up on a run.

HOW: The bulk of a runner's diet (about 50 per cent) should consist of carbohydrates from unrefined sources, such as brown rice, whole wheat bread, and fruits and vegetables. Another 25 per cent of calories should consist of protein from lean meat sources, fish or beans and pulses. The remaining calories should come from fat (healthy unsaturated versions – olive or rapeseed oil, nuts and fish). While it's important for runners to keep fluid levels high, drinking too much water during a long run or race can put you at risk for hyponatraemia, a condition that occurs when an athlete consumes so much water that sodium levels become dangerously low. Two hours before a long run, drink 480ml of sports drink. While on the run, take in around 240ml every 20 minutes. Afterwards, rehydrate with at least 480ml of sports drink.

RULE 9: MIX IT UP

WHY: Cross-training develops endurance and maintains fitness during rehabilitation, while giving your body a break from the repetitive forces of running. For new runners, supplementing running with another activity until the body can handle more running is an excellent strategy. Serious runners who are already covering as much mileage as their bodies can handle but want to increase training volume can take it up a notch, without risking injury, by cross-training. (You'll see specific cross-training recommendations for runners in the next section.)

HOW: New and injury-prone runners can devote 50 per cent of their overall workout time to cross-training by running every other day and doing other activities on the off days. Or you could run for 15 minutes, then hop on an elliptical trainer or spin bike for 15 minutes. It's best to choose non-weight-bearing activities, such as pool running or cycling. As you become a more experienced runner, you should cross-train once or twice a week. Use it to add some conditioning work on days off from running, or do it after a run as a way to build strength in other areas of the body.

RULE 10: INCREASE YOUR FLEXIBILITY AND STRENGTH

WHY: Although research hasn't proved conclusively that stretching reduces the incidence of injuries among runners, anecdotal evidence points strongly to the virtues of stretching. If you put enough miles on your legs without stretching, you'll feel it: range of motion will be reduced, and running will feel strained. When your body is that rigid and inflexible, you simply won't be training at optimal capacity. Also, strengthening your upper body and core counteracts the force and stress on your legs when you run and helps you maintain proper form.

HOW: Adopt a 5-minute 'no excuses' stretching routine that focuses on the areas of your body in which tightness is most likely to inhibit your stride: calves, hamstrings, quadriceps and inner thighs. (See 'Flexibility Training' on page 121 for sample routines.) Make a commitment to strength train twice a week on days when you're running easy or cross-training. Trying to do lunges or squats the day of a long run or hard workout will make you vulnerable to injury, which defeats the whole point of strength training. For a runner-specific lifting programme, see 'Strength Training' on page 108.)

CROSS-TRAINING

When you're preparing for a road race, it's only natural for running to be the focus of your workout time. After all, slaving away on the stairclimber or rowing machine isn't going to get you race ready like an elliptical trainer will, but that doesn't mean you should completely shun all other types of exercise. In fact, runners who *only* run are more prone to injury than those who mix other activities into their training schedule. That's because cross-training can strengthen muscle groups that running neglects, and rebalance muscles that running overworks. 'Cross-training will make you a stronger and healthier runner,' says www.TriEndurance.com multisport coach Kris Swarthout. 'Low- and non-impact sports like biking and swimming will help build supporting muscles used in running, while also giving your primary running muscles a rest.' Here's information on the top three cross-training activities for runners.

SWIMMING

In the last sweaty miles of a hot summertime run, nothing seems more inviting than a dip in a cold pool, lake or the sea. But does swimming offer anything besides a way to cool your heels? Absolutely, according to Dan Bullock, a former competitive swimmer and founder of www.swimfortri.com. Swimming is a great workout for runners because it builds strength in often-neglected muscles and promotes recovery. 'Swimming enhances functional strength in the upper body and core muscles,' Bullock says. This is the kind of strength you need for maintaining an upright running form at the end of races and hard workouts, when runners have a tendency to hunch forward. And runners who swim regularly may recover from their road miles faster than landlubbers do. 'Swimming gives you "active recovery", free of the impact forces of running,' Wilson says. The hydrostatic pressure and coolness of water promote bloodflow, which carries waste products away from sore muscles, according to research in the American Journal of Physiology.

Whether you're in a pool or the sea, swimming is a technique sport, like golf or skiing. So unless you're a natural in the water, you'll get the most out of your swimming workouts if you take lessons to learn how to stroke, kick and breathe properly. 'Swimming with the head high and lifting it to breathe are common mistakes, and cause the legs to sink,' explains Bullock. 'This position increases drag and will tire you out, even if you're fit. Always keep the head and neck neutral and comfortable when you're swimming, except when you're turning your head sideways to breathe.' An adult swimming class is the best place to learn the basics of proper technique.

POOL RUNNING

Lap swimming isn't the only way to increase your fitness in the water. In fact, aqua running is probably the best of all cross-training options for runners because of the direct impact it can have on your running performance. 'Done right, it's a full-body workout involving the legs, arms, shoulders and core muscles,' says British cross-country coach Nick Anderson of www.fullpotential.co.uk. That's because water is 773 times more resistant than air, so it serves to strengthen all key running muscles, thus increasing your land-running turnover and stride length. Also, water exercise is isokinetic – the water resists you only as much as you resist it – so you can work out as hard or as easy as you like.

Studies have shown that runners who pool run improve their hip extension and even run faster 5-K times. 'Many of the runners who take pool-running classes become faster on the roads,' says Anderson. And they do so without increasing their risk of injury one bit, as pool running is completely non-impact (you don't touch the bottom). Aqua runners can also maintain aerobic fitness for up to 6 weeks when not running on land, making it a great injury-recovery activity. A whole host of injuries – shin splints, stress fractures and plantar fasciitis among them – won't keep you from pool running. Therefore, you won't lose one iota of fitness during your healing period. What's more, research has shown that injured runners who pool run can reach the same positive mood state as when they run. No surprise here. You're not sitting around sulking; you're staying fit and recovering from your injury. Pool running is as simple as land running: you jump into the water and start running. If you know how to run, you know how to pool run.

I started pool running a few years ago when I was recovering from a stress fracture. At first I was apprehensive of trying it. Would I be bored out of my mind? Would I look silly? Would it even feel like a workout? But when you can't run, you quickly become willing to try anything. Once I tried it, I loved it and continued to pool run even after my injury healed. Here are some tips that helped me.

1. **GO WITH FRIENDS.** I was lucky and found another injured runner to join me. Pool running with a friend or group helps the time pass more quickly.

2. **TAKE TUNES.** Lots of pools have PA systems with music on, which is great. But if yours doesn't, or if the music they play doesn't motivate you, bring your own. Check out www.swimmer.co.uk for waterproof MP3 players and containers – mine became my saviour on my solo pool runs.

3. **RUN FOR TIME.** Commit to spend as much time in the water as you'd spend on a normal run.

4. **DO REGULAR RUNNING WORKOUTS.** Vary the pace, the tempo, the length of time. Simulate a favourite running workout. Some type of fartlek workout, whereby you're constantly changing speeds, works best.

5. **EXPERIMENT WITH ACCESSORIES.** AquaJogger belts – available from www.aquarunning.com – are flotation devices worn around the waist to help keep legs moving at a quick pace. Special waterproof footwear that's slightly weighted will add resistance to your workout – you'll slow down but work harder.

CYCLING

You can become just as fit on your bike as you do in your running shoes. Joe Friel, a pro-cycling coach who works with runners, cites a study in which moderately fit runners ran 4 days a week, while another group ran twice and did two hard bike workouts. 'After 5 weeks,' says Friel, 'there was no difference between the two groups in maximal oxygen uptake and running performance.' But did you notice that word – *hard*? A casual spin around the block may be an excellent recovery workout, but to challenge the cardiovascular system and reach peak fitness, you have to invest a little more energy. As with running, that means quality workouts like tempo rides, intervals and hills. 'Doing intervals at 80 per cent of your maximum heart rate on the bike is the same to your heart and lungs as doing them running,' says Terrence Mahon, who coached Deena Kastor to victory in the 2006 London Marathon. 'The muscles and motor skills involved in each sport are what differentiate them.'

Moreover, bicycling enhances running because it works the major muscles. 'The bike develops power muscles like quads, glutes and calves,' Mahon says. Cycling also gives runners' bodies a break from the pounding, allowing for faster recovery. Add up all these benefits, and they equal this: cycling lets you add another high-intensity but non-impact workout to your week, thus reducing stress on the joints, risk of injury and the cumulative fatigue of high mileage.

STRENGTH TRAINING

It's no secret that weight training isn't your top priority. If it were, you'd be reading a different book (and probably spending more time flexing in front of the mirror). But if it's not part of your programme at all, you're missing out on more than toned biceps. Strength training is a smart supplement to a runner's race preparations because it strengthens muscles and joints, which can improve race times and decrease injury risk. 'Running faster is easier if your whole body is working with you,' says Anderson. 'A runner with strong legs but weak arm muscles and weak core muscles will always be slower than a runner with total-body fitness.'

The trouble is that when runners adopt a strength-training programme, they tend to do the standard gym-rat routine – that is, bench presses, biceps curls and leg presses. While these moves might make you look good, they're virtually useless for making you a better runner. Think about it: how does pushing a weight away from your chest help you run a faster 10-K? It doesn't. In fact, lifting weights the way everyone else does may even increase your injury risk because typical workouts often lead to strength imbalances between muscle groups and around joints.

That's why runners need a strength-training workout that targets key muscle groups and keeps them balanced. The following programme is based on four basic principles that make it distinct from training plans that don't benefit running. The result? Big pay-offs – decreased injury risk, increased performance – in little time. It takes less than 30 minutes, 2 days a week.

THE PRINCIPLES

1. WORK THE BACK OF YOUR BODY. People tend to neglect the muscles they can't see. They focus on their quadriceps and chest and overlook their hamstrings and back. But building the posterior chain is especially important for runners. The muscles at the back of your lower body propel you forward, and the muscles at the back of your upper body help you maintain an upright running stance. Slumping forward decreases your ability to run efficiently, requiring you to exert more energy. Many runners work their quads more than their hamstrings, creating a strength imbalance, which is the primary reason for recurrent hamstring injuries. Weak hamstrings also transfer stress to the knee joint.

2. TARGET YOUR CORE. Core training is as trendy today as aerobics was in the '90s. But this is one fitness fad runners should embrace. Your core is the foundation from which all movement is initiated. It includes all the muscles of your midsection and hips that support your spine and allow you to flex, extend and rotate your trunk and hips. A strong core gives you more than the confidence to race in a vest; it improves your performance. Exercises that involve twisting your torso not only work your abs, they also strengthen your hips, enabling you to fire up a powerful stride and finish-line kick when the rest of the pack is fading.

3. MIX IT UP. People tend to gravitate towards workouts that emphasize their natural abilities. Since runners are masters of endurance, it makes sense that in the weight room, we'd adopt the classic formula for building muscular endurance – light weights, high repetitions. But lifting heavier weights for fewer reps is necessary for increasing strength. Strong muscles enhance the stability of joints, which reduces the wear and tear on ligaments and makes you a better sprinter and hill climber. This programme incorporates both lower-repetition (six to eight) and higher-repetition (10 to 15) sets. Afraid of bulking up? Don't be. Adding a significant amount of muscle requires a steady surplus of calories (which few runners have) and workouts that focus on muscle size, not performance.

4. MULTITASK. You've got a race to prepare for, so you need a lifting programme that won't infringe on your road time. The key to an efficient workout is emphasizing compound movements – exercises that require you to move more than one joint at a time. For instance, rows and lunges give you greater benefits in less time than single-joint isolation exercises such as biceps curls and triceps extensions. Another way to get the most from a workout is to combine two movements into one. For example, rotating your torso as you perform a shoulder press doubles your gains.

THE PLAN

Do Workout A and Workout B each once a week, resting at least a day between each session. Each workout includes five exercises. Perform the first three (numbers 1, 2 and 3) as a circuit: do one set of each and move to the next without resting in between. When you've completed one circuit of the three exercises, rest for 60 seconds. Repeat once or twice, for a total of two or three circuits. Alternate between the final pair of exercises: do one set of number 4 followed by 30 seconds of rest, then one set of number 5 followed by 30 seconds of rest. Repeat until you've done two or three sets. Use the heaviest weight that allows you to complete every repetition of every set. You shouldn't finish the last set feeling like you could have done five more repetitions.

WORKOUT A

1. OVERHEAD LUNGE

Hold a pair of dumbbells straight above your shoulders, your arms straight and elbows locked. Step forwards with your left leg and lower your body until your front knee is bent 90 degrees. Return to the starting position, and repeat with your right leg. That's 1 repetition.

Modification: To make it easier, hold dumbbells at shoulder level.

Repetitions: 6 to 8

Muscles worked: quadriceps, hamstrings, glutes, shoulders, core

2. MIXED-GRIP CHIN-UP

Grab a chin-up bar overhand with your left hand and underhand with your right, and hang with your arms completely straight. Pull yourself as high as you can without allowing your body to rotate. With each set, alternate grips. (Mixing grips forces your core muscles to contract to stabilize your torso so that your body stays straight throughout the movement. This means you strengthen your arms, back and abs in one move.)

Modification: To make it easier, place a bench underneath the bar. Jump up to the top position, then lower yourself slowly.

Repetitions: 6 to 8

Muscles worked: back, biceps, core

3. SCORPION

Get into a press-up position, but with your feet on a bench. Raise your right knee towards your left shoulder as you rotate your hips up and to the left as far as you can. Then reverse directions, rotating your hips up and to the right, and try to touch your right foot to the back of your left shoulder (you won't be able to do it). That's 1 repetition. Continue for 30 seconds with your right leg, then switch legs.

Modifications: To make it easier, do step one of the exercise, twisting in just one direction. To make it harder, instead of putting your feet on a bench, do the exercise with your shins on a stability ball.

Repetitions: as many as you can in 30 seconds

Muscles worked: shoulders, core

4. STABILITY BALL JACKKNIFE

Get into a press-up position, but instead of placing your feet on the floor, rest your shins on a stability ball. Pull the ball towards your chest by raising your hips and rounding your back as you roll the ball forwards with your feet.

Modification: To make it easier, pull your knees as close as you can to your chest without lifting your hips into the air, and return to the starting position.

Repetitions: 10 to 12

Muscles worked: shoulders, core

5. BACK EXTENSION WITH LOWER TRAP RAISE

Grab a pair of dumbbells and position yourself in a back-extension station, hooking your feet under the leg anchors. Lower your upper body until it's just short of perpendicular to the floor – allow your back to round – and let your arms hang straight down from your shoulders, your palms facing each other. Without moving your arms, raise your upper body until it's in line with your hips. Holding that position, raise your arms at 45-degree angles to your body (so they form a Y) until they're in line with your torso. Lower your arms slowly, then repeat the entire move.

Modifications: To make it easier, do the back extension without the arm lift. To make it harder, place one leg under the leg anchors and the other on top.

Repetitions: 10 to 12

Muscles worked: lower back, glutes, middle back, shoulders

WORKOUT B
1. STABILITY-BALL HIP EXTENSION/LEG CURL

Lie on your back and place your calves on a stability ball. Extend your arms to your sides to help support and balance your body. Push your hips up so that your body forms a straight line from your shoulders to your knees. Without allowing your hips to sag, roll the ball as close as you can to your hips by bending your knees and pulling your heels towards you.

Modifications: To make it easier, do only steps one and two, and skip the leg curl. To make it harder, do the exercise with just one leg, holding the other leg in the air above your hips.

Repetitions: 6 to 8

Muscles worked: hamstrings, glutes, core

2. ROTATIONAL SHOULDER PRESS

Stand holding a pair of dumbbells just outside your shoulders, your palms facing each other. Press the dumbbells overhead as you rotate to your left. Lower the dumbbells as you rotate back to the centre, then rotate to the right as you press the weights upwards again. That's 1 repetition.

Modification: To make it easier, do half of the repetitions without the rotations.

Repetitions: 6 to 8

Muscles worked: shoulders, triceps, core

3. STABILITY-BALL KNEE DRIVE

Place your hands on a stability ball and get into a press-up position, your body form-ing a straight line from your shoulders to your ankles. Keeping your arms straight, quickly raise your right knee as close as you can to your chest. Lower it and repeat with your left leg.

Modification: To make it easier, perform the move in a regular press-up position with your palms on the ground, not the ball.

Repetitions: as many as you can in 30 seconds

Muscles worked: shoulders, core

4. ALTERNATING DUMBBELL ROW

Hold a pair of dumbbells at arm's length in front of you, palms facing your thighs. Keeping your back naturally arched, bend at the hips and lower your torso until it's nearly parallel to the floor. Keep your arms straight as you bend your hips so that the dumbbells hang straight down. Pull the dumbbell in your right hand by bending your elbow and raising your upper arm towards the middle of your back. Lower and repeat with your left arm. That's 1 repetition.

Modification: To make it easier, perform the move with both hands at once, which requires less core stability.

Repetitions: 10 to 12

Muscles worked: middle back, biceps, core

5. LOWER-BODY RUSSIAN TWIST

Lie on your back with your upper legs perpendicular to the floor and your knees bent 90 degrees. Without changing the bend in your hips or knees, lower your legs to the right side of your body while keeping your shoulders in contact with the floor. Lift them back to the starting position, and repeat to the left side. That's 1 repetition.

Modification: To make it harder, keep your legs straight.

Repetitions: 10 to 12

Muscles worked: core

FLEXIBILITY TRAINING

When runners start training for a race, they focus on building endurance and speed. Improving flexibility never seems to be part of the strategy. Yet a flexible body is more efficient, sees more gains in strength and endurance, enjoys more range of motion, is less injury prone, recovers more quickly and simply feels better. 'Runners who work to increase their flexibility can enhance their performance without increasing their mileage or spending more time on the track,' says Jim Wharton, a musculoskeletal therapist and co-author of *The Whartons' Stretch Book*.

While most experts agree that improving range of motion is a good thing – especially for runners, who are notoriously inflexible – how you develop it is a subject of debate. There are several different ways to increase flexibility, and one method hasn't been shown to be better than the others. So while it would be great to be able to give you an exact, one-size-fits-all recommendation, the only way to find the best method for you is to experiment.

STATIC STRETCHING

You've seen this classic method a million times – it's the runner trying to touch his toes, the runner leaning over an extended leg, the runner lowering her heel off a curb. This method involves stretching a muscle to its furthest point and then holding it from 30 to 60 seconds.

Static stretching has come under fire in recent years, being blamed as a cause of injuries rather than as a way to prevent them. But when static stretching leads to an injury, it's usually because a cold, tight muscle was forced into a position too quickly and too aggressively. If too much tension is placed on a muscle, it will contract (defeating the purpose of stretching) and could become strained or torn. But if the muscle is stretched gradually and after it's been warmed up, this method is generally considered safe and effective.

Here is a static stretching programme recommended by Stephen Pribut, sports podiatrist who specializes in running injuries and author of popular sports medicine website www.drpribut.com. It specifically targets the muscles you'll use while training for your next race. It's safest to do the stretches after a run, once your muscles are warmed up. If you want to loosen up before a run, do a 5-minute walk or easy jog, stretch and then run. Be sure to stretch gently, and if a specific area of your body is painful (beyond simple soreness), bypass that muscle group until you get the sign-off from your doctor – not every running injury responds well to stretching.

WALL PRESS-UP

Target: calves, Achilles tendon

Technique: Stand facing a wall, with one foot close to the wall and the other foot approximately 2 to 3 feet from the wall. With your hands on the wall and keeping your heels on the ground, lean forwards with your hips, bending your front leg's knee but keeping your back leg straight. Hold for 10 seconds, switch legs and repeat 10 times.

KNEE CLASP

Target: hamstrings, lower back

Technique: Lie down on a firm surface. Bring both of your knees to your chest. Hold for 10 seconds, and repeat 5 times.

HEEL HOLD

Target: quadriceps

Technique: Stand sideways to a wall, one hand against it for support. Reach down with your other hand and grasp your ankle, pulling the heel of that foot against your buttocks. Hold for 10 seconds, and repeat on the other side.

BUTTERFLY

Target: adductor, or inner thigh, muscles

Technique: Sit on the floor with your back straight. Pull your legs together so the soles of your feet are touching. Your knees will be pointing to each side. Wrap your hands around your feet and press outwards with your arms against the inside of your thighs, extending the stretch. Hold for 10 to 30 seconds.

PLANTAR STRETCH

Target: plantar fascia

Technique: Sit down barefoot and cross your right leg so that your ankle rests on your left thigh. Hold your toes and bend them back towards your shin, stretching the band of tissue that runs along the arch of your foot. Hold for 10 to 30 seconds, then switch feet.

SIDE STRETCH

Targets: iliotibial band

Technique: Stand with your left foot crossed in front of your right. Reach overhead and lean towards your left. Lean as far as you can without bending your knees. Hold for 10 to 30 seconds, then repeat on the other side.

ACTIVE-ISOLATED STRETCHING

This method was developed as an alternative to static stretching. Active-isolated stretching aims to lengthen muscles, filling the area with blood and oxygen, which repatterns the neurological pathways, restores muscles that have become torn and realigns imbalances. It differentiates itself from static stretching in two ways. First, it's active: instead of holding a stretch for 10 to 30 seconds, you hold positions for just a second or two. When you feel slight tension on the muscle, you release, and then you repeat the entire motion 10 times. This active movement (rather than a static hold) allows you to gradually warm up your muscles. With each repetition, you'll be able to stretch further; there will be a noticeable difference in how much you can bend or reach between your first and your 10th stretch. Because of this, active-isolated stretching serves as a warm-up, and it can be done safely before and after a run.

The second way active-isolated stretching differs from static stretching is that it isolates the muscles you are stretching by contracting the opposing muscle group. So if you are stretching your hamstrings, you contract your quadriceps. If you are stretching your quads, you contract your hamstrings first. This relaxes the targeted muscle group so that it can lengthen more effectively.

Here is an active-isolated routine Jim Wharton, co-author of *The Whartons' Stretch Book*, designed specifically for runners. Some of the moves require a stretching rope – if you don't have one, you can use a towel, belt or dog lead.

DOUBLE-LEG PELVIC TILT

Target: lower back and buttocks

Contract: abdominals and muscles in the front of the hips and thighs

Technique: Lie down on your back with both knees bent. Place your hands behind your knees. Lift your legs towards your chest. Gently assist with your hands; don't pull. Hold for a second or two, release, and repeat for a total of 10 repetitions.

STRAIGHT-LEG HAMSTRING

Target: back of thighs

Contract: front of thighs

Technique: Lie with your non-exercising knee bent and your other leg straight. Place your foot into the loop of a stretching rope. Lift your leg as far as you can. Grasp the ends of the rope with both hands and 'climb' up it, hand over hand, as your leg lifts. Hold for a second or two, release, and repeat for a total of 10 repetitions. Repeat with the other leg.

HIP ADDUCTORS

Target: inner thighs

Contract: outer thighs, buttocks

Technique: Place one foot inside the loop of a rope, and wrap it around the inside of the ankle. Lock your knee, rotating your leg inwards. Extend your leg out to the side, leading with your heel. Hold for a second or two, release, and repeat for a total of 10 repetitions. Repeat on the other leg.

HIP ABDUCTORS

Target: outer thighs, hips

Contract: inner thighs

Technique: Place your foot into the loop of a rope and wrap it around the outside of your ankle. Rotate the exercising leg outwards, knee locked. Extend your leg across the midline of your body, leading with your heel. Hold for a second or two, release, and repeat for a total of 10 repetitions.

QUADRICEPS

Target: front of thighs

Contract: buttocks, back of thighs

Technique: Lie on your side with your knees against your chest and your head on the floor. Slide your bottom arm under the thigh of your bottom leg, placing your hand around the outside of your foot. Grasp the shin of your upper leg with your upper hand. Move your upper leg back as far as you can. Hold for a second or two, release, and repeat for a total of 10 repetitions.

GLUTEALS

Target: lower back, hips, piriformis, buttocks

Contract: abs, front of thighs

Technique: Lie with one leg straight, toes pointed inwards, and the other leg bent. Lift your bent knee towards the opposite shoulder. Keep your pelvis on the ground, and use your hands for a gentle assist. Hold for a second or two, release, and repeat for a total of 10 repetitions.

ACHILLES TENDON

Target: the 'cord' that attaches your heel to your lower leg

Contract: front of lower leg

Technique: Sit on the floor with one leg straight and one leg bent, your bent leg's heel close to your buttocks. Grasp the bottom of your foot with both hands. Raise the ball of the foot up, keeping your heel on the floor. Hold for a second or two, release, and repeat for a total of 10 repetitions.

GASTROCNEMIUS

Target: calves

Contract: muscles in front of the lower legs

Technique: Sit on the floor with both legs straight. Loop the rope around one foot and grasp the ends of the rope with both hands. Flex your foot, aiming your toes towards your knee while keeping your knee locked. Hold for a second or two, release, and repeat for a total of 10 repetitions.

YOGA

While stretching after every run is ideal, sometimes it's difficult to fit in – especially if your runs are followed by a mad dash to get to work or pick up the children. Runners who always find themselves pressed for time and barely manage to fit in a run, let alone stretching, would benefit from signing up for a yoga class – a predetermined time to focus on flexibility. This way, you know that Tuesdays and Thursdays, for instance, you'll manage an hour of much-needed flexing time.

Yoga isn't just for people who can already bend like a contortionist. In fact, inflexible runners with tight muscles stand to gain the most. 'Tight muscles create imbalances, and every step you take makes the situation worse,' says personal trainer and massage therapist Suzi Hall (www.innovatefitness.com). 'Because yoga focuses on balance, flexibility and proper alignment and can relax and elongate the muscles, I would absolutely recommend it as part of a training programme for runners.'

This simple yoga-for-runners routine will make you stronger, fitter, faster and less injury prone. It was developed specifically for runners by certified instructor Jeff Logan. Each pose strengthens and stretches muscle groups that will benefit your running. Unless otherwise noted, hold each pose for 30 to 60 seconds, and repeat each one right after the other. Do this sequence two or three times a week.

BOUND ANGLE POSE (BADDHA KONASANA)

Benefit: stretches and 'opens' hips and groin, improving range of motion and creating a more efficient running stride

Technique: Sit on the floor with your back against a wall and the soles of your feet together. Move your heels towards your groin as much as you can. Exhale, and press down with your legs. Keep your 'sitting bones' grounded and your arms and shoulders relaxed as you hold the pose. (This pose can be held for up to 5 minutes.)

DOWNWARD-FACING DOG (ADHO MUKHA SVANASANA)

Benefit: stretches glutes, hamstrings and Achilles tendon; opens shoulders and chest to enhance breathing; stretches and loosens shoulders so they can be more relaxed while running

Technique: Sit on your heels with your arms extended and forehead on the floor. Spread your fingers and press your palms into the floor. Keep your hands in this position. Lift your hips, tuck your toes and extend your legs. Turn your buttocks up towards the ceiling and stretch your heels towards the floor.

CHAIR POSE (UTKATASANA)

Benefit: stretches and strengthens legs, particularly quadriceps and ankles; stretches and strengthens shoulders and chest

Technique: From a standing position, with feet hip-width apart, extend your arms over your head, keeping your shoulders relaxed. Exhale as you bend your legs until your thighs are nearly parallel to the floor. (Visualize yourself sitting in a chair.) Keep your heels flat on the floor.

HERO POSE (VIRASANA)

Benefit: stretches quadriceps; relieves stiffness in knees

Technique: Kneel on the floor with your knees nearly together and your feet hip-width apart, toes pointing straight back. Exhale as you sit on the floor between your feet. (If you can't do that, place a prop such as a block, thick book or folded blanket between your feet and sit on that.) Place your hands on the top of your thighs, your palms facing down. Relax your shoulders and upper body, keeping your chest lifted. Feel the stretch in your thighs.

TRIANGLE POSE (UTTHITA TRIKONASANA)

Benefit: strengthens legs; expands rib cage, enabling you to breathe more deeply and easily when you run

Technique: Stand with your legs about 4 feet apart. Lift your chest and stretch your arms at shoulder height, palms down. Turn your left foot in and your right foot and leg out 90 degrees. Stretch your legs; on an exhalation, extend your upper body to the right, placing your right hand on your right shin, your right ankle or the floor. Stretch your left arm up with your palm facing forwards. Look up at your left hand, keeping your spine straight and your neck relaxed.

WIDE-LEGGED FORWARD BEND POSE (PRASARITA PADOTTANASANA)

Benefit: strengthens and stretches legs, particularly hamstrings, one of the tightest muscle groups in runners

Technique: Stand with legs about 5 feet apart, feet parallel and toes pointing straight ahead. Exhale as you bend forwards from your hips, keeping your heels on the floor. Place your fingertips on the floor shoulder-width apart, chest parallel to the floor. (If you can't reach the floor, rest your hands on two blocks.) Exhale and lower your upper body towards the floor. Let your head hang.

MOUNTAIN POSE (TADASANA)

Benefit: helps achieve proper posture to improve running form

Technique: Stand tall, feet together and planted into the ground with your heels, tailbone and base of skull in a straight line. While in this position, try to extend your legs, lift your chest and roll your shoulders back and down. The first time you try this, it may feel awkward, especially if you have poor posture. You should practise this position and try to maintain it throughout the day. 'Be conscious of standing this way in your daily life and while you're running,' Logan says. 'Runners that plod along tend to roll their shoulders forward. Elite runners, by contrast, are in Tadasana, whether they know it or not.'

YOGA DECODED

There are several major yoga styles or schools, which share a common lineage. Almost all fall under hatha yoga, which seeks to achieve a balance of mind, body and spirit through the practice of specific asanas (poses) and breathing. The differences between the styles are more a matter of emphasis – on breathing, alignment, coordination of breath and movement, holding the posture or the speed with which the practitioner flows from one posture to another. As yoga has become Westernized, the differences between the 'brands' are vanishing. 'No one type of yoga is better than another,' says Sherry Roberts of www.yogamovement.com. 'It is simply a matter of personal preference.' Here's a list of some of the more common types of yoga.

Ananda: a gentle and inward-focused style that's not as athletic or aerobic as other styles

Ashtanga: a more challenging workout (Power Yoga is one form), in which the practitioner moves from one posture to another rapidly to build strength and flexibility

Bikram: involves a set series of 26 asanas practised in a room that may be as hot as 37°C in the belief that the body will be more flexible in heat

Iyengar: pays attention to the precise alignments of the postures and uses props, such as belts and blocks, to help the flexibility-challenged do poses correctly

MASSAGE THERAPY

Sports massage isn't an indulgent spa treatment, nor is it reserved for hard-core elite athletes. It's a method of flushing out the lactic acid that's produced when we run, says massage therapist Suzi Hall (www. innovatefitness.com. This waste can build up in muscles and cause soreness over time. Removing it speeds recovery and increases flexibility, both of which can improve performance. 'If you have the right shoes and training plan and you eat and hydrate well, massage is the one extra thing that will make a difference in how well you train and race,' says Hall. Sports massage combines other massage techniques, including deep-tissue and Swedish. What sets it apart is that it targets and reduces tension in muscles and joints that are affected by athletic use and injury.

A study in the *British Journal of Sports Medicine* found that massage therapy administered 2 hours after exercise reduced the intensity of muscle soreness 48 hours later. An Australian study showed similar findings: post-exercise massage lessened soreness 24 hours later. Scientific evidence linking massage with injury prevention isn't as strong, but runners who have regular massages say their injury-free limbs are all the proof they need. 'I used to get sidelined from calf strains,' says Elizabeth Cartwright of Sale, Manchester, who runs 30 miles a week and gets a massage every other Thursday. 'Since I started having regular massages, the chronic tightness in my calves has disappeared, and I'm not becoming injured.' The practice has medical-community support as well. 'Massage is probably the best way to prevent delayed-onset muscle soreness,' says Dr Lewis Maharam, MD, author of *The Exercise High: How to Get It, How to Keep It.* 'And as far as injuries go, massage is icing on the cake. Massage can supplement physiotherapy as an effective injury treatment.'

All runners can benefit from massage, but it's especially useful for runners training for marathons or covering more than 35 miles a week. Not only are their bodies subjected to a greater amount of stress, but high-mileage runners tend to have an intense commitment to their training schedules – and don't deviate from them. 'Some runners plough through runs and ignore aches and pains, and that can create problems down the road,' Hall says. Massage therapists get to know their clients' bodies by taking full inventories of their muscles and how they respond to training. 'If there's something lurking in that hamstring,' says Hall, 'we'll find it.'

Massage therapy also works on a psychological level. Clearing metabolic waste from the muscles helps the entire body function optimally. And when your body is performing at its best, you feel less of the anxiety that could otherwise affect your gait, breathing and posture, Hall says.

Even if you're training for a shorter event, like a 5-K or 10-K, you'll see long-term results from regular massage. 'You're maximizing your ability to enjoy running for years to come,' says Hall.

Therapists usually recommend a weekly hour-long massage, but that depends on individual need. For some runners, once every 6 weeks is enough. Just be sure to never get a deep sports massage just before or after a race, warns Hall: 'Sports massage changes muscle tissue at a deep, structural level, and that can have a huge impact on your performance.' Allow at least 48 hours between your last intensive massage and a race.

Finding a massage therapist who understands all of this is key, so see a licensed practitioner who specializes in sports massage and has experience with runners. Visit the British Massage Therapy Council website (www.bmtc.co.uk) for a listing.

RECOVERY

Recovery is an important – but often neglected – part of training plans. Most runners don't have a problem pushing themselves. But when you're focused on building endurance and speed, it's easy to forget how important rest is. 'It's when you're not running that the muscle rebuilds itself and becomes stronger,' says physiotherapist Bryan Heiderscheit, a contributor to Evidence-based Sports Medicine. 'If recovery is insufficient, you'll break down more than you build up.' Recovery is vital, whether you want to run the race of your life or just get to the starting line. Here's how to make the most of your downtime.

EASE UP. If you stop seeing positive gains or your legs feel sluggish or especially sore, you're overdoing it. 'Don't wait for aches or pains to take a recovery day,' Heiderscheit says. 'That's a sign of overtraining.' Take at least 1 rest day per week and additional days as needed. Check your pulse for 60 seconds before getting out of bed. If it's 20 per cent higher than normal, you're due for a rest day.

If you're training for a marathon, your long-run pace should be 1 to 2 minutes slower than the pace you plan to race at, says Heiderscheit. So if you are planning to run 26.2 miles at an 8:30 minute-mile pace, your long runs should be run at a 9:30 to 10:30 pace. Alternate hard efforts (speedwork, hill repeats, long runs) with easy ones: 3- to 4-mile easy-pace recovery runs, cross-training or complete rest. Make your rest days count for more than just a day off by doing something you enjoy that you don't have time for while training. A film or a dinner out serves as more than a reward because relaxation helps you heal. A study published in *Psychosomatic Medicine* found that a distraction can lower stress levels and raise levels of cytokines, hormones that help tissue regenerate.

REFUEL. If you don't eat within 15 to 30 minutes after every run, you risk delaying your recovery for up to 24 hours, which leads to diminished performance, says Leslie Bonci, co-author of *Total Fitness for Women*. Researchers who had athletes consume carbs and protein immediately after exercise or 3 hours later found that protein synthesis was three times greater in the group that refuelled right away. Bonci recommends 50 grams of carbohydrates and 10 grams of protein post-workout. Yogurt and muesli or an energy bar and sports drink will do the trick.

BABY YOUR BODY. Act like an elite runner. 'When we aren't running, we're doing everything we can to recover,' says Bob Kennedy, a two-time Olympian who is a devotee of post-workout ice baths and weekly sports massages. Ice baths (sit in a cold bath for 10 to 20 minutes) and sports massages improve circulation and flush out waste products, reducing inflammation and soreness. A weekly sports massage is ideal, but those of us without sponsorship deals can do well with one every 4 to 6 weeks. Self-massage using foam rollers is an at-home alternative (see 'Do It Yourself' on page 150).

DO IT YOURSELF

Using a foam roller can provide similar benefits as deep-tissue massage – at a fraction of the cost. By increasing flexibility and decreasing muscle tension, a foam roller can help prevent injury and improve performance. Make the following exercises part of your regular running routine – run, roll then stretch. Place your body on the roller (find one at physique.co.uk) and slowly roll up and down (for about 10 to 15 seconds) along the muscle group you're targeting. If you find a particularly tight area, pause on that spot. Applying pressure can help release the tissue.

1. GLUTEAL MUSCLES, PIRIFORMIS (BUTTOCKS)

Lie on your left side with the foam roller under your left gluteal area and your left leg extended straight out. Bend your right knee. Take your right leg and cross it over your left with your right foot on the ground. Place both hands on the floor for support. Roll your left gluteal muscles, then repeat on the other side.

2. ILIOTIBIAL BAND (OUTER THIGH)

Lie on your left side with the foam roller just below your hip bone. Extend your left leg straight out, and bend your right leg and place it in front of your left leg. Place both hands on the floor for balance, and roll along your outer thigh from below your hip bone to just above your knee. Repeat on the other side.

3. QUADRICEPS

Lie face-down with the foam roller under your right thigh. Put your forearms on the ground. Keep your left foot off the ground by stacking your feet on top of each other (toe of left foot on heel of right foot). Supporting your body weight with your forearms, roll up and down from the bottom of the hip to the top of your knee. Repeat on the other side.

4. HAMSTRINGS

Sit with the foam roller under your left thigh. Place the palms of your hands on the ground (fingers pointing towards your body). Keep your right foot off the ground by stacking your feet on top of each other (heel of right foot on toe of left foot). Supporting your body weight with your hands, roll up and down from the bottom of your hip bone to the top of your knees. Repeat on the other side.

5. GASTROCNEMIUS (CALF)

Sit with the foam roller under your left calf. Place the palms of your hands on the ground (fingers pointing towards your body). Keep your right foot off the ground by stacking your feet on top of each other (heel of right foot on toe of left foot). Supporting your body weight on your hands, roll up and down along your calf. Repeat on the other side.

INJURY TREATMENT

Diagnosing injuries early is the key to a fast recovery. Here are the five most common running injuries, how to spot them and how to get relief quickly.

PLANTAR FASCIITIS

A runner's foot hits the ground about 750 times per mile, and the heel and its attaching tissues bear the brunt of that force, says Richard Braver, a sports podiatrist and contributor to *Podiatry Today* Magazine. The plantar fascia is the connective tissue that runs from the heel to the base of the toes. It may look like a series of fat rubber bands, but it's made of collagen, a rigid protein that's not very stretchy. The stress of overuse, overpronation or overused shoes can rip tiny tears in it, causing pain and inflammation, also known as plantar fasciitis.

CAUSES: Drastic or sudden increases in mileage, poor foot structure and inappropriate running shoes can overload the plantar fascia.

SYMPTOMS: Sufferers feel a sharp stab or deep ache in the middle of the heel or along the arch. Another sign is the 'morning hobble'. The foot tries to heal itself in a contracted position overnight, explains osteopath and runner Dr Gavin Burt of www.backsandbeyond.co.uk. Taking that first step causes sudden strain on the bottom of the foot. The pain can recur after long spells of sitting. But it tends to fade during a run, once the area is warmed up.

TREATMENT: To prevent plantar fasciitis, run on soft surfaces as much as possible, keep mileage increases to less than 10 per cent per week, and visit a specialist running shop to make sure you're wearing the proper shoes for your foot type and gait. It's also important to stretch the plantar fascia and Achilles tendon. Plantar fasciitis can be a nagging problem, which becomes worse and more difficult to treat the longer it's present. At the first sign of soreness, massage (roll a golf ball under your foot) and apply ice (roll a frozen bottle of water under your foot). What you wear on your feet when you're not running also makes a difference. Arch support is key, and walking around barefoot or in flimsy shoes can delay recovery. If pain is present for more than 3 weeks, see a sports podiatrist. Treatments such as orthotics, foot taping, cortisone injections, night splints and anti-inflammatories decrease symptoms significantly within 6 weeks in about 95 per cent of sufferers, says Burt. For more stubborn cases, physiotherapy may be prescribed; 6 months of chronic pain may benefit from shock-wave therapy or low-level laser treatments. While it's typical to experience pain in just one foot, massage and stretch both feet. Do it first thing in the morning and three or four times during the day.

ILIOTIBIAL BAND SYNDROME

Iliotibial band (ITB) syndrome is one of the most common overuse injuries among runners. Because the most notable symptom is typically swelling and pain on the outside of the knee, many runners mistakenly think they have a knee injury, but it actually involves the ligament that runs down the outside of the thigh from the hip to the shin. 'When the band comes near the knee, it becomes narrow, and rubbing can occur between the band and the bone. This causes inflammation,' says Dr Freddie Fu, an orthopaedic surgeon and author of *An Atlas of Shoulder Injury*.

CAUSES: ITB syndrome can result from any activity that causes the leg to turn inwards repeatedly, such as wearing worn-out shoes, running downhill or on banked surfaces, running too many track workouts in the same direction or simply running too many miles. Unlike many overuse injuries, however, ITB pain afflicts seasoned runners almost as much as beginners. 'Also, ITB syndrome is much more common in women,' says John Pagliano, a podiatrist who specializes in sports medicine and a one-time 2:26 marathon runner. 'It could be the way some women's hips tilt, which can cause their knees to turn in.'

SYMPTOMS: The best way to tell if you have ITB syndrome is to bend your knee at a 45-degree angle. If you have an ITB problem, you'll feel pain on the outside of the knee. 'Sometimes an MRI can confirm it,' says Dr Fu. 'An x-ray is usually negative, but an MRI can show a partial thickening of the band, which results from inflammation.'

TREATMENT: Once you notice ITB pain, the best way to get rid of it for good is to rest immediately. That means fewer miles or no running at all. 'In the majority of runners – 85 per cent – once they rest, the pain doesn't come back,' Dr Pagliano says. 'But I'm not talking about the guy who finally decides to rest after feeling pain for 6 months during 90-mile weeks. You have to rest immediately.' While you're backing off on your mileage, you can cross-train. Swimming, pool running, cycling and rowing are all fine. Side stretches will also help, as will ice or heat, ultrasound or electrical stimulation with topical cortisone. This last method is useful 'particularly in the acute phase,' says Dr Fu. If your ITB problem doesn't get better after several weeks, seek help from a sports medicine professional.

RUNNER'S KNEE

Forty-two per cent of all overuse injuries affect the knee joint, and patellofemoral pain syndrome (PFPS) – runner's knee – is the most common overuse injury among runners. It occurs when a mistracking kneecap (patella) irritates the femoral groove in which it rests on the thighbone (femur).

CAUSES: Pinpointing a single cause is difficult, says Dr Stephen Pribut, a sports podiatrist who specializes in running injuries and author of popular sports medicine website www.drpribut.com. It could be a biomechanical problem – the patella may be larger on the outside than it is on the inside, sit too high in the femoral groove or dislocate easily. Also, worn cartilage in the knee joint reduces shock absorption, high-arched feet provide less cushioning and flatfeet or knees that turn in or out excessively can pull the patella sideways.

There are also muscular causes. Tight hamstrings and calf muscles put pressure on the knee, and weak quadriceps can cause the patella to track out of alignment. Just the repetitive force of a normal running stride alone can be enough to provoke an attack.

SYMPTOMS: Symptoms include tenderness behind or around the patella, usually towards its centre. You may feel pain towards the back of the knee, a sense of cracking or that the knee's giving way. Steps, hills and uneven terrain can aggravate PFPS, which can affect one or both knees. It strikes mostly younger, recreational runners and twice as many women as men, according to the *British Journal of Sports Medicine*. (Women tend to have wider hips, resulting in a greater angling of the thighbone to the knee, which puts the kneecap under more stress.)

TREATMENT: To prevent PFPS, run on softer surfaces, keep mileage increases less than 10 per cent per week and gradually increase hill work in your programme. Visit a specialist running shop to make sure you're wearing the proper shoes for your foot type and gait. Also, strengthening your quadriceps will improve patellar tracking, and stretching your hamstrings and calves will prevent overpronation. At the first sign of pain, cut back your mileage. The sooner you lessen the knee's workload, the faster healing begins, says Dr Pribut. Avoid knee-bending activities, cambered surfaces and downward stairs and slopes until the pain subsides. As you rebuild mileage, use a smaller stride on hills. Consider orthotics if new shoes don't fix the problem. 'If your feet have good form, your knees will follow,' says Dr Pribut. If pain persists, see a doctor to rule out another condition.

SHIN SPLINTS

The nature of shin splints most often can be captured in just four words: *too much too soon*. This is usually a problem for either new runners or runners starting afresh. 'Shin splints' is the catch-all term for lower-leg pain that occurs below the knee either on the front outside part of the leg (anterior shin splints) or the inside of the leg (medial shin splints).

CAUSES: Shin splints often plague beginning runners who do not build their mileage gradually enough, or seasoned runners who abruptly change their workout regimes, suddenly adding too much mileage, for example, or switching from running on flat surfaces to hills. There can be other factors at work as well, such as overpronation (a frequent cause of medial shin splints), inadequate stretching, worn shoes or excessive stress placed on one leg or hip from running on slanted roads or always running in the same direction on a track.

SYMPTOMS: You'll feel tenderness, soreness or pain along your lower leg. Initially, the pain might be present only while you're exercising. Eventually, however, it can be continuous. The most common site for shin splints is the medial area, according to Burt. Anterior shin splints usually result from an imbalance between muscles in the calf and the front of the leg and often afflict beginners who either have not yet adjusted to the stresses of running or are not stretching enough.

TREATMENT: Experts agree that when shin splints strike, you should stop running completely or decrease your training, depending on the extent and duration of pain. Then, as a first step, ice your shin to reduce inflammation. If you continue running, wrap your leg before you go out. Use either tape or an elastic bandage, starting just above the ankle and continuing to just below the knee. Keep wrapping your leg until the pain goes away, which usually takes 3 to 6 weeks. 'What you're doing is binding the tendons up against the shaft of the shin to prevent stress,' Burt says. Consider cross-training for a while to let your shin heal. When you return to running, increase your mileage slowly, no more than 10 per cent weekly. Make sure you wear the correct running shoes for your foot type. Overpronators should wear motion-control shoes, and severe overpronators may need orthotics. Avoid hills and excessively hard surfaces until the pain goes away completely, then re-introduce them gradually to prevent a recurrence. If you're prone to developing shin splints, stretch your calves and Achilles regularly as a preventive measure.

ACHILLES TENDINITIS

The Achilles is the large tendon connecting the two major calf muscles – the gastrocnemius and soleus – to the back of the heel bone. Under too much stress, the tendon tightens and is forced to work too hard. This causes it to become inflamed (that's tendinitis) and, over time, can produce a covering of scar tissue, which is less flexible than the tendon. If the inflamed Achilles continues to be stressed, it can tear or rupture.

CAUSES: Tight or fatigued calf muscles transfer too much of the burden of running to the Achilles. This can be brought on by not stretching the calves properly, increasing mileage too quickly or simply overtraining. Excessive hill running or speedwork, both of which stress the Achilles more than other types of running, can also cause tendinitis. Inflexible running shoes, which force the Achilles to twist, are responsible in some cases. Runners who overpronate (feet rotate too far inward on impact) are most susceptible.

SYMPTOMS: Dull or sharp pain anywhere along the back of the tendon, but usually close to the heel; limited ankle flexibility; redness or heat over the painful area; a nodule (lumpy build-up of scar tissue) that can be felt on the tendon; and a cracking sound (scar tissue rubbing against the tendon) when the ankle moves signal Achilles tendinitis.

TREATMENT: Stop running, take an anti-inflammatory and ice the area for 15 to 20 minutes several times a day until the inflammation subsides. Self-massage may also help. 'I have every therapeutic machine available for the treatment of Achilles tendinitis, and the treatment of choice is massage with a heat-inducing cream or oil,' says Marc Chasnov, a physiotherapist and author of *Healing Sports*

Injuries. He suggests rubbing semicircles in all directions away from the knotted tissue three times a day. Once the nodule is gone, stretch the calf muscles. Don't start running again until you can do toe raises without pain. Next, move on to skipping, then star jumps, and then gradually begin running again. You should be back to easy running in 6 to 8 weeks. If your injury doesn't respond to self-treatment in 2 weeks, see a physiotherapist or orthopaedic surgeon.

HOT OR COLD?

Ice packs and heating pads can provide relief when you're hurt. Here's how to put them to use.

ICE

Best use: Apply immediately after sustaining an acute injury, such as an ankle sprain, or after irritating a chronic injury, such as shin splints or plantar fasciitis.

How: You can use a commercial ice pack, frozen water bottle or bag of frozen veggies. Never apply directly to skin – always lay a barrier such as a towel or piece of clothing against your skin.

Duration: Research has shown that icing in 10-minute increments (10 minutes on, 10 minutes off, then repeat) is more effective than icing for 20 minutes straight. Also, icing three to five times a day produces better results than just once or twice.

HEAT

Best use: Applying heat to a tender spot before you run can help loosen tissues and relax the injured area.

How: Heating pads or hot wet towels (hold a facecloth under hot tap water) both work well.

Duration: Apply heat for 5 to 10 minutes before a run.

OTHER NUISANCES

WEATHER EXTREMES

One of the simple joys of running is the connection it gives us to the outdoors. Breathing in fresh air, witnessing a sunrise and experiencing the changing seasons keep us coming back for more – well, most of the time. It's tough to be enthusiastic about running outdoors when the mercury drops below zero or shoots up beyond 30°C. Even if you are lucky enough to live in an area of mild temperatures year-round, you may be racing in a location that isn't so temperate. Even runners at the London Marathon have faced less-than-ideal racing weather. In 2007 temperatures reached 25°C. The April average is just 13°C. To help you prepare for whatever Mother Nature dishes out, here's expert advice for training and racing in unfriendly conditions.

Rules for Running in the Heat

1. DRESS FOR SUCCESS. Wear light-coloured, lightweight apparel that has vents or mesh. Microfibre polyesters, such as CoolMax and Drifit are good fabric choices. Also, be sure to apply sunscreen with an SPF of 30 or higher.

2. JUST SAY NO. Alcohol, antihistamines and antidepressants can all have a dehydrating effect. Using them just before a run can cause you to have to go to the bathroom, compounding your dehydration risk. Anti-inflammatories affect kidney function, so they should also be avoided before long, hot runs or races.

3. DRINK EARLY AND OFTEN. Top up your fluid stores with 450ml of sports drink an hour before you head out, then toss down 200ml to 700ml about every 20 minutes while running. And remember: sports drinks beat water because they contain glucose and sodium (sugar and salt), which increase your water-absorption rate, replace the electrolytes you lose in sweat and taste good, encouraging you to drink more.

4. MAKE ADJUSTMENTS. Don't do long or higher-intensity runs during the heat of the day. And when you do run at midday, try to pick a route that affords some shade. Nick Anderson, a British cross-country coach, has his runners adjust the pace when race day is warm. 'I tell them to start up to 30 seconds slower than their goal pace,' Anderson says. 'Then, if they're feeling good at the halfway point, they can gradually speed up.' Use the same pacing strategy when the temperature rises during your training runs.

5. DETERMINE YOUR LOSSES. Rehydrate with 100ml of sports drink for every 100g of body weight you lose during exercise. Because sweat rates vary enormously, you can get an idea of your own sweat rate by weighing yourself naked before and after a couple of runs (see page 218). If, for example, you lose 100g during a 40-minute run, it means you sweat about 100ml of fluid. Going forward, you can then try to replenish your fluids at a rate of about 100ml per 40 minutes of running.

HOW HEAT CAN HURT

HEAT CRAMPS

Cause: Dehydration leads to an electrolyte imbalance.

Symptoms: Severe abdominal or quad, hamstring or calf cramps

Treatment: Restore salt balance with foods or drinks that contain sodium.

Prevention: Don't run hard in the heat until acclimatized, and stay well hydrated with sports drink.

HEAT FAINTING

Cause: Often, a sudden stop interrupts bloodflow from the legs to the brain.

Symptoms: Fainting

Treatment: Elevate legs and pelvis to help restore bloodflow to the brain.

Prevention: Cool down gradually after a workout, with at least 5 minutes of easy jogging and walking.

HEAT EXHAUSTION

Cause: Dehydration leads to an electrolyte imbalance.

Symptoms: Core body temperature of 39° to 40°C, headache, fatigue, profuse sweating, nausea, clammy skin

Treatment: Rest and apply a cold pack on the head and neck, and restore salt balance with sodium-rich foods and drinks.

Prevention: Don't run hard in the heat until acclimatized, and stay well hydrated with sports drink.

HYPONATRAEMIA

Cause: Excessive water intake dilutes blood-sodium levels; usually occurs after running for 4 or more hours.

Symptoms: Headache, disorientation, muscle twitching

Treatment: Emergency medical treatment is necessary; hydration in any form can be fatal.

Prevention: When running, don't drink more than about 800ml per hour, and choose sports drink over water.

HEATSTROKE

Cause: Extreme exertion and dehydration impair the body's ability to maintain an optimal temperature.

Symptoms: Core body temperature of 40°C or above, headache, nausea, vomiting, rapid pulse, disorientation

Treatment: Emergency medical treatment is necessary for immediate ice-water immersion and IV fluids.

Prevention: Don't run hard in the heat until acclimatized, and stay well hydrated with sports drink.

Rules for Running in the Cold

1. DRESS UP. Experts agree that you can ward off hypothermia and frostbite by covering skin with clothing that wicks moisture and repels rain and snow. Richard Donovan, an Irish ultra runner and organizer of the North Pole Marathon and Antarctic Ice Marathon, recommends running in a balaclava when the temperature plummets. He also recommends layering kit so you can vary the amount of warmth your kit provides with the changing conditions. Damp clothes increase heat loss, so after a run change into warm, dry clothes as soon as possible.

2. MAINTAIN A STEADY PACE. Windy weather and treacherous surfaces can slow you down, lowering your metabolic heat production and increasing your risk of hypothermia or frostbite. 'Don't venture too far from home in cold or icy conditions.' says Donovan. Run loops in your neighbourhood – if you get tired, slip on ice or get wet, you can quickly escape the elements. If you're a morning or evening runner, consider switching to midday runs during the winter. You could even consider getting on the treadmill at the gym if conditions outside make running impossible.

3. KNOW WHAT YOU'RE UP AGAINST. Don't just consult the thermometer – windchill is actually more important. It can be a tolerable 1°C outside, for example, but if the winds are gusting at 20 miles per hour, the resulting sub-zero windchill could make you reconsider an outdoor run. If you do venture out, take note of the wind's direction. Donovan suggests that you start off running into the wind. 'If the wind is at your back, it'll push you along, so you'll pick up your pace and warm up quickly,' he says. 'But when you turn around to head back, you'll be running into the wind. Your temperature will drop, and your risk of hypothermia or frostbite will increase.'

4. REMEMBER TO DRINK. 'Because runners don't see their sweat losses in the winter, they're not attentive to their drinking,' says

Lawrence Armstrong, author of *Performing in Extreme Environments*. But it's possible to sweat just as much as you do on a warm day – especially if you're wearing layers. Fill your water bottle with sports drink so its contents don't freeze (the sugar content lowers its freezing point).

5. **LOCATION, LOCATION, LOCATION.** Even soft surfaces like grass or muddy trails can freeze and become hard in the winter. If you've got a bad knee or, say, a history of shin splints, it's probably best to alternate outside runs with treadmill running or cross-training activities. Also, consider relocating your running route. On the coldest days, you might find that the hills are warmer than low-lying areas. Avoid running alongside lakes and rivers, where winds can really bite because of a lack of tree cover. And remember, while running in harsh weather can earn you bragging rights, there's no shame in sticking with the treadmill – especially if you want to train hard. You're more likely to reach your race goal, after all, if you run whatever the weather.

LEG CRAMPS

Muscle cramps are one of the most common medical complaints from athletes during endurance events, especially marathons and triathlons, according to Dr Martin Schwellnus, professor of sports medicine at the University of Cape Town in South Africa. No one knows for sure what causes them, and there's ongoing debate on the subject. The varied theories range from excessive heat, dehydration, and the loss of electrolytes to muscle fatigue, insufficient training and poor stretching habits. The newest theories focus on the interaction between nerves and muscles. Experts do agree on several steps you can take to reduce your cramping risk. Try these five strategies.

1. **TAKE TIME TO STRETCH.** Pay particular attention to the muscles that are most prone to cramping. Stretch them gently but thoroughly.

2. TRAIN APPROPRIATELY FOR EVERY EVENT. This is especially important for marathon runners. On race day, running much faster or further than you've trained will simply overwhelm your muscles and make you susceptible to cramps.

3. PREPARE YOUR BODY FOR THE ELEMENTS. If you live in a dry climate, for example, don't decide to run a marathon in an extremely humid city, unless you give yourself ample time – a week or more – before the race to become accustomed to the steamy conditions.

4. KEEP SPORTS DRINK HANDY. Though experts don't know for sure if dehydration causes cramping, it's still important to stay well hydrated when you run. Plus, it may lessen the severity of any cramps you do develop. An hour or two before you run or race (depending on your tolerance), top up your tank with 450ml of fluid. Then take in 150ml to 350ml every 15 to 20 minutes during the run. Make sure your fluid of choice contains electrolytes; these salts can help prevent cramps.

5. TRY PLYOMETRICS. Make leaping, hopping or skipping drills – otherwise known as plyometrics – part of your regular training. Such exercises can improve muscle–nerve coordination and strength and help loosen tight muscles (see 'Hop To It', below, for drills).

HOP TO IT

Plyometrics – bounding, jumping and hopping exercises – generate explosive muscle power and can help you become a faster runner. Diane Vives, a contributor to the plyometrics book *Training for Speed, Agility, and Quickness* and president of Vives Training Systems, describes 12 plyometric drills geared specifically for runners. You'll want to gradually introduce these into your training, no more often than twice a week, and take a 2-week break from all plyometric work every 8 weeks.

To warm up for a plyometrics workout, jog for at least 5 minutes, followed by 5 minutes of light skipping and gentle star jumps. It's best to perform the jumping drills on grass so you have some cushioning. A football pitch is ideal so you can use the lines, but any stable, cushioned surface like a track will provide the give you need. After the drills, do an easy run to finish your workout. Launch into each drill with your feet shoulder-width apart and knees slightly bent. Perform two to four sets of each drill.

BALANCE DRILLS

The payoff: improves balance; strengthens ankle, knee and hip joints

1. JUMP AND STICKS

Jump from and land on the balls of both feet. Jump high, not far. Land with knees bent and hold 2 to 3 seconds before jumping again. Alternate jumping 10m forward and sideways.

2. TWO-WAY HOPS

Start balanced on your right leg. Hop roughly 1 metre forwards onto your left leg. Hold for 2 seconds to regain balance. Stay facing forwards and hop back to the starting position onto your right leg. Now hop onto your left again, but move sideways, then back. That's 1 set. Do 3 more, then repeat the drill starting on your left leg.

ELASTICITY DRILLS

The payoff: strengthens all lower-body muscles; improves the spring-like ability of muscles and tendons around the joints

3. SKIP-UPS

This is an exaggerated skipping motion. Drive your leading knee high, until the thigh is parallel to the ground, while popping off the ground, with your toes pointed.

4. STANDING LONG JUMPS

Swing your arms back, then forwards as you leap. Jump as far as possible, landing on both feet.

POWER DRILLS

The payoff: improves stride power, or the force of each push-off

5. JUMP AND SPRINT

Do a standing long jump (drill 4), but at the moment you land, sprint for about 10 metres.

6. TRIPLE JUMPS

Start with a standing long jump (drill 4), but land on your right foot, quickly hop forwards onto your left, then hop and land on both feet. Aim for maximal distance the whole way.

CHAFING

Nothing is more irritating and painful than skin rubbed raw. Runners are most prone to chafing during long runs or races. 'During a marathon, every moving body part that can chafe will chafe,' says Dr William Roberts, author of *Bull's Sports Injuries Handbook*. And if you think it will make your racing experience uncomfortable – just wait for your post-race shower. Warm water beating down on chafed skin is pretty painful (trust me). To prevent this, make sure your shoes, socks and clothing have no raised seams that will rub against skin. Also, use Vaseline, Bodyglide or another lubricant product in key locations, including armpits, nipples and inner thighs. If you're chafing mid-race and have no lube, rinse the area with water or saliva. Sweat residue causes friction.

BLISTERS

When road racers share war stories, the villain is often a throbbing blister. Annoying and painful, blisters are caused by friction, usually shoes or socks rubbing against skin. Anything that intensifies rubbing can start a blister, including a faster pace, poor-fitting shoes and foot abnormalities such as bunions, heel spurs and hammertoes. Heat and moisture intensify friction by making feet swell, which explains why many runners suffer blisters only during races, especially marathons. You're perspiring more, running faster and longer, sloshing through water stations, and – if it's warm – pouring water over your head. The body responds to friction by producing fluid, which builds up beneath the part of the skin being rubbed, causing pressure and pain. A blood blister occurs when friction ruptures tiny blood vessels. While most blisters don't pose a serious health risk, they should be handled with care.

Prevention

1. MOISTEN YOUR FEET. Just like sweaty skin, dry skin is more prone to friction. Use skin creams and lotions liberally on a daily basis to maintain proper moisture.

2. RUN WITH SLICK SKIN. Coat your feet with Vaseline or Bodyglide before you run. These products form a protective shield between your skin and sock.

3. WEAR HIGH-QUALITY SOCKS. Synthetic socks wick moisture away from the skin. Cotton may be lighter, but it retains fluid. Socks with reinforced heels and toes also help reduce friction.

4. DOUBLE UP. Wear two pairs of socks so the friction occurs between the layered socks, rather than between the sock and skin. If your shoe now feels too tight, go up half a size, as long as your foot doesn't slide around, making blisters a possibility.

5. WEAR SHOES AND SOCKS THAT FIT. Shoes that are too small will cause blisters under the toes and on the ends of the toenails. There should be a thumb's width of space between your toes and end of the toe box. Your socks should fit smoothly, with no extra fabric at the toes or heels.

Treatment

SMALL BLISTER: Cover it with an adhesive bandage or a blister-specific product like Compeed, which provides cushioning and works like a second skin. If you're hurting mid-run or mid-race, it's worth stopping to take off your shoe and check for any loose debris that might be causing the blister. If there's an aid station nearby, apply some lubricant to the sore area before setting off again.

SUPERSIZE BLISTER: It's beyond help – from bandages, anyway. If a blister is large enough that you can see the fluid inside, it's better to drain it. Otherwise, you risk a painful pop while you're running. Here's how to safely drain a blister.

- Wash the blistered area with soap and water.

- Sterilize a needle by rinsing it in ethanol or putting the point in a flame until it's red hot. Make a small hole in the blister, and squeeze out the clear fluid.

- Do not remove the skin over a broken blister; the new skin underneath needs this protective cover.

- Apply hydrogen peroxide to prevent infection, and wrap the area with antibiotic ointment and a sterile bandage.

- If the blister swells, reddens or discharges thick yellow/green fluid, it may be infected; see your GP.

BLACK TOENAILS

While they make a pedicurist squirm, black toenails generally aren't harmful and are considered by many runners to be a rite of passage. Toenail injuries increase with training miles, so they're pretty common among marathon runners and ultra runners. It will take a few weeks or months, but the black nail will be raised up and pushed off the nail bed as the new healthy nail grows below. The discolouring is caused by pooled blood under the nail, which makes it an attractive place for fungal growth. So as the toenail starts to grow, clean underneath it with soap and water, and keep it clipped short to make it harder for fungus to get underneath it. You can also try a silicone toe sleeve or tube to help protect it until it grows out. You'll reduce the chance of your nails turning black in the future if you make sure that you have enough room in the toe area of your shoes. Also, remember that as your mileage increases, your feet tend to swell, so you may want to consider going up half a size in your favourite pair for the second half of your training programme.

STOP PAIN IN ITS TRACKS

Certain types of mid-race discomfort (chest pain, a torn muscle) warrant an immediate trip to the medical tent. But there are less severe but still irritating points of tension that can crop up during a race. Here are five 'quick release' moves that can ease your pain while keeping you in the running.

1. **Calf cramp:** Stand on the side of the road, with feet below your shoulders, and raise the ball of the cramped leg's foot while keeping the heel on the ground. For a deeper stretch, lean forwards, keeping the knee of the stretched leg locked and the opposite knee bent. Hold for 2 seconds; repeat 10 times or more as necessary.

2. **Stiff neck:** Slow down or walk. Look straight ahead; slowly lower your right ear towards your shoulder. Press gently on your temple with your right hand. Hold for 2 seconds, then release. Repeat 10 times or more on each side as needed.

3. **Tight shoulders:** Slow your pace or walk. Looking straight ahead, turn your head to the right 45 degrees and drop your head forwards, bringing your ear down towards your chest. Place your left hand on top of your head and press down gently. Hold for 2 seconds, release and repeat 10 times or more on each side as needed.

4. **Side stitch:** While running, contract your abdominal muscles, and lean forwards and into the side where you feel tightness. Push your hand against the point of pain. If the pain persists, make a quick pit stop. Stand with your feet shoulder-width apart and gradually lean into the cramp. Hold for 2 seconds, release and repeat 10 times or more as needed.

5. **Back tension:** While running, focus on the feeling of pulling your navel in and up. If this doesn't relieve the pain, stop running. Place your hands on your hips and lean forwards. Hold for 2 seconds, release and repeat 10 times or more as needed.

THE MENTAL SIDE OF TRAINING

Any experienced runner will tell you that racing is as much mental as it is physical. Your legs, heart and lungs can be in great shape, but if your brain isn't prepared for race day, you're not going to perform your best. Runners are realizing the role the mind plays in performance. Some elite runners now employ two trainers: one to help prep the body and another to train the brain. Recreational runners are also starting to take advantage of this expertise. The two-pronged approach makes sense, says coach Nick Anderson of www.fullpotential.co.uk. 'You might have lots of race potential, but without training your mind, you won't tap it.' Here's how to get over the four most common mental roadblocks runners face.

1. MENTAL HURDLE: You start off your training programme with boundless energy, but within a few weeks just lacing up your shoes feels like a chore.

CLEAR IT: Throwing all your energy into the beginning of a training plan is like starting a race at a full sprint. You're not going to have enough juice to finish strong – or finish at all. 'Initial excitement is good,' says sports psychologist and runner Dr Robert Udewitz, 'but you need to harness those feelings and divide them up throughout your training.' If you're on a 16-week marathon plan, for instance, 4 months is a long time to wait for a finish-line reward. Schedule a half-marathon midway through your training to help you stay focused and motivated. Also, there's no shame in self-bribery. Promise yourself a massage after your long run. Download new songs into your iPod to help you through a track workout.

2. MENTAL HURDLE: You get so stressed-out with performance anxiety that you aren't able to relax and enjoy the race experience.

CLEAR IT: 'Runners who feel this way are usually caught up in time goals,' says Dr Kate Hays, a sports psychologist and author of *Working it Out: Using Exercise in Psychotherapy*. 'Don't lose sight of all the other reasons you run – health, sense of accomplishment,

VISUAL ART

You've probably heard that visualization techniques and mental imagery can help your race results, but how exactly do you paint a picture of success? Sports psychologist Dr Kate Hays offers three ways to improve your visualization skills.

1. TAKE AN INSIDE-OUT APPROACH

When you imagine your body running, take an internal perspective. Before a race, think about how your muscles feel when you're tired and you still have a mile to go. 'Getting your mind prepared for those sensations will help you handle them on race day,' Hays says.

2. VISUALIZE HELPFUL PROPS

If you find tackling hills particularly challenging, pump your arms and imagine that you're using imaginary ropes on either side of you to haul yourself up the incline.

3. INCLUDE ADDITIONAL SENSES

Tuning in to your other senses provides more dramatic results, Hays says. If you become anxious before a race, for example, you can imagine sensations that have a calming effect, such as 'feeling' a cool sea breeze. During a rough patch in a race, you could 'hear' a loved one giving you encouragement.

connection to others.' To ease race-day pressure, she recommends setting three levels of goals: your ideal scenario, results that would make you happy and an outcome you could live with. And keep your ideal to yourself, so you don't face additional pressure from well-meaning family and friends.

3. MENTAL HURDLE: You struggle to balance running, work and family.

CLEAR IT: You might have been able to devote 15 hours a week to running – when you didn't have three children and a senior management job. Setting goals that don't reflect your current lifestyle sets you up for disappointment, says Hays. There's no need to give up running. But switching to a 3-day-a-week marathon-training plan or temporarily focusing on shorter-distance races could make you feel more successful in all areas of your life. Also consider ways in which running can bring you closer to your family. 'Some runners isolate themselves and push away others when they are training,' says Udewitz. 'Make your training more of a team effort by getting your family involved.' For instance, ask your partner to bike alongside you during a long run or your children to make you signs for race day, and then treat them to dinner at their favourite restaurant or take them to see a film of their choice. And make sure you're their top supporter at their next event.

4. MENTAL HURDLE: You're locked into a training plan, no matter what.

CLEAR IT: Runners are notoriously inflexible – and not just in their hamstrings. 'Part of the appeal of running is that it's an element of our lives we can control,' Hays says. 'If other areas of our lives are chaotic, a regimented routine can be comforting.' This is fine, but many runners obey their plans over their own bodies, putting themselves at risk of injury. To loosen this mind-set, Hays recommends visualizing a more flexible schedule. Imagine what it would be like skipping a run to rest an achy muscle. Then picture yourself running stronger the next day because you took time off. Or create an internal self-coach. Runners tend to be harder on themselves than a coach would be. A coach doesn't push you when your body needs a break or recommend completely unrealistic goals. 'Ask yourself if a coach would approve of what you're doing,' Udewitz says. 'Or if you were coaching another runner, what would you advise in this situation?'

SO HAPPY TOGETHER

We brush it off when our non-running friends call us addicts because we'd rather run than sleep in or join them for all-you-can-eat pizza. But there's a fine line between commitment and unhealthy obsession. 'Running to a point where you're losing performance or where your health suffers isn't healthy,' says sports psychologist Dr Rob Udewitz. Take this quiz to see if your attitude is putting you at risk for burnout or injury.

My main motivation for running:

A. Running makes me feel good. (1 point)

B. Running burns calories; it's a means to an end. (2 points)

C. Running is all about competition and performance. (3 points)

D. It's high-intensity; I need to continually test the limits of my body. (4 points)

When I run, I think mostly about:

A. Nothing in particular; I daydream and let my thoughts flow. (1 point)

B. My workouts for the rest of the week. (2 points)

C. Whether I'm running fast enough and far enough. (3 points)

D. My own shortcomings and ways to train harder. (4 points)

If I'm feeling under the weather:

A. I'll skip my workout; my body needs rest. (1 point)

B. I'll run; I can't miss a day. (2 points)

C. I'll run; I'm on a strict training plan and have to get in a set number of weekly miles. (3 points)

D. I'll run; I think it will make me stronger and help me feel better. (4 points)

If I'm hoping for a PB in a race and I don't get it:

A. I'm disappointed, but it doesn't ruin my day. (1 point)

B. I sign up for another race straight away. (2 points)

C. I berate myself and keep replaying it in my head. (3 points)

D. I start planning an even higher-intensity training schedule. (4 points)

After my run:

A. I bask in the post-run mood boost. (1 point)

B. I'm too exhausted to think about anything. (2 points)

C. I'll immediately review my splits to determine if it was a good run.
(3 points)

D. I'm usually already planning or thinking ahead to my next workout.
(4 points)

If another runner passes me during a training run:

A. I barely notice. (1 point)

B. It irritates me; it makes me feel inferior. (2 points)

C. I try to catch him. (3 points)

D. I take it as a sign that I need to do more speedwork. (4 points)

RESULTS

6 to 9 points: The Balanced Runner

You have a healthy attitude toward running. 'When you're balanced, you don't depend solely on running for your happiness and overall well-being,' says Dr Greg Dale, author of *The Fulfilling Ride: A Parent's Guide to Helping Athletes Have a Successful Sports Experience*.

10 to 14 points: The Addict

You're letting yourself be consumed by exercise. 'If your entire life is orchestrated around exercising, take a step back,' Dale says. You don't have to stop running, but take 2 days off every week and find a running partner who can help you enforce it. Keep an exercise log; instead of writing down calories burned or time and distance, record how the run made you feel, physically and emotionally.

15 to 20 points: The Number Cruncher

'When you focus too much on outcome goals, you lose the bigger picture,' Udewitz says. Reacquaint yourself with the joy of running: leave the watch at

(continued)

SO HAPPY TOGETHER (CONTINUED)

home every other run, enter some different types of races where fun is the goal, or volunteer to pace someone slower than you and be their coach and supporter.

21 to 24 points: The Overtrainer

There's a good chance you're overtraining – a recipe for injury and burnout. Udewitz recommends using the 80/20 rule: 80 per cent of your running should be comfortable; 20 per cent can be uncomfortable. Use a heart-rate monitor as a guide to when you can push it and when you should take it easy.

FUEL

When you're training for a race, what you put in your mouth becomes just as important as what you put on your feet. When you increase your mileage or intensity, your body needs more energy (calories) to power you through your runs and more nutrients to help you recover so that you stay strong and injury free. But not just any fuel will do. Think of your body as a high-performance car. Filling your tank with quality fuel will keep you running smoothly, not stalling or sputtering on your way to the finish line. By staying away from fad diets (low-carb plans especially) and understanding what your body needs, you can build an eating plan that fits you and helps you reach your goals.

THE RUNNER'S DIET

The first thing to consider is your calorie intake. Adult men and women need about 2,000 to 2,500 calories a day. To estimate your daily calorie needs for maintaining your weight, take your present kg and multiply by 34. That number covers your metabolic needs for the day, factoring in a bit of light activity. So if you weigh 65kg, you need about 2,210 calories per day. The rule of thumb is that running burns about 100 calories per mile. If you run 6 miles, you'll burn about 600 calories – that's 600 extra calories you'll need to consume to maintain your current weight. If you're looking to shed a few pounds (training for a race is a great way to do so), then you need to create a calorie deficit, meaning that you burn more than you consume. So in this example, you would want to keep your daily calorie intake below the 2,810 you are burning. Whether you are trying to lose weight or maintain, approximately 50 per cent of your daily calories should come from carbohydrates, 25 from protein, and 25 per cent from fat. Here's info on each component from nutritionist Dr Liz Applegate, a long-time contributor to *Runner's World*.

CARBOHYDRATES

Carbohydrates are the body's fuel for speed and power and, therefore, are essential to a runner's diet. Once ingested, carbs are either converted to glucose, an immediate energy source, or stored in the muscles and liver as glycogen, which is tapped later for energy. When glycogen stores are depleted, you'll feel it. Your legs will feel heavy, your body will feel sluggish, and you'll have difficulty keeping up your pace. So not surprisingly, nutritionists caution runners about popular low-carb diets, which can negatively affect a runner's health and performance. Training in a glycogen-depleted state causes the body to struggle to maintain even low-intensity exercise, making it difficult to improve fitness.

But not all carbohydrates are created equal. Some provide your body with a slow and steady stream of energy, while others deliver fast but short bursts of fuel. The difference between these two types of carbohydrates is revealed in the glycaemic index (GI), which assigns a number from 1 to 100 to a food based on how quickly its carbohydrates enter your system (see 'GI Guide' on page 181). If the carbs are quickly digested, with sugar rapidly entering your circulation, the GI is high: 70 plus. Many complex carbohydrates such as breads, pasta and potatoes have moderate to high GIs. If your digestive system has to wrestle with the carbs a bit before the sugar makes its way throughout your system, the food's GI is low: less than 55. Most fruits and other fibre-packed foods such as beans and porridge oats have low GIs, because the fibre trips up the sugars before they are absorbed into your system.

The addition of fat or protein also changes a food's GI. Both of these nutrients slow digestion and, therefore, lower the GI of a food or meal. So a slice of whole wheat bread smeared with peanut butter has a lower GI than the bread alone.

All of the popular weight-loss plans that recognize the difference between low- and high-GI carbohydrates strongly recommend eating low-GI foods to maintain weight and health. But it's not that easy for runners, who need to include a mix of both in pre-run and post-run meals to achieve maximum performance. High-GI foods can help boost speed and aid recovery, while low-GI foods extend endurance. So here's what to eat – and when.

Before you run: Go low. Studies have shown that eating low-GI foods about 2 hours before a workout helps maintain steady blood sugar levels during exercise, compared with high-GI foods. Therefore, you're able to run longer. In one study, cyclists were given either a high- or low-GI meal a few hours before a hard 2-hour ride. They were then instructed to pedal at full exertion for as long as they could. Cyclists pedalled almost 60 per cent longer after the low-GI versus the high-GI meal, and they also maintained higher blood sugar levels. The researchers attribute this to the slow and steady release of carbohydrates from the low-GI meal. Fruit, porridge and low-fat yogurt are great foods to eat about 2 hours before you run to help sustain you for the long haul (for more suggestions, see 'Adapt Your Snack' on page 183). But if you fuel up just minutes before you hit the road, reach for a higher-GI energy bar or sports drink so the carbs enter your system faster.

While you run: Time to get high to boost performance. The quickly digested carbohydrates in high-GI sports drinks, gels and energy bars (most bars have moderate to high GIs) offer an immediate source of sugar for your hard-working muscles. The quick-release carbohydrates also keep you feeling alert, as your brain thrives on sugar for fuel.

After you run (30 to 60 minutes later): High-GI foods are essential for restocking your glycogen stores. A study with cyclists demonstrated that eating high-GI foods following an exhausting session boosted glycogen stores almost twice as much as equal amounts of low-GI foods. So after your runs, fuel up with foods such as potatoes, cereals or bagels.

Of course, there are 23 or so hours in the day when you're not running or recovering from a run. During that time, should you reach for low- or high-GI foods? Research suggests that eating mostly low-GI foods is the best way to maintain health and weight. Here's why: when you eat a high-GI food, your blood sugar levels soar. Your insulin levels then surge in response as your body works to send the sugar to your muscles. While this sugar–insulin dance is okay on occasion, repeated spikes take a toll on your health. Countless research studies link a predominantly high-GI diet to obesity, diabetes, heart disease and cancer.

These examples of low-, moderate- and high-GI foods may help guide your menu choices.

GI GUIDE

LOW GI (LESS THAN 55)

Low-fat yogurt: 31

Pear: 36

Apple: 36

Tomato juice: 38

Lentil soup: 44

Baked beans: 48

Porridge oats: 49

Banana: 51

MODERATE GI (55 TO 70)

Sweet potato: 55

Brown rice: 55

Popcorn: 55

Honey: 55

Spaghetti: 60

Sweetcorn: 60

Muesli bar: 61

White or brown bread: 70

HIGH GI (MORE THAN 70)

Bran-flakes cereal: 71

Bagel: 72

Baked potato: 78

Energy bar: 83

Sports drink: 89

White rice: 91

Rice cakes: 91

Cornflakes: 92

PROTEIN

With all due respect to carbohydrates, protein is particularly important for runners because of its role in transporting carbohydrates throughout the body. Protein is especially crucial after a run. Recent evidence shows that adding protein to your high-carbohydrate post-workout meal enables the carbs to move more quickly into the muscles for faster refuelling. Runners need more protein than sedentary people because it builds and repairs muscles and tendons, which is key to recovery and injury prevention. Eating a post-run meal with a protein–carbohydrate combination – whether it's a fruit smoothie or a turkey sandwich – will provide what you need for a speedy recovery. When you choose proteins, lean is always best. Fat adds flavour – but also calories. So be sure to limit the number of calories in the protein sources you choose. A good rule of thumb: the fattier the protein, the smaller the serving.

FAT

There's a reason nutritionists always praise fish, particularly salmon. It contains a very powerful, almost panacea-like nutrient called omega-3 fat. When eaten regularly, these fats improve physical and mental health and prolong life. Often called good fats, omega-3s are found mostly in seafood and flaxseed and, to a lesser extent, certain oils and nuts. Omega-3 fats are considered essential fats because the body cannot manufacture them; we can get them only from the foods we eat. Besides salmon, top sources include tuna, cod, flaxseed (or oil), pumpkin seeds and walnuts. In fact, a very low-fat diet is as harmful as a very high-fat one. While cutting out fatty food is a good idea, healthy fats reduce the risk of heart disease and arthritis, as well as helping us feel full and satiated.

ADAPT YOUR SNACK

Drop that bagel. Before you instinctively reach for the same old pre-run snack, consider its glycaemic index (GI). The carbs you eat 2 hours before a run should be low GI, to provide your body with a slow but steady stream of sugar to enhance endurance. Thing is, many common pre-run snacks are actually high-GI carbohydrates. Here are five of them, with ways to lower their GI value so they'll sustain your energy levels throughout your entire run. Of course, if your run is only a few minutes away, keep the GI high.

Go from high: 1 bagel
To low: ½ bagel topped with 1 tablespoon peanut butter

Go from high: 1 bowl of instant porridge
To low: 1 bowl of porridge topped with dried fruit and nuts

Go from high: 240ml sports drink
To low: 240ml tomato juice

Go from high: 30g pretzels
To low: 30g pretzels dipped in yogurt

RUNNING FOR WEIGHT LOSS

While running is one of the most effective activities for burning calories, it's still a lot easier to eat 25 calories (a mintcrisp chocolate) than it is to run them off (at least 400m). And that's why runners who spend months training for a marathon might still be carrying a few extra pounds as they cross the finish line. 'There's also a big variable in the energy cost of running – which differs between genders, ethnicities, age, weight – that can result in 10 to 15 per cent variances in how much weight two different runners might lose,' says exercise physiologist Ralph La Forge. If you've always relied on the notion that 35 miles of running will burn exactly 3,500 calories and, therefore, result in the loss of 500g of body weight, you're missing out on an important part of the equation.

As La Forge explains, that 100-calories-per-mile standard (which is built into the readouts on your gym's treadmills) is the gross energy cost of running – strictly how many calories you burn going from point A to point B. But runners who are trying to lose weight need to also know the net energy cost of their runs so that they can more accurately calculate their entire calorie burn for the day. For example, if you go for a 3-mile run and it takes half an hour, you need to subtract however many calories you would have burned during those 30 minutes even if you'd been just sitting at your desk (about 80 calories). That means the true net energy cost of your run over the course of the day is more like 220 calories than 300.

It's also important for weight-conscious runners to factor in what La Forge calls energy conservation. 'About a third of us wipe out almost half of the energy expenditure of a workout by conserving energy afterwards,' he says. If your long run leaves you so exhausted that you spend the rest of your Saturday on the sofa watching TV rather than cleaning the house or working in the garden, you may end up burning fewer calories throughout the day than if you did a slightly shorter run but still had the energy to take the children to the park or take the dog for a walk in the afternoon. And, of course, you have to beware of 'energy compensation' – better known as eating more calories after a workout than you burned off during the run. 'I met a guy who ran purely because he liked ice cream,' says Dr Brian Wansink, author of *Mindless Eating: Why We Eat More Than We Think*. 'But to equal his daily fix, he needed to run 12 miles every day.' Most of us don't (or can't) do that.

'If you're exercising primarily for health, none of this matters that much,' says La Forge, who takes note of the many benefits of exercise, including its link to a reduced risk of chronic diseases such as diabetes and heart disease. But if you're running to lose weight, you have to keep in mind all the variables. 'I believe in exercise,' says Wansink. 'But I also know how quickly you can eat many more calories than you will run off in a normal workout.'

In fact, it takes only 100 extra calories a day to gain 4.5kg a year. That's one high-calorie pre-run snack you didn't need, or one unnecessary bottle of sports drink. The extra weight many runners carry around is simply the result of eating for energy or performance – with little regard for total calories. To lose 500g a week, you must create a calorie deficit of 500 calories a day (3,500 calories equals 500g). How many calories you can cut depends a lot on how much you're eating right now. There's a big difference between cutting 500 calories if you're eating 1,500 a day than if you're eating 3,000. But remember: weight loss is a lot easier when you factor in your running mileage (1 mile = 100 calories). So your calorie deficit can – and should – be created by eliminating some calories from your daily diet and increasing the number you burn per day through running.

After you've determined the total number of calories you should be consuming per day to meet your weight-loss goals, divide those calories so that 50 per cent come from carbohydrates, 25 per cent from protein and 25 per cent from fat. For example, if you've determined that your daily calorie goal is 1,800 calories, then 900 of those calories should come from carbohydrates, 450 from protein and 450 from fat. Remember: you're not striving to have every food you eat meet this ratio. You're simply aiming to get your total daily calorie intake to fall within these guidelines.

Also, don't go too many hours without eating or your brain will signal starvation mode and stimulate your appetite. So go ahead and have a morning, afternoon and evening meal, along with snacks. Just make sure that when you tally it all up, you're still within your calorie range.

EATING FOR PERFORMANCE

Just like a car, the human body can't run on empty. Running and racing performance are limited by four fuelling factors.

1. Loss of body fluids: losing more than 2 per cent of your weight as sweat during a run can hamper your performance. Dehydration hurts your running because it thickens the blood, decreases the heart's efficiency, increases heart rate and raises body temperature.

2. Drop in blood sugar levels: your brain relies heavily on a steady supply of sugar (glucose) for fuel. Running drains your blood glucose stores, which eventually gives you that light-headed, woozy feeling.

3. Depletion of muscle carbohydrate stores: your muscles also suck up stored glucose (glycogen) as fuel. Depending on the intensity and distance of your run, you'll deplete your glycogen stores in as little as 60 minutes. Once this happens, you experience that leaden feeling in your legs.

4. Altered amino acid levels: researchers also believe there is a chemical component to fatigue. For example, levels of circulating amino acids have been shown to change during endurance exercise. And research shows that endurance may be improved with specially formulated foods or beverages that modify amino acid levels and, in a sense, keep your brain thinking you're not tired.

Fortunately, you can easily avoid performance problems by eating properly before and during training runs and races. Here are the guidelines.

1. **Find *your* perfect meal.** Although many runners do go with the traditional 'last supper' of pasta, there is no one-size-fits-all pre-race meal. Your training runs should be a dress rehearsal for not only

what you'll wear and what pace you'll race, but also what you'll eat the night before and day of your race. It's not a great time to try a new Thai restaurant. And it's not wise to visit a coffee shop on your way to the start – unless a pre-run caffeine hit was part of your training routine.

2. **Carbo-load (kind of).** It's not necessary to go for all-you-can-eat pasta and garlic bread. Your last big meal should be eaten 12 hours before your race to ensure that the food's been digested and you don't head to the starting line feeling stuffed. Aim for a meal that's 65 to 75 per cent carbohydrates. Avoid eating meals that are high in fat, protein or fibre, because these take longer to digest and could contribute to GI distress and multiple loo stops during the race.

3. **Don't eat and run.** Chomping down a banana as the starting gun fires doesn't give your body the opportunity to absorb and use the nutrients and carbs – which defeats the purpose of eating it in the first place. Always eat your pre-race meal (about 100 to 200 calories) about 2 hours before the race is scheduled to start. This will also give your body time to digest it so you don't feel full as you run. Stick with familiar, easy-to-digest foods that are high in carbohydrates and low in protein, fat and fibre. Some runners prefer liquids, such as meal-replacement shakes or even chocolate milk, which are absorbed into the stomach faster and also help with hydration.

4. **Refuel properly.** During shorter events, such as a 5-K, a cup of water from an aid station is probably all you'll need to get yourself to the finish (for more details, see 'What to Drink When' on page 213). For races that are longer than 1 hour, you'll benefit from an endurance boost, such as sports drinks, energy gels or energy bars.

····⊱ **Sports drinks:** Offering a mix of water and carbohydrates, sports drinks are an excellent on-the-run source of fuel. For exercise lasting anywhere from 60 minutes to several hours, they significantly boost endurance, compared with drinking plain water. Most sports drinks offer a blend of carbohydrates such as the sugars sucrose, glucose, fructose and galactose. A few also add maltodextrin, a complex carbohydrate made of several different glucose units. Research suggests that the body can absorb more carbohydrates from sports drinks that offer a blend than from drinks with a single carbohydrate source. The researchers believe this is because the various sugars combined can be absorbed via different routes. Sports drinks also come with added electrolytes (the vital minerals we lose when we sweat). Sodium is the most important of these, as studies show that drinks with added sodium help maintain fluid balance in the body and promote the uptake of fluid in the intestines. In plain English: you stay better hydrated when you drink beverages that contain sodium. Stick with sports drinks that contain 13 to 19 grams of carbohydrate per 225ml. Drinks with higher-carb concentrations hamper fluid absorption and give you that sloshing feeling in your stomach, while drinks with lower-carb concentrations won't refuel your muscles fast enough. Aim to drink 250ml to 750ml of sports drink per hour of exercise (the bigger you are and the faster you run, the more you need) to get both the fluid and carbohydrates required for endurance.

···❭ **Energy gels:** Carbohydrates don't get any more convenient than this. Gels come in small, single-serve plastic packets that can fit into that tiny key pocket in most running shorts. (Go ahead and try that with a sports drink – actually, don't.) Gels contain mainly sugars and maltodextrins, which make them similar to sports drinks without the water. Some gels, such as Lucozade Sport Body Fuel, also come with added electrolytes. There are also gels with extras such as ginseng and other herbs, amino acids, vitamins and co-enzyme Q10 (a non-essential substance found in the body). Some have caffeine; check the label or consult the manufacturer's website for specific amounts, as some gels contain as much caffeine as half a cup of coffee. That's not a problem if you normally use products with caffeine, but it can cause nervousness if you're not accustomed to it. If you're a fan of honey – nature's original carbohydrate gel – but not into fitting that little plastic jar into your running shorts, check out Honey Stinger gel packs. Research by Dr Richard Kreider, co-author of the book *Overtraining in Sport*, suggests that honey boosts endurance just as well as the high-tech carb gels. Most gels contain about 100 calories and 25 grams of carbohydrate. Depending on the intensity and duration of your run, take in one to three gels for every hour you're out there. Remember to wash each down with ample water.

···⟩ **Energy bars:** With all the new bars on the market, you might need to eat one for some quick energy before you try to work out which is best for you. Given all the versions, including women-only, high-protein and meal-replacement bars, try to read labels carefully if you want to fuel up properly. The standard high-carbohydrate bars, such as PowerBar and High 5's Energy Bar, are great for fuelling both before and during a run because, as with sports drinks and gels, they facilitate a rapid release of carbohydrate into the bloodstream. About 70 per cent of their carb calories come from sugars (brown-rice syrup and sucrose) and grains (oats and rice crisps). Some bars also contain fruit, another source of easily digestible carbohydrates for your working muscles. The best bars for before and during a run contain about 25 grams of carbohydrate and fewer than 15 grams of protein, which is not a crucial fuel source during exercise. Also, check labels for fat content. Some bars pack a hefty dose, which will slow your digestion. Eat one bar about an hour before a run. If you're running for more than an hour, eat one high-carb bar per hour of running, along with ample water.

EATING FOR *PEAK* PERFORMANCE

If you're tackling an endurance event, such as a half-marathon or marathon, you might want to experiment with your diet. Certain tweaks – namely, increasing your carb intake – could boost your performance. In the months leading up to the Tour de France, every aspect of cyclist Lance Armstrong's training regime had a purpose – including eating. He upped his calorie intake from 3,000 to 6,000 a day. The percentage of carbohydrates in his diet also increased (from 60 to 70 per cent of calories), while he slightly decreased his protein and fat intake. This finely tuned nutritional balancing act, which helped him win seven consecutive Tours, was designed by Chris Carmichael, Armstrong's long-time coach, nutritionist and friend.

As an Olympic trainer and a former competitive cyclist, Carmichael, the founder of Carmichael Training Systems, has learned that athletes, including runners, need to match nutritional intake to training demands in order to achieve peak performance. According to Carmichael, runners need to take a holistic approach to eating and training. 'Diet and training are so closely intertwined, they can't be separated,' he says. Runners' diets, therefore, must evolve throughout the year to correspond with particular workouts. Essentially, Carmichael takes the training technique known as periodization (you break your training year into 'periods' with different goals, then concentrate on specific training) and extends it to the training table.

The concept of periodization naturally translates to nutrition, because the amount of energy you burn changes as you go through weeks, months and a full year of training. If you're eating the same number of calories all year, there is most likely a portion of the year when you're eating more than you need. Likewise, there will be times

PERIODIZATION FOR IDIOTS

How do you apply the principles of periodization to your diet without complex nutrient calculations? Remember that the concept of eating more carbs during your heaviest training is more important than trying to adhere to specific numbers. But when you're upping the miles, adding just one of these mini-meals per day gives you the extra carbs you need to keep running strong.

240ml vanilla yogurt + 145g fresh fruit (60g carbs)
Bonus benefit: provides over 40 per cent of your daily calcium needs

8floz (240ml) orange juice + 1 banana (52g carbs)
Bonus benefit: packs almost 200 per cent of your recommended daily amount (RDA) of vitamin C

1 slice banana bread + 240ml skimmed milk (about 45g carbs)
Bonus benefit: gives you 25 per cent of the RDA for calcium

1 PowerBar energy bar + 240ml PowerBar Endurance sports drink (62g carbs)
Bonus benefit: provides plenty of sodium and potassium to keep you well hydrated

Smoothie of 480ml skimmed or soya milk + 200g strawberries + 2 tablespoons soya protein (about 50g carbs)
Bonus benefit: contributes about 5g of fibre

200g multigrain cereal + 350ml skimmed milk (54g carbs)
Bonus benefit: contains over 100 per cent of the RDA for iron

1 bagel + 1 banana + 1 tablespoon peanut butter (about 75g carbs)
Bonus benefit: provides 12g of protein

when your training burns more calories and demands more nutrients than you're consuming. So just as your training focuses on different goals in different months, you need to make sure you're eating enough – and the right kinds of foods – to support your workouts.

But it isn't as simple as eating an extra muesli bar or two when you're running longer or harder. 'Carbohydrates, proteins and fats are tied together and linked to how you perform,' says Carmichael. So on top of eating more calories as your training intensifies, the ratio of carbohydrates to fats to proteins needs to change as well. 'If you are training for a half-marathon, for example, you need a greater percentage of carbohydrates in your diet than if you're just running for fitness,' he explains. When you're at the peak of your training, it's important to increase the percentage of carbs in your diet from about 60 to 70 per cent to ensure you're giving your body enough fuel to enhance your workouts. For tips on how to do this, see 'Periodization for Idiots' on page 191.

EATING FOR RECOVERY

If you're like a lot of runners, your post-workout routine goes something like this: stretch, drink water, shower and get on with your day. Food? That can wait until you're hungry, right? Not if you want to feel your best on your next run. When you run, you burn mostly glycogen, a fuel stored in your muscles. Your mission straight after a run, therefore, is to eat, even if you don't feel hungry. And make it quick. No matter what time of day you run, the enzymes responsible for making glycogen are most active immediately postworkout, leaving you a 60-minute window in which they're at maximum capacity to produce glycogen.

'After exercise, especially following intensive or prolonged bouts, the body is primed to reload muscle glycogen,' says Suzanne Girard Eberle, author of *Endurance Sports Nutrition*. Wait more than an hour to refuel and your body's ability to make glycogen out of what you consume drops by an astounding 66 per cent. And the longer you wait, the more likely you are to feel sluggish. 'Everything runners do is about how well we recover,' says Lisa Dorfman, a sports nutritionist and marathon runner. 'That's when the gains from training come.'

In that crucial first hour, aim to consume 300 to 400 calories, ideally containing 3 grams of carbs to every 1 gram of protein. Your body's already primed to make glycogen out of simple carbs, and a little protein helps repair muscle-tissue microdamage. Of course, what you'll feel like eating (or drinking, or not) after a 7:00 a.m. run will probably differ from what you'll want after a run at lunch time or between work and dinner. Here's how to maximize the refuelling window, whatever time of day you run.

EARLY RISERS: Many breakfast foods have the perfect post-run carb–protein mix. 'Cereal with skimmed milk is a great recovery meal,' Dorfman says. Choose a cereal with a few grams of protein. If you have time to cook, she recommends egg whites on toast. If you eat on the way to work, choose easily transported foods, such as energy bars or a bagel with cheese.

THE LUNCH SHIFT: You've spent your lunch break running. Now you have to eat, but you have limited time. Use the office fridge and microwave for tasty leftovers with the right nutritional balance (a small serving of pasta with tomato sauce, or a turkey sandwich on whole grain bread). Of course, if high noon means high temperatures, the heat might have zapped your appetite. 'Drink your carbohydrates and protein,' says Girard Eberle. 'Chocolate milk, a fruit smoothie, a meal-replacement beverage or a post-workout sports drink are good options.'

AFTER OFFICE HOURS: If you can't sit down to your evening meal within an hour of your run, graze on raw veggies, crackers, bread and a little cheese to tide you over until your fully restorative dinner. You'll want more of a glycogen-reloading plan if you run from the office and still have a long commute in front of you. 'This would be the perfect scenario for a sports drink,' says Dorfman. 'Then you have dinner.'

NIGHT MOVES: Finding good recovery-window foods after late-night running will involve some experimentation. 'Try a carbohydrate-rich drink,' Girard Eberle suggests. 'Or eat half of your dinner before and the other half after. The key is to end up not starving at dinnertime or after the run. This will easily lead to over-eating.'

AFTER THE RACE: Most races are held in the morning, so it's likely that you'll receive a banana or cereal bar in your goody bag. These high-carbohydrate foods are great for replacing your glycogen stores, which are as wiped out as you are. But it's important to get your protein, too. Chocolate milk is one of the most popular post-run recovery aids; it'll go down easy if your stomach is feeling off or you don't have much of an appetite. Cans of Slim-Fast or other meal-replacement drinks are easily portable. You can freeze one the night before, take it with you to the race, and drink it during your drive home.

STOCKING UP

Most supermarkets stock more than 30,000 items, yet every time we race up and down the aisles, we throw the same 10 to 15 foods into our trolleys. Which isn't such a bad thing, as long as you're taking home the right foods – ones that will keep you healthy, fuel peak performance and readily cook up into lots of delicious meals. So before your next food-shopping trip, add the following 15 items to your must-buy list.

1. ALMONDS

Nuts, especially almonds, are an excellent source of vitamin E, an antioxidant that many runners fall short on because there are so few good food sources of it. Studies have shown that eating nuts several times a week lowers circulating cholesterol levels, particularly the artery-clogging LDL type, decreasing your risk for heart disease. And the form of vitamin E found in nuts, called gamma-tocopherol (a form not typically found in supplements), may also help protect against cancer.

ADD TO YOUR DIET: Runners should eat a small handful of almonds at least three to five times per week. Add them (and other nuts) to salads or pasta dishes, use as a topping for casseroles or throw them into a bowl of hot cereal for extra crunch. Combine almonds with chopped dried fruit, mixed nuts and chocolate chips for a healthy and tasty trail mix. Almond butter is great spread on whole grain toast, or slather it on a whole wheat tortilla, top with raisins, and roll it up. Store all nuts in jars or zip-lock bags in a cool, dry place away from sunlight and they'll keep for about 2 to 4 months; frozen, they'll keep an extra month or two.

2. EGGS

One egg fulfils about 10 per cent of your daily protein needs. Its protein is the most complete food protein short of human breast milk, which means egg protein contains all the crucial amino acids your hardworking muscles need for promoting recovery. Eat just one of these nutritional powerhouses and you'll also get about 30 per cent of the RDA for vitamin K, which is vital for healthy bones. Plus, eggs contain choline, a brain nutrient that aids memory, and leutin, a pigment needed for healthy eyes. Choose omega-3-enhanced eggs and you can also increase your intake of healthy fats. Don't worry too much about the cholesterol: studies have shown that egg eaters have a lower risk for heart disease than those who avoid eggs.

ADD TO YOUR DIET: Whether boiled, scrambled, poached or fried (in a non-stick frying pan to cut down on the need for additional fats), eggs are great any time. Use them as the base for meals such as frittatas, or sub them for meat in sandwiches, salads or wraps. Add eggs to casseroles and soups by cracking one or two in during the last minute of cooking.

3. SWEET POTATOES

This colourful alternative to the potato should be a staple in your diet. Just a single 100-calorie sweet potato supplies more than 250 per cent of the RDA for vitamin A in the form of beta-carotene, a powerful antioxidant. Sweet potatoes are a good source of vitamin C, potassium, iron and the two trace minerals manganese and copper. Many runners fail to meet their manganese and copper needs, which can affect performance, because these minerals are crucial for healthy muscle function. New sweet-potato varieties have purple skin and flesh and contain anthocyanidins, the same potent antioxidant found in berries.

ADD TO YOUR DIET: Sweet potatoes can be baked, boiled or microwaved. You can fill them with bean chilli, low-fat cheese and your favourite toppings or incorporate them into stews and soups. Baked as wedges or disks, sweet potatoes make delicious oven chips. Don't store sweet potatoes in the fridge or they'll lose their flavour. Instead, store them in a cool, dark place, and they should keep for about 2 weeks.

4. WHOLE GRAIN CEREAL WITH PROTEIN

Look for whole grain cereals that offer at least 5 grams of fibre and at least 8 grams of protein. For example, one serving of Vogel's UltraBran cereal contains 15g of fibre (that's more than 50 per cent of your RDA) and also contains linseed which provides omega-3 and omega-6 polyunsaturates. If you're looking for a cereal that packs a protein punch, Vogel's Vita-Pro is a protein-rich soya cereal that's high in fibre and has a pleasant honey-roast flavour. Each serving provides a hefty 10g of protein and it's also low in salt and sugar.

ADD TO YOUR DIET: Of course whole grain cereal is excellent for breakfast – a meal you don't want to skip, as research indicates that those who eat breakfast are healthier and trimmer and manage their weight better than non-breakfast-eaters. With its mix of carbohydrates and protein, cereal also makes a great post-run recovery meal. Or you can sprinkle whole grain cereal on yogurt, use it to add crunch to casseroles, or put some in a zip-lock bag for a snack.

5. ORANGES

Eat enough oranges and you may experience less muscle soreness after hard workouts such as downhill running. Why? Oranges supply over 100 per cent of the RDA for the antioxidant vitamin C, and a recent study in Medicine and Science in Sport and Exercise showed that taking vitamin C supplements for 2 weeks prior to challenging arm exercises helped alleviate muscle soreness. This fruit's antioxidant powers also come from the compound herperidin, which is found in the thin orange-coloured layer of the fruit's skin (the zest) and has been shown to help lower cholesterol levels and high blood pressure.

ADD TO YOUR DIET: Add orange segments to fruit and green salads, or use the juice and pulp in sauces to top chicken, pork or fish. To benefit from the herperidin, use the zest in baking and cooking. Select firm, heavy oranges, and store them in the fridge for up to 3 weeks. Orange zest can be stored dried in a glass jar in a cool place for about a week.

6. TINNED BLACK BEANS

200g of these beauties provides 30 per cent of the RDA for protein, almost 60 per cent of the RDA for fibre (the majority of it as the cholesterol-lowering soluble type), and 60 per cent of the RDA for folate, a B vitamin that plays a key role in heart health and circulation. Black beans also contain antioxidants, and researchers theorize that this fibre-folate-antioxidant trio is why a daily serving of beans appears to lower cholesterol levels and heart-disease risk. In addition, black beans and other beans and pulses are low-GI foods, which help control blood sugar levels and may enhance performance because of their steady release of energy.

ADD TO YOUR DIET: For a quick, hearty soup, open a can of black beans and pour into chicken or vegetable stock along with frozen mixed veggies and your favourite seasonings. Mash beans with salsa for an instant dip for crudites or spread them onto a whole wheat tortilla for a great recovery meal. Add beans to cooked pasta or rice for extra fibre and protein.

7. MIXED SALAD GREENS

Rather than selecting one type of lettuce for your salad, choose mixed greens, which typically include several colourful delicate greens such as radicchio, rocket and watercress. Each variety offers a unique blend of phytonutrients that research suggests may fend off age-related diseases, such as Alzheimer's, cancer, heart disease and diabetes. These phytonutrients also act as antioxidants, warding off muscle damage brought on by tough workouts. You can usually buy mixed greens in bulk or pre-washed in bags.

ADD TO YOUR DIET: Toss a mixed-greens salad with tomato, cucumber, spring onions and an olive oil-based dressing (its fat helps your body absorb the phytonutrients). You can also stuff mixed greens in sandwiches, wraps and pittas. Or place them in a heated pan, toss lightly until wilted, and use as a bed for grilled salmon, chicken or lean meat. Greens store best in a salad spinner or crisper drawer in your fridge. They'll keep for up to 6 days – as long as you don't drench them in water.

TRAINING TABLE: WHAT THE ELITES EAT

'I eat whenever I'm hungry because I burn calories easily with the high mileages I'm running. I'll have a couple of slices of toast and a cup of coffee before my first run of the day, then Cornflakes and some more toast when I get back. I snack on yogurt with chopped fruit. I live with Kenyan runners so I've learnt to eat ugali – it's their secret weapon, a food made from maize flour, which is packed with carbs.'

Mo Farah, second fastest Briton ever over 5,000m

'Running around 100 miles a week, I don't go more than a couple of hours without eating. I'm not particularly scientific but I try to eat healthily. I eat a lot of homegrown fruit and veg, and eggs from my chickens. Marathons are usually in the morning so it can be a challenge getting up three hours before the race. I have a pint of water as soon as I'm up. Then three slices of toast with honey, a banana and an energy bar.'

Dan Robinson, 13th in the 2008 London Marathon

'If I have a hard session ahead of me, I'll have brown toast with peanut butter. For lunch I often have a tortilla wrap stuffed with chicken, spinach and tomatoes, followed by yogurt and berries. I've started eating a lot of turkey for dinner – it's low in fat and the beta alanine helps muscles recover quickly from hard sessions. I eat steak once a week to boost my iron levels.'

Steph Twell, Junior European Cross-Country Champion

'If my morning run is 40 minutes or more, I eat porridge with a banana first, otherwise I'll just have a coffee and go. I have a balanced lunch of carbs and protein, then coffee and a piece of carrot cake before my second session of the day. I usually have salmon or chicken for dinner, with steamed or stir-fried vegetables and rice or pasta. I eat fruit for dessert and chocolate to boost my energy levels. I always have a recovery drink within 20 minutes of training and a good meal within two hours to further aid recovery.'

Jo Pavey, fourth in the 10,000m at the 2007 World Championships

(continued)

8. SALMON

Nutritionwise, salmon is the king of fish. Besides being an excellent source of high-quality protein (about 30 grams in a 115g serving), salmon is one of the best food sources of omega-3 fats. These essential fats help balance the inflammation response, a bodily function that, when disturbed, appears to be linked to many diseases, including asthma. In a recent study, people with exercise-induced asthma reported improved symptoms after 3 weeks of eating more fish oil. If you've been limiting seafood due to possible mercury or PCB (polychlorinated biphenyl) contamination, simply aim for a variety of farm-raised and wild salmon for maximum health benefits.

ADD TO YOUR DIET: Bake, grill or poach salmon with fresh herbs and citrus zest. Gauge cooking time by allotting 10 minutes for every 2cm of fish (steaks or fillets). Salmon should flake when done. Leftover or tinned salmon is great in salads and soups, tossed with pasta or on top of pizza. Fresh fish keeps for 1 to 2 days in the fridge, or you can freeze it in a tightly sealed container for about 4 to 5 months.

9. WHOLE GRAIN BREAD

Runners need at least three to six 30g servings of whole grains per day, and eating 100 per cent whole grain bread (as opposed to just 'brown' bread, which may contain refined grains and flours) is an easy way to meet this requirement: one slice equals one serving. Whole grain bread may also help weight-conscious runners. One study showed that women who eat whole grain bread weigh less than those who eat white bread and other refined grains. Whole grain eaters also have a 38 per cent lower risk of suffering from metabolic syndrome, which is characterized by tummy fat, low levels of the good cholesterol and high blood sugar levels, all of which raise the risk for heart disease and cancer.

ADD TO YOUR DIET: Spread bread with peanut butter or stuff a couple of slices with your favourite sandwich fillings and plenty of sliced veggies for a satisfying recovery meal. Coat with a beaten egg for French toast, or use it as layers or crumbled in a casserole. Just be sure the label says '100 per cent whole grain' (all the grains and flours in the ingredients should be listed as whole, not milled or refined). And don't just stick with popular whole wheat. Try different varieties of whole grains such as barley, buckwheat, bulgur, rye and oat.

10. FROZEN STIR-FRY VEGETABLES

Research shows that eating a combination of antioxidants, such as beta-carotene and vitamin C, may ease muscle soreness after hard interval workouts by reducing the inflammation caused by free-radicals (molecules containing oxygen atoms that attack cells in our bodies). Most ready-to-use stir-fry veggie combos offer a potent mix of antioxidants with red and yellow peppers, onions, pak choi and soya beans. And frozen vegetables save lots of prep time but still provide the same nutrition as their fresh counterparts.

ADD TO YOUR DIET: Toss frozen vegetables straight into a hot wok or frying pan; add tofu, seafood or meat and your favourite stir-fry sauce; and serve over brown rice. Or add them to pasta water during the last few minutes of cooking, drain and toss with a touch of olive oil. You can also stir frozen veggies into soups or stews at the end of cooking, or thaw them and add to casseroles. Vegetables store well in the freezer for about 4 months, so make sure you date your bags.

11. WHOLE GRAIN PASTA

Pasta has long been a runner's best friend because it contains easily digestible carbs that help restock spent glycogen (energy) stores. Whole grain versions are a must over refined pastas because they contain more fibre to fill you up, additional B vitamins that are crucial to energy metabolism and disease-fighting compounds such as lignans. Try a fortified pasta, such as Buitoni's Fibre Rich and Pasta Lensi's Fibre Plus.

ADD TO YOUR DIET: Pasta makes a complete one-pan meal – perfect for busy runners – when tossed with veggies, lean meat, seafood or tofu. Or combine pasta with a light sauce and a bit of your favourite cheese to turn it into a satisfying casserole.

12. CHICKEN

Runners need about 50 to 75 per cent more protein than non-runners do to help rebuild muscles and promote recovery after tough workouts. And just one 115g serving of chicken can supply about half a runner's daily protein needs. Chicken also contains selenium, a trace element that helps protect muscles from the free-radical damage that can occur during exercise, and niacin, a B vitamin that helps regulate fat burning during a run. New studies also suggest that people who get ample niacin in their diet have a 70 per cent lower risk of developing Alzheimer's disease. Don't eat meat? See 'The Vegetarian Runner' on page 205 for other protein options.

ADD TO YOUR DIET: Chicken's versatility makes it perfect for runners with little time to cook. You can bake, grill or poach chicken. Leftovers work well on top of salads, mixed into pasta or packed into sandwiches, wraps and pittas. Fresh chicken stores safely for 2 days in the fridge but can be frozen for 6 months or more.

13. FROZEN MIXED BERRIES

The colourful compounds that make blueberries blue, blackberries deep purple and raspberries a rich shade of red are called anthocyanins – a powerful group of antioxidants that may help stave off Alzheimer's and some cancers. Anthocyanins may also assist with post-run recovery and muscle repair – not bad for a fruit group that contains a mere 60 calories or so per 150g. And remember: frozen berries are just as nutritious as fresh but keep far longer (up to 9 months in the freezer).

ADD TO YOUR DIET: Frozen berries make a great base for a smoothie, and there's no need to thaw them. Eat thawed berries on their own, add them with chopped nuts to vanilla yogurt, or liven up hot or cold cereal with a big handful. You can also bake berries with a nutty topping of oats, honey and chopped almonds for a sweet treat after a long weekend run.

14. DARK CHOCOLATE

You deserve at least one indulgence – especially one you can feel good about. Chocolate contains potent antioxidants called flavonoids that can boost heart health. In one study, a group of football players had lower blood pressure, lower total cholesterol levels and less artery-clogging LDL cholesterol after just 2 weeks of eating chocolate daily. Other research suggests that chocolate's flavonoids ease inflammation and help prevent blood substances from becoming sticky, which lowers the risk of potential blood clots. But not just any chocolate will do. First off, dark chocolate (the darker the better) generally contains more flavonoids than milk chocolate. Also, the way the cocoa beans are processed can influence the potency of the flavonoids. Processing at lower than 42°C retains much of the anti-oxidant powers of the flavonoids with the result that the cocoa retains its nutritional attributes. Check out www.consciouschocolate.co.uk for a healthy version.

ADD TO YOUR DIET: Besides the obvious (just eat it!), you can add dark chocolate to trail mix, dip it in peanut butter, or combine it with fruit for an even greater antioxidant punch. Just keep track of the calories. Buy chocolate wrapped in small pieces to help with portion control.

15. LOW-FAT YOGURT

Besides being a good source of protein and calcium (240ml provides 13 grams of protein and 40 per cent of the RDA for calcium), low-fat yogurt with live cultures provides the healthy bacteria your digestive tract needs to function optimally. These good bacteria may also have anti-inflammatory powers that can offer some relief to arthritis sufferers. Look for the live-culture symbol on the yogurt carton.

ADD TO YOUR DIET: Low-fat yogurt is great topped with fruit, muesli or nuts or used as a base for smoothies. Plain yogurt can be mixed with diced cucumber and herbs like dill and spread over grilled tofu, chicken, fish and other meats. Yogurt can also double as a salad dressing with vinegar and herbs or be mixed with fresh salsa to stand in as a dip for veggies and baked potato wedges.

THE VEGETARIAN RUNNER

Endurance athletes need more protein than sedentary people in order to repair small, exercise-induced tears in the muscle fibres. The protein recommendation for athletes is 1.2–1.45g per kg of body weight per day (so a 65-kg runner should consume about 78–91g of protein per day). And because it is the most concentrated source, animal protein (including eggs and cheese) is the easiest way to make sure you get the protein you need: A 170g serving of chicken, for instance, has 42g.

It's possible to get 75 to 105g of protein a day by eating a variety of soya products, beans and pulses, nuts and whole grains, as long as you pay close attention to what you're eating. 'The trick for athletes is to think about protein-rich plant foods at every meal,' says sports nutritionist Dr D. Enette Larson-Meyer, author of *Vegetarian Sports Nutrition*. 'Add a little peanut butter to your bagel, toss some lentils [150g has 18g] into your pasta sauce or add chickpeas to a salad. And remember that protein in bread, cereal and grains can add up to a considerable amount.' Using meat substitutes like soya burgers and mince in dishes such as lasagna can provide up to 10 to 13g of protein.

Certain nutrients are harder to get without eating meat – including omega-3 fatty acids, vitamin B_{12}, zinc and iron. When you do eat fish, poultry and meats, choose sources that pack the most nutritional punch, such as fatty fish (like salmon, mackerel and trout) for omega-3s and lean cuts of beef for iron and zinc.

If you're looking to eat less meat, make changes slowly, says Larson-Meyer – a hummus, cheese and veggie sandwich one day, a turkey sandwich the next; cottage cheese or yogurt for breakfast on Tuesday, low-fat bacon on Wednesday. A gradual switch will help keep your energy levels high – and your race times fast.

AVOIDING A GUT REACTION

Studies suggest that as many as 60 per cent of runners experience some degree of nausea and unpleasant stomach trouble during or following a run. These stomach issues can make finishing a workout or race painful or, worse, impair or interrupt your performance. The problems are said to be caused, in part, because blood is diverted from the gastrointestinal tract to the muscles during exercise, which can cause cramping and limits the body's ability to absorb fluids, potentially leading to dehydration. 'Stops at the Porta-loo can also accelerate dehydration, which can end a race,' says Bobby McGee, a distance-running coach in Colorado and author of best-selling book *Magical Running*.

The main culprit of stomach distress, however, is running itself. When you ride a bike, blood is also diverted from the gut, but cyclists report half the number of problems as runners. That's because running has twice the force of impact. 'All the pounding jostles the GI tract,' says runner and general practitioner Dr Roger Henderson. That, in turn, speeds up the need for a pit stop.

Why do some runners suffer and others don't? Because the amount of bacteria in the stomach, digestion time and even hormone and stress levels affect digestion and vary from person to person. Also, running compounds pre-existing conditions such as irritable bowel syndrome, says Dr Henderson. Some runners experience difficulty only during speedwork and races (at higher intensities, more blood is diverted, increasing the likelihood of distress). The solution is to experiment with your diet the day before workouts that give you trouble. 'Test different foods,' says McGee. 'You'll find what works for you.'

In the late 1980s, gastrointestinal specialist Dr Mervyn Danilewitz reported curing a number of runners' stomach ailments by having them eliminate dairy 24 hours before running. Milk, cheese and ice cream can trigger stomach pain because they contain lactose, a sugar that's hard for some people to digest. If you just can't skip your glass of milk, try soya, rice or almond milk; these generally don't contain lactose. Or choose acidophilus milk and yogurts with 'probiotics' (look for the seal), added bacteria that help break down lactose.

EASY TO TAKE

Sidestep stomach aches with these foods.

Digestible dairy: Soya, rice and almond milks generally don't contain lactose, a sugar that can be tough to digest. Acidophilus milk and yogurt with live cultures (look for the seal) are also good choices because they contain bacteria that aid digestion.

Low-fibre produce: Courgettes, tomatoes, olives, grapes and grapefruit all have less than 1g of fibre per serving.

Refined carbs: Processed white foods, such as regular pasta, white rice and plain bagels, come with the whole grain broken down, so your stomach's job is easier. (Remember, whole grains are healthier and should be part of your overall diet. But if you are prone to stomach issues, opt for refined carbs the day before a race.)

Healing herb: Mint stimulates digestion and eases intestinal cramps. Sip mint tea 30 minutes before a run or take peppermint-oil capsules on long runs. Avoid mint if you're prone to heartburn, however; it can exacerbate the condition.

Root remedy: Anthea Schmid, an ultra runner, the female winner of the 2002 Leadville Trail 100-mile run, carries a bag of ground ginger while she runs. By neutralizing acid, ginger – ground or in teas and supplements – can help relieve nausea and gas.

Another option is to reduce your fibre intake – its indigestibility cleans out your system but also increases the risk for trouble. 'When fibre gets low in the tract, bacteria feast on it, producing gas and sometimes cramping,' says Bob Seebohar, author of *Nutrition Periodization for Endurance Athletes*. Replace high-fibre fruits and veggies like pears and green peas with lower-fibre cantaloupe melons and tomatoes (see 'Easy to Take' above). Save the bran cereals and other high-fibre foods for after your run.

Certain sweeteners can also lead to problems. Check the ingredients in your energy bar for anything ending in 'ol' – sorbitol, mannitol and so on – and avoid gels with fructose as the first sugar on the ingredient list. 'These sweeteners can cause GI trouble,' says Seebohar. And take gels slowly. 'Suck a little, sip some water, and then swallow,' says Seebohar. 'Otherwise, the gel could just sit in your stomach.'

Other solutions include avoiding cruciferous vegetables, like broccoli, cauliflower and cabbage; they contain raffinose, a gas-inducing compound also found in – you guessed it – beans. And limit hard-to-digest foods like protein and fats. The night before or morning of a run, aim for a meal that is 80 per cent carbs, 10 per cent protein and 10 per cent fat.

Finally, watch the timing of your meals. Allow 3 hours between big meals and your run; eat dinner at least 2 hours before bed. And, of course, try to empty your system before a run. Coffee and tea can help move things along, but limit your intake to a cup, says Seebohar: 'Caffeine can trigger GI complaints when taken in large quantities.' Runners with frequent heartburn should skip caffeine altogether because it can increase acid in the stomach.

Most of all, don't let gastrointestinal trouble keep you from your run. As you become fitter, the muscles divert less blood, and there's more for the stomach. The effect on the gut improves. And so does your running.

HYDRATION

The second part of a runner's fuel plan is hydration. Water plays an important role in the body. It's used to digest, absorb nutrients from food, dispose of wastes and regulate temperature. Being well hydrated is especially critical for runners. As we exercise, our bodies produce more heat, and we sweat in order to cool ourselves. We need to replace the fluids we are sweating out in order to keep our core temperatures down. Electrolytes such as sodium and potassium that are lost in sweat also need to be replaced so our bodies can maintain proper functioning.

As important as it is to stay well hydrated, some runners go above and beyond their intake needs, drinking at every water station in a race. But drinking too much can result in more than just a few extra pit stops; it can cause a dangerous overhydration condition called hyponatraemia (see 'Hypo What?' on page 210). But no need to worry. This section will tell you everything you need to know about hydration – including when to top off and when to hold off – so that you can have a strong and safe race experience.

HOW MUCH DO I NEED?

The old formula – everyone needs eight glasses of water a day – is out. It's been replaced by formulas based primarily on gender and calorie expenditure. (See page 177 to work out your daily calorie requirement.)

2,000 calories requires 2 litres
2,500 calories requires 2.5 litres
3,000 calories requires 3 litres

So a 60kg woman, who consumes 2,040 calories per day, should drink around 2 litres of water a day. She'll get the rest of her daily fluid supply from food and metabolic processes. Runners need to drink extra to cover their daily sweat losses. And how much is that, exactly?

Well, it basically comes down to thirst.

In 2006, the International Marathon Medical Directors Association (IMMDA) released its long-awaited hydration guidelines, which concluded that runners should, simply, drink when thirsty. 'The new scientific evidence says that thirst will actually protect athletes from the hazards of both over- and underdrinking,' says the IMMDA announcement. The concept of drinking according to thirst may seem too simple to be an accurate barometer of fluid needs. In fact, for years runners have been urged to drink ahead of thirst – the message being that by the time you feel thirsty, you're already on the road to dehydration. Despite the controversy, there is increasing

HYPO WHAT?

Hyponatraemia occurs when your fluid intake exceeds your rate of fluid loss from sweating, which results in low blood-sodium levels. Symptoms – nausea, disorientation, muscle weakness – can be similar to dehydration. Giving additional liquids to hyponatraemic runners only exacerbates the problem by diluting their blood-salt levels even more, which can lead to coma and, in the worst cases, death.

Experts hypothesize that hyponatraemia has become more of an issue in the past few years because so many inexperienced runners are attempting marathon and ultramarathon distances. This means people are on the course for 5 or 6 hours or even longer. 'Slower, back-of-the-pack runners who aren't sweating as much don't need to drink as much fluid as front runners,' says Dr Neil Walsh, Reader in Physiology at the School of Sport, Health and Exercise Sciences, Bangor University.

Women, smaller runners, slower runners and those who are not as well trained, face the greatest risk of hyponatraemia. 'Based on the lab data we have, women tend to overdrink, and they typically have a lower sweat rate than men,' says Dr Craig Horswill, senior research fellow at the Gatorade Sports Science Institute. The idea that every runner needs to down a cup at every drinks' station can be a dangerous one because such a rigid fluid-replacement strategy doesn't account for differences in body size, running pace, terrain, climate, metabolic rate and sweat rate.

Not every runner needs to worry about hyponatraemia, but if you're training for a marathon and plan to run it in 4-plus hours, your risk increases. Here are specific drinking guidelines to follow.

scientific evidence to support the notion that thirst is actually the ideal way to gauge hydration needs.

Thirst is the basic physiological instinct that the body uses to maintain normal thickness of body fluids. 'Humans evolved the thirst mechanism over millennia,' says Dr Timothy Noakes, a professor of exercise

1. Don't drink obsessively in the several days before a marathon. Drink when you're thirsty; that will get the job done.

2. Don't take NSAIDs (nonsteroidal anti-inflammatory drugs) such as aspirin, ibuprofen or naproxen sodium before, during or immediately after your race. NSAIDs can possibly cause water retention and hyponatraemia in marathon runners.

3. Weigh yourself before the marathon, and write your weight on the back of your race number. If you need help at the finish line, the marathon medical staff will find this pre-race weight very helpful.

4. During the marathon, drink when you're thirsty, understanding that water, sugars and electrolytes will help you feel and perform your best. But don't force yourself to drink.

5. Be particularly careful if you expect to run over 4 hours and if you have an unusually small or large body size. Drink less if you begin to get a queasy, sloshy feeling in your stomach.

6. Drink sports drinks rather than water.

7. Don't down fluids immediately after the marathon. This is a time, according to a 2003 London Marathon report, when the risk of hyponatraemia can be quite high, as stomach fluids are absorbed into the bloodstream. Nibble on solid foods and sip a variety of drinks slowly until you feel well recovered.

and sports science at the University of Cape Town, South Africa, and author of *Lore of Running*. 'It is the only system used by all other creatures on this earth. Why should it not also be ideal for humans?' Dr Noakes and his colleagues completed a study looking at the connection between thirst and sports performance. They found that drinking less than what thirst dictated resulted in a 2 per cent drop in cycling performance during an 80-kilometre time trial and that drinking more than thirst dictated did nothing to enhance performance. 'We concluded that if you drink according to the dictates of thirst, your performance will be optimized,' says Dr Noakes.

The IMMDA has found the latest body of research on thirst so compelling that the group dismissed its own advice that runners stay ahead of dehydration by using an mls-per-minute fluid-replacement strategy and instead strongly endorsed thirst in its groundbreaking new fluid recommendations. 'We're used to hearing that thirst follows too far behind what you really need, but that doesn't hold true scientifically,' says Dr Lewis Maharam, chairman of the board of governors for the IMMDA. 'Your body's thirst mechanism is giving you real-time feedback on your internal fluid balance.'

This feedback can be especially important when running on steamy summer days. According to Dr Noakes's research, your body will respond to the heat by increasing your thirst. And on the flip side, when you aren't sweating as much or losing as much fluid, your thirst will guide you to drink less.

Dr Maharam suggests listening to your instincts. 'If you come up on a water station and you're ambivalent about downing a cup, you're not thirsty and you don't need to drink,' he says. For instance, having a dry mouth – which can be the result of nerves or heavy breathing – doesn't necessarily mean you're thirsty. 'But if you see the water at the station and crave it,' says Dr Maharam, 'then you're truly thirsty and should have a drink.'

When it comes to determining your own hydration needs, it's still important to remember that you are an experiment of one, since there is such individual variation in sweat rates among runners. 'Thirst is simple, and it's based on good, strong research,' says Dr Maharam. But he adds that if you feel you can't rely on thirst alone, you might want to determine your own sweat rate (see 'Know Thy Sweat Rate' on page 218). This will give you an estimate of your fluid losses during a run so that you can calculate your own rate of fluid replacement.

Another way to assess your level of hydration is to pay attention to the colour of your urine. If it's totally clear, you may be drinking too much. If it looks dark yellow, you're definitely not drinking enough. Your bathroom scales can also help. If you gain any weight on a run, you're taking in too many fluids, but if you lose more than 2 per cent of your body weight on a single outing, you probably need to drink more.

In the end, much of the hydration debate comes down to listening to your body – a concept quite familiar to runners. So when you're thirsty or sweating by the bucketful on a long run, go ahead and drink. Otherwise, feel free to pass by that next water stop.

WHAT TO DRINK WHEN

As you approach the first water stop along the racecourse, you see sports drink in some of the cups and water in others. Which should you reach for? That depends. Running time and distance, level of intensity, individual fitness, environmental conditions and even personal preference all factor in to what you should drink – and when you should drink it.

Having to decide between the array that lines the supermarket's drinks aisle is even more daunting. Just about all those drinks – even the ones that have caffeine or are high in sugar – count towards your fluid needs. But some options are simply better than others, especially when you're striving for peak performance and optimal hydration. 'Runners need to make informed beverage choices that fit their individual needs,' says sports nutritionist Anita Bean, author of *The Complete Guide to Sports Nutrition.*

Taste is certainly key, since research has shown that we're likely to stay better hydrated if we enjoy what we're drinking. But runners also need to read labels closely to find out the intended use of each product, says Carmichael. 'A runner out on a 30-minute jog won't be hurt by using one of the new endurance sports drinks,' he says, 'but he'd really be just fine with plain water, since endurance drinks become more important as workouts become longer.'

This drinking guide can help you navigate the waters (and drinks and juices). Here are the most popular drinks categories and expert recommendations on how they are best used. Whatever you choose, drink it cold and in frequent small amounts. This proven strategy ensures that your fluids will be absorbed much more quickly – leaving you properly fuelled and well hydrated.

1. The Simplest Choice: Water

With so many thirst-quenching options, plain old water may seem rather pedestrian. But water is least expensive, most available – and calorie free. While tap water may seem less pure than bottled, it's often subject to more stringent safety regulations and is generally richer in minerals. But drink whichever you think tastes better to ensure that you drink enough. Just remember that water won't refuel your carbohydrate (energy) reserves or replace electrolytes lost through sweat.

DRINK IT on runs under 30 minutes. 'The person out for a 3-mile jog typically has enough stored energy to meet the demands of the workout and can simply rely on water for hydration,' says Carmichael. Drinking water is also a great way to stay hydrated throughout the rest of the day.

PASS IT BY on runs over 30 minutes, since you need to replace spent carbs and electrolytes. Those who find the taste of water boring may want to experiment with flavoured drinks to ensure that they drink enough to meet their hydration needs.

2. Get Some Carbs: Sports Drink

The carbohydrate-electrolyte-fluid potion that Gatorade launched back in 1965 has spawned an entire drinks industry based on the theory that athletes need more than just water to stay properly fuelled and well hydrated during strenuous aerobic exercise. Ideally, sports drinks have a 6 to 8 per cent carbohydrate concentration (14 to 20 grams of carbs per serving), which allows them to be absorbed by the body up to 30 per cent faster than water and provide a steady stream of carbs to restock spent energy stores. They also contain the electrolytes sodium and potassium, minerals that are lost through sweat and are important for fluid retention. Some runners – particularly weight watchers – avoid sports drinks because of the calories. That's a mistake, says Girard Eberle. 'When you're training long and hard, you shouldn't minimize your calorie intake. Don't work against your body while you're asking it to perform.' Besides, research indicates that consuming carbohydrates during exercise may suppress appetite later in the day.

DRINK IT on runs over 30 minutes. Sports drinks are ideal before, during and after such workouts

PASS IT BY on runs under 30 minutes. During such short workouts, runners don't need the extra calories and are well served by water. People with sensitive stomachs may need to experiment with different brands and flavours during training.

3. Just a Little Extra: Enhanced Water

Also known as fitness waters, most of these drinks, which typically contain less than 50 calories per 240ml serving, list water as the first ingredient, followed by a sweetener – either real or faux. Many are also enhanced with vitamins and minerals and come in a wide variety of flavours. But don't expect the extra vitamins and minerals to boost your running. 'There is no evidence that the small amount of vitamins and minerals added to these drinks will aid performance,' says Girard Eberle. 'And there's no evidence that we need them during exercise.' These waters also won't properly fuel long workouts because of their low carbohydrate content.

DRINK IT on runs under 30 minutes. It also can be used for hydrating throughout the day by those who don't want a lot of extra calories or when drinking plain water seems too dull.

PASS IT BY on runs over 30 minutes. You need the extra carbs in traditional sports drinks to support longer workouts.

4. A Lot of Extra: Energy Drink

What puts the 'energy' in energy drinks? Most contain a potent mixture of caffeine and sugar, both proven to enhance performance. But all that sugar (between 110 and 160 sugar calories per 240ml serving) actually prohibits them from being a good fluid choice during exercise. That's because the dense carbohydrate content slows fluid absorption and can give some runners an upset stomach. Other stimulants often found in these drinks, such as guarana, ginseng, taurine and L-carnitine, may boost performance but can also increase blood pressure and heart rate and make you feel shaky – particularly if taken on an empty stomach. (Some traditional sports drinks have so-called energy formulas, but they're often not the same as energy drinks like Red Bull, since they usually aren't as high in sugar or caffeine.)

DRINK IT if you're well fed, well hydrated, and looking to boost alertness and energy before or after a run, not during.

PASS IT BY if you have a sensitive stomach or a history of heart palpitations, or you're watching your weight.

5. When It's Over: Recovery Drink

Research indicates that adding a little protein to the carbs you consume post-run helps speed the restoration of your glycogen (energy) stores and facilitate muscle repair. Consequently, most recovery drinks contain 30 to 60 grams of carbs and 7 to 15 grams of protein – roughly a four-to-one ratio. 'Recovery drinks can significantly improve any athlete's ability to have a quality workout tomorrow and the day after that,' says Carmichael.

DRINK IT after a race or workout, especially if you have no appetite after running. A recovery drink can also serve as a pre-run meal if you can't tolerate solids when fuelling up. Ultra runners might want to experiment with these drinks during exercise to help meet their high need for calories.

PASS IT BY if you're logging easy miles and don't need or want the extra calories.

6. Traditional Sip: Juice or Soft Drink

Both juice and soft drinks can help keep you hydrated, although their relatively dense carbohydrate concentrations (10 to 14 per cent) slow fluid absorption in the intestinal tract and can cause stomach distress or nausea in some runners when taken during exercise. If you're looking to fulfil some of your fruit quota for the day, check the label of your favourite fruit drink and make sure it's made with 100 per cent real fruit juice. Soft drinks offer no real nutrition, but those that are caffeinated can serve as an occasional pick-me-up.

DRINK IT when hydrating or fuelling before or after runs.

PASS IT BY when hydrating or fuelling during runs or if you don't need the extra calories.

KNOW THY SWEAT RATE

1. Weigh yourself naked right before a run.

2. Run at race pace for 1 hour, keeping track of how much you drink (in ml) during the run.

3. After the run, strip down, towel off any sweat and weigh yourself naked again.

4. Subtract your weight from your pre-run weight and convert to grams. Then add to that number however many ml you drank. (For example, if you lost 500g and consumed 1 litre of fluid, your total fluid loss is 500ml.)

5. To determine how much you should be drinking about every 15 minutes, divide your hourly fluid loss by 4 (in the example above, it would be 250ml).

6. Because the test only determines your sweat losses for the environmental conditions you run in that day, retest on another day when conditions are different. You should also redo the test during different seasons, in different environments (such as higher or lower altitudes) and as you become faster, since pace also affects your sweat rate.

NEED NUMBERS?

For runners who love numbers, the new hydration recommendation to drink when thirsty is too simple. So *Runner's World* created its own Healthy Hydration Guidelines for Runners, devised from a review of medical studies on runners and their sweat rates and from sweat-rate testing conducted at the magazine. These guidelines are designed to replace not all but most of the fluid you lose while running. And as with any guidelines, these will not work for everyone, so follow at your own risk. It's still important to weigh yourself before and after workouts to see if you are losing or gaining weight and adjust your drinking accordingly.

Below are some numbers that will show you the amount of fluid you should consume for each mile you run.

Weight: 45kg

Outdoor temperature and fluid needs (ml per mile):

10°C, 90; 15°C, 95; 21°C, 100; 27°C, 110; 32°C, 120; 38°C, 140

Weight: 55kg

Outdoor temperature and fluid needs (ml per mile):

10°C, 110; 15°C, 115; 21°C, 120; 27°C, 130; 32°C, 150; 38°C, 160

Weight: 63.5kg

Outdoor temperature and fluid needs (ml per mile):

10°C, 125; 15°C, 130; 21°C, 140; 27°C, 150; 32°C, 170; 38°C, 190

Weight: 72.5kg

Outdoor temperature and fluid needs (ml per mile):

10°C, 140; 15°C, 150; 21°C, 160; 27°C, 170; 32°C, 190; 38°C, 220

Weight: 81.5kg

Outdoor temperature and fluid needs (ml per mile):

10°C, 160; 15°C, 170; 21°C, 180; 27°C, 190; 32°C, 210; 38°C, 250

Weight: 90kg

Outdoor temperature and fluid needs (ml per mile):

10°C, 180; 15°C, 190; 21°C, 200; 27°C, 210; 32°C, 240; 38°C, 275

Weight: 100kg

Outdoor temperature and fluid needs (ml per mile):

10°C, 200; 15°C, 210; 21°C, 220; 27°C, 230; 32°C, 260; 38°C, 300

Weight: 109kg

Outdoor temperature and fluid needs (ml per mile):

10°C, 210; 15°C, 220; 21°C, 230; 27°C, 250; 32°C, 290; 38°C, 330

PRE-RACE DIET TIPS

Getting the balance right with your eating is always challenging, but even more so when you are training for a race: your food intake should mirror the intensity of your training schedule: as your training increases or tapers, your food intake should take this into account. Here are some dos and don'ts to help you.

Do increase your calorie intake. Whenever you up the intensity of your training or your weekly mileage, you'll need to make sure your calorie intake reflects the greater energy output. If you're feeling weak and your legs feel heavy, increase your carbs: a morning bowl of porridge, a mid-afternoon bagel or an extra portion of potatoes at dinner can make a big difference to muscle glycogen levels.

Do eat two to four hours before training. Choose cereal with milk, a turkey sandwich or a jacket potato with tuna. If you can't stomach very much, have a banana, a few almonds or a pot of yogurt half an hour beforehand, to give you an energy boost and keep you going. Drink plenty of water or a sports drink to replenish lost fluid immediately after a run. Have a carb-rich snack with a little protein ideally within 30 minutes and no later than two hours after you run, perhaps sardines on toast or a chicken sandwich.

Do eat often. To keep your energy levels high you should ideally eat every three hours, so make sure you graze through the day. Plan your mealtimes, and take nutritious snacks or smoothies with you if you have to eat on the move.

Don't eat less on rest days, or skip meals. Your muscles are still working hard to repair themselves and strengthen even when you're not running, so you need to feed them plenty of carbs and protein. Leaving longer than four hours between meals depletes energy reserves and in the long term can affect your muscles as your body goes into starvation mode and turns to protein for fuel. If you're pushed for time, have a smoothie or some nuts and raisins to stay fuelled.

Don't over-indulge. You do need to take on a lot of calories when you're training hard, and balance the energy you take in with what you are expending. Focus on natural food rather than processed, and don't overdo it: gaining unwanted extra weight might affect your fitness levels.

Don't drink too much alcohol. Alcohol contains empty calories with no real nutritional benefits, can put stress on the liver and slow down your recovery during training.

THE BIG DAY

Race day – the day you've been anticipating is here. There were days during your training when you didn't feel like running. There were workouts that were tough and made you wonder what you were doing. But you hit the roads and you stuck with the programme. You made an investment in yourself, putting in time, miles and sweat, and now it's time to cash in and reap your reward – a successful race and the pride that comes with it. Whether it's your first event or your 15th, whether you're running 3.1 miles or 26.2, this chapter will help you with all the last-minute preparations and give you all the expert advice you'll need for getting across that finish line healthy, strong and – most important – happy.

RACE EVE

VERIFY LOGISTICS: Double-check the start time of the race. If you're driving, make sure you know where the starting area is and where you can park. Bigger races often have road closures, which could affect your commute, so give yourself extra travel time. If you're taking part in a big-city marathon, check the arrangements for getting to the start. Shuttle buses may be provided.

GET OFF YOUR FEET: The longer the race, the more important it is to conserve energy the day before. Marathon runners, especially, should try to stay off their feet. Go to the expo to pick up your race pack, but don't linger around checking out all the latest energy gel flavours. This can be a challenge when you're in a new city where there's lots to see and do. But try to remember the reason you are there – you don't want to spend your race-day energy on sightseeing. The day before I ran the New York City Marathon, my training partners and I opted to see a Broadway show. It was a great way to relax our minds as well as our feet.

EAT SMART: The night before a race is not the time to experiment with new cuisine. Don't eat anything different or unusual the night before, the morning of or during a race. Your training runs offered the opportunity to experiment with meals and snacks to see what provides you with enough energy to perform well without irritating your stomach; now stick with what you know. Many marathons host pre-race pasta-party dinners. Most usually serve basic spaghetti dishes (meat and vegetarian sauces are available), salads and bread. These parties also give you the chance to mix and mingle with other runners. Other people prefer having a low-key meal on their own. Whatever you decide to do is fine, of course. Just remember to stick with a simple, familiar meal and avoid overeating. Eat a reasonable portion of 65 to 75 per cent carbohydrates. Avoid foods that are high in fat or protein because both take longer to digest and will sit in your stomach longer, possibly contributing to GI distress and multiple loo stops. For the same reason, hold off on that bran muffin until after the race.

MAKE FINAL PREPARATIONS: Lay out everything you plan to wear on race day: shoes, socks, top, shorts/tights, sports bra, lube, sunglasses and visor/brimmed hat (warm weather) or gloves and hat (cool weather). (For more on what to wear, see 'Dress Code' on page 224.) If you are running a big race, you'll probably already have your

CHASING ZS

Most of us wish our bodies would race in a competition as well as our minds do the night before. Because counting sheep and projected split times will get you only so far, here are fall-asleep-fast tips from some top runners.

'I stick to my usual routine, because that's the best way to enjoy a good night's sleep. I like watching wildlife documentaries because they are absorbing and help me to switch off. If I am anxious about the race it can be useful to write down all the things I've done to prepare – from the training, carbo loading and hydration to formulating a race plan and wearing in my shoes – as that helps me to feel positive.'

Mara Yamauchi, sixth woman in the 2007 London Marathon

'I always have Horlicks before going to bed and make sure I take some with me if I'm travelling abroad to compete so my body has its normal pre-sleep routine. It doesn't always send me to sleep but if I am still awake, I know that everything is organized for race-day and it's just a case of get up and go.'

Sharon Gayter, Great Britain's top female 24-hour runner

'I always make sure I sleep well the night before the night before a race. That way I feel as though I have some sleep in the bank if I have a restless night before the race. I eat early and sometimes have a glass of red wine to relax. I try not to think about the race – everything should be organized by that point. If I don't sleep well, I don't worry about it as I know adrenaline will keep me going on race day.'

Heidi Wilson, English international ultra runner

'I never have trouble sleeping before a big race because I know I'm totally pre-pared. Roughly 12 weeks before a marathon I make sure my training is on track so by the time the night before the race arrives, there is nothing left that has not been planned.'

Huw Lobb, the first man ever to beat the horse at the annual Man versus Horse 22-mile cross-country race in Wales race number, safety pins and ChampionChip – a timing device that attaches to your shoe; it's used in large races to give participants a more accurate finish time. Having everything out and ready to go will prevent you from having to rummage through your drawers or luggage the next morning and will give you peace of mind, which will help you sleep more soundly. Set multiple alarms – your alarm clock and your watch or mobile phone alarm. If you're staying at a hotel, arrange for a wake-up call.

REST EASY: If you can't sleep the night before a big event, don't panic. The *Journal of Sports Medicine and Physical Fitness* has reported that it's the sleep you get 2 nights before a race that matters.

DRESS CODE

Check the weather, and dress for your race as if it's about 10 degrees C warmer than the thermometer actually reads. This rule of thumb helps you dress for how warm you'll feel at mid-run, not the first mile, when your body is still heating up. This doesn't account for significant windchill, however, so on very windy days, you may need to dress warmer. If it's a chilly morning and you may be standing at the starting line for a while (the case at the London Marathon and Great North Run), you might want to bring an extra layer that you can leave at the starting area. Many big races offer a baggage service, which allows you to put your clothes in a bag and pick them up at the finish. Some runners keep it simple and opt for throwaways that race organizers collect from the roadside and donate to charity.

TEMP	BASIC APPAREL
21°C+	Lightweight/light-coloured vest, shorts
15°–20°C	Tank top or vest, shorts
10°–14°C	T-shirt, shorts
4°–9°C	Long-sleeved top, tights or shorts
-1°–-3°C	Long-sleeved top, tights
-6°–-2°C	2 upper-body layers, 1 lower-body layer
-12°–-7°C	2 upper-body layers, 1 lower-body layer
-17°–-13°C	2 or 3 upper-body layers, 1 or 2 lower-body layers
-18°C and below	3 upper-body layers, 2 lower-body layers

The study found that athletes' VO_2 max (an indicator of aerobic fitness) wasn't adversely affected after 1 sleepless night; it was lowest 2 days after sleep deprivation. That's why Olympian Dan Browne arrives at a big race at least 2 days early. And to counteract jet lag when travelling abroad, Browne tries to adjust to his destination's schedule as soon as he can. Dr James B. Maas, author of *Power Sleep*, also says you can gradually shift your body clock, starting the week before the event. If you're travelling from London to Hong Kong, start getting up progressively earlier after going to bed earlier and eating dinner slightly earlier. Don't take any sleep medications, which can leave you feeling hungover on race morning. These pills, especially over-the-counter antihistamines, can linger in your body for hours after you wake up.

RACE DAY

EAT EARLY. As you slept, your brain was active and used the glycogen (stored carbohydrate) from your liver. Breakfast restocks those stores, so you'll be less likely to run out of fuel. Chomping down a banana minutes before the start doesn't give your body the opportunity to absorb and use the nutrients and carbs, however. Always eat your pre-race meal about 2 hours before the scheduled start. This will also give your body time to digest it so you don't feel full while running. Stick with familiar, easy-to-digest foods that are high in carbohydrates and low in protein, fat and fibre. Aim for 100 to 200 calories, such as half a bagel, a banana, toast or a sports bar.

ARRIVE EARLY. This is especially important if you haven't pre-registered. Give yourself more time than you think you need. Even if you are already registered, it's good to arrive about an hour early to warm up, visit the toilet, collect yourself, check out the finish and avoid the stress of feeling rushed.

WARM UP. About 25 minutes before the start, do some walking or slow jogging. Don't overdo it – you need to preserve your glycogen stores and keep your core body temperature down. If you're a faster runner with a goal pace significantly quicker than your training pace, do no more than 10 minutes of light jogging, finishing 15 minutes before the start.

CHECK IN WITH YOURSELF. Try to get rid of any lingering all-or-nothing big-race anxiety by using relaxation techniques. Inhale strength and confidence through your nose and exhale nervousness and tension through your mouth. Review your race strategy and goals. Setting mini-goals you can achieve mid-race – like running an even pace – will ease the burden of an ultimate goal such as finishing in a specific time. Remind yourself that fear and anxiety are common emotions that every runner experiences. Pick a mantra, or positive phrase, that you can repeat to yourself when the going gets tough. Instead of thinking *I can't do it* or *I'll never finish*, pick a positive statement or word to override those negative thoughts (for ideas, see 'Choice Words' on page 228).

START SLOW. Position yourself appropriately at the start according to your projected pace, and remind yourself to start easy. You'll be glad you did when late in the race you're able to pass all those runners who started too fast.

THINK LAPS, NOT MILES. 'Instead of obsessing about each of the 26 miles, I look at each 3-mile segment as a lap,' says 2:13 marathon runner Keith Dowling. 'That makes it more manageable mentally. To concentrate on every mile would be like paying attention to the odometer throughout a 5-hour drive.' This trick is especially helpful for longer races but can be used for shorter distances as well.

PLAY GAMES. 'To take my mind off the big task ahead, I sing songs in my head,' says Jean Arthur, a 3:21 marathon runner. 'I pick a song and try to sing it from start to finish. Usually I don't know all

FIRST TIMERS

Toeing the line for the first time? You're bound to feel more comfortable if you're aware of certain established race procedures.

Expect a crowd. Don't be discouraged by the queues at the Portaloos; they move pretty fast. Hint: the longest queues occur 20 to 30 minutes before race start, so go earlier or later to beat the rush.

Pin your number on front. In track meets, athletes often wear numbers on their backs; in road races, they wear numbers on the front.

Get to the back. Clear the way for faster, more experienced runners by lining up closer to the back of the pack at the start. This is not to make you feel like a second-class citizen. It's just that lining up towards the front increases the chances that you will start at a pace that's faster than you can maintain for the duration of the race. It's always best to start conservatively at a relaxed, comfortable pace, then perhaps pick it up later – and maybe even pass some of those who started out ahead of you. If you're taking walk breaks, stay to one side of the road or on the pavement.

Pace yourself. One reason for starting at the back is to avoid running the first mile too fast, either because of enthusiasm or because faster runners pull you along. Once you cross the starting line, settle into your normal training pace – or run even slower. You'll enjoy your first race more if you run comfortably and see what's happening. Save personal bests for later races.

Pass politely. Unless you're at the front vying for prize money, it's best to show courtesy as you pass people. Very early in the race, you may feel boxed in by a slower group. Be patient. Soon there will be openings that will allow you to gradually weave your way through the crowd without elbowing fellow racers.

Navigate aid stations. At most races, each fluid station has several tables – some with water and others with sports drink. Race volunteers are usually very good about calling out which tables are which. If the first table you approach is crowded, run past it to a less crowded one. When you get your cup or bottle, quickly move past the tables to the side of the road. Leave the middle of the road clear for runners who aren't stopping for fluid.

the words, so I sing it and try to work out what the artist is saying.' Arthur also becomes an on-the-run mathematician. 'I calculate exactly what percentage of the race I have done,' she says. 'That's good for me in two ways: first, it occupies my mind, and second, I love the point at which I can tell myself I've done more than 50 per

CHOICE WORDS

Mantras – short power bytes you play over and over in your head – can help you stay focused and centred. They can be your inner motivation when you need it most. Finding a mantra isn't hard: it can pop into your head as you're listening to your iPod or while chatting with training partners.

One way to develop your inner strength is to remember thoughts you have while running well. If you're feeling especially strong or light on your feet, recognize those sensations and try to translate them into a saying. Dr Gloria Balague, an internationally acclaimed sports psychologist and contributor to *The Sport Psych Handbook*, recommends jotting down your post-run thoughts in a training log or journal. 'You may start to find a pattern of things that occur when you're doing well,' she says. 'Motivational sayings may emerge that will help you replicate that optimal state.'

Dr Barbara Walker, a sports psychologist and seven-time marathon runner, advises keeping mantras as simple as possible. 'Repeating two words can become part of the rhythm of the run,' she says. Walker often uses 'tall and strong' and 'light and focused'.

Balague advises having a stash of phrases or images that you call upon based on your mood or race. 'You're looking for different sensations, depending on what you have to overcome,' she says. For a marathon, for example, you might want a phrase that keeps your pace nice and steady and helps you endure the distance. When you are racing a 5-K, on the other hand, you'd want something that will help you push harder and tap your inner superhero or speed demon.

Ever wonder what's running through the minds of top athletes? Here, they share the mantras and techniques that keep them going.

In races that can last for days, top ultra runner Sharon Gayter needs to be able to talk herself through a bad patch. 'I repeat to myself: "You are the best, it's time to go, GO GAYTER GO."'

Sharon Gayter, Great Britain's top female 24-hour runner

'Instead of chanting a mantra, I visualize myself running strong, and focus on my stride to distract me from any fatigue or pain I might be feeling.'

Heidi Wilson, English international ultra runner

'Before I won the Chicago Marathon in 2005, my coach, Terrence Mahon, said, "Today, define yourself,"' Kastor says. 'This was so powerful; the entire race I repeated, "Define yourself." I've also used "Go faster" and "Push harder"'

Deena Kastor, 2004 Olympic Marathon bronze medalist and former London Marathon winner

'I find longer events to be quite emotional at times: I have intense thoughts and feelings about those close to me. I also sometimes end up repeating the most daft things to myself like "Just keep swimming" from Finding Nemo!'

Mark Hartell, holder of the record for the most number of summits completed (77) on the Bob Graham Round 78-mile ultra

'I think of a song and play it through in my mind. Sometimes I also try to enjoy the pain of the tough parts of a race!'

Jo Pavey, fourth in the 10,000m at the 2007 World Championships

'I use visualization techniques at certain stages in races. For example, with 13 miles to go, I always visualize my favourite 13-mile morning run and this puts me into a comfort zone.'

Martin Rea, ultra runner and top-30 finisher at the World 100-K Championships 2007

'I try to focus on things that will help me to stay positive, such as relaxing, reminding myself that I'm running well, or that I'm on course for a personal best. Towards the end of races when it becomes really tough, I focus on short-term goals such as the next mile marker or drinks station and break the remaining distance down into smaller chunks.'

Mara Yamauchi, sixth woman in the 2007 London Marathon

cent because, at that point, I know I can't quit.' Repeat a mantra to yourself, write it on your arm as a reminder or have your friends shout it out as you run past.

GO HARD LATE. Keep things under control until you're past halfway. Then you can become aggressive. Focus on a runner who is 100 metres ahead of you, pass him or her, then move on to your next 'victim'.

YOUR BEST MARATHON EVER

You've run hundreds of miles in training, you've tapered well and now it's race day. You're on the starting line and you're thinking: what have I got myself into? Don't worry. Here's the plan.

FIRST 3 MILES

SET YOUR PACE: Most races have start-area signs that refer to expected mile pace, such as '9-minute pace', so position yourself accordingly. Resist the temptation to move up.

TIME IT RIGHT. Start your watch when you cross the line. Each mile may be marked, but times may not be available at all of them. Also, you might want to wear a marathon pace band that shows the times you should be hitting at each mile mark. (You can get your own customized band at www.runnersworld.co.uk.)

WATCH THE FIRST MILE. Aim for a first mile that's 10 to 15 seconds slower than your goal pace. This lets your body become warm and loose as your breathing and heart rate rev up. Besides, the crowds at many marathons are likely to dictate a slow pace anyway.

BE PRUDENT. After a slow first mile, you'll be eager to make up for lost time by changing into another gear. Don't. Instead, gradually accelerate until you're running right at goal pace, even if this takes a few miles.

DRINK AND DOUSE. Start taking in fluids at the first aid station, especially if the weather's hot. But there's no need to eat yet. Splash water over your head, trunk and upper legs if it's a warm day.

MILES 3 TO 13

CRUISE CONTROL. This is the time to settle into the pace you want to run. It should feel easy. If it's a flat course, make a game of trying to run as close as possible to identical mile-split times. Most experts agree that maintaining an even pace from start to finish – within a span of 10 to 15 seconds per mile – is the best way to run a marathon. Make adjustments, of course, for uphills (a little slower), downhills (a little faster), headwinds (slower) and tailwinds (faster).

DON'T BANK. The idea of 'banking' time – getting several minutes ahead of goal pace so you can draw on that time later if needed – is bankrupt. The opposite usually occurs. Every minute you get ahead of goal pace will probably cost you 2 minutes due to fatigue by the end. An even pace is best, or slightly slower than race pace.

KNOW PACK TACTICS. Taking up with a runner or group may be tempting. But if they're not running your pace, ignore them. If they are at your pace, you can tuck in behind and 'draft' against headwinds, like a bike racer. Pack running also offers psychological advantages because you can feed off the energy of the group and join in the banter. But the minute the rhythm bogs down or speeds up, say goodbye.

MILES 13 TO 20

WATCH YOUR STRIDE. Even if you've run conservatively, your body will start to become stiff and more fatigued during this stretch. Aches and twinges may occur, and it will become increasingly difficult to stay on goal pace as you near the 20-mile mark. Don't panic; this is normal! Try to maintain an efficient stride length and cadence, and keep your face and upper body relaxed. The only reason to drop out is if a sharp, specific pain forces you to alter your stride.

WALK ON. A short walk can relieve and revive those sore and tired muscles, as well as eliminate a side stitch. In fact, walking breaks throughout the race are an effective part of many marathon pro-grammes because they let your body recover and extend the distance you can go before fatiguing. Walking can be limited to aid-station strolls for faster marathon runners. Beginners might need as much as 1 minute of walking for every 3 minutes of running.

STAY FOCUSED. There's a tendency during these miles for the mind to drift, but fight it, or you'll slip off goal pace. It won't be easy to get the time back in the last 10-K. Maintain concentration by aiming to run each mile as fast as the last one or by mentally latching on to runners around you.

ADD SOLIDS. Energy gels and bars, sweets such as jelly beans, and bananas are good choices, but try them first on long runs. Tak-ing in carbs is so important because stored carbs are replaced by stored fat as the body's main energy source from about the 20-mile mark on in a marathon – and fat isn't nearly as efficient as carbs at delivering energy.

MILES 20 TO 26.2

ALMOST THERE. Stay positive by focusing on the shrinking dis-tance to the finish line. Think about running from one mile marker to the next, and, if you're feeling good enough to pass runners, focus on catching one at a time. When you hit mile markers, don't say those numbers (21, 22, 23 . . .). Rather, count down the number of miles to go (5, 4, 3 . . .).

KEEP DRINKING. Don't bother eating during the last couple of miles because solid food won't help now (it takes too long to be absorbed). But keep drinking, and pour water over your head to cool you down if it's a hot day.

CHEER UP. Runners adore the London Marathon for its noisy spectators, but how do you keep your spirits up at smaller marathons? Use self-talk. Repeat messages such as 'Stay smooth' and 'Run tall'. Or visualize the spectators or your family cheering for you at the finish.

DIG DEEP. Keep reminding yourself that you only have to endure this fatigue and stiffness just a little longer. It's practically nothing compared with the hours of training you put in. You wouldn't want to waste that or throw away the chance to run a time you'll treasure for years. Don't forget that until you cross the finish line.

FINISH LINE AND BEYOND

RECOVER. To restore your body to its pre-race state, recovery needs to start as soon as you cross the finish line. Here's a post-race guide.

- **Zero to 10 minutes:** Walk slowly. 'It prevents blood from pooling in your legs, which can cause light-headedness,' says Janet Hamilton, author of *Running Strong & Injury Free*.

- **10 to 15 minutes:** Drink 240ml to 480ml of sports drink. To avoid overhydration, which is a risk for marathon runners, wait to drink again until after you go to the toilet.

- **15 to 25 minutes:** Put on warm clothes. After a race, your core temperature will drop. The colder you are, the harder it is for bloodflow to get to the heart.

- **25 to 30 minutes:** Refuel. Stomach feeling unsettled? Try chocolate milk. It has a replenishing combo of protein and carbs and will go down easy if your stomach's not ready for solid food.

- **30 to 45 minutes:** Stretch, focusing on hamstrings, quads and hip flexors. Spend more time on your quads if a large portion of the race was downhill.

- **When you get home:** Take a 'contrast bath'. Hamilton recommends 5 minutes in a cool bath and 5 minutes in a warm shower, repeating the sequence twice.

- **Remainder of race day:** Refuel and relax. Eat carbs and protein. Drink plenty of water. Sleep if you're tired, and don't stay out too late celebrating.

CREATE A HAPPY ENDING. After the race, evaluate how well you stuck to your race plan. Focusing on what you achieved can help you refine your strategy for next time and feel successful, even if you were disappointed in the final outcome. 'If you didn't run your best race, give yourself 10 minutes to assess what went wrong, then move on,' advises

PLAN B

Runners dutifully train for weeks or months, and when the day doesn't go as planned, they want to make up for it right away. But is that smart? It depends on the distance, says Mike Gratton, coach and winner of the 1983 London Marathon, who cites conventional wisdom of 1 day of recovery for every mile raced. If you have a bad 5-K or 10-K, you could race again the following weekend – so long as you recover well during the days in between.

But because of the toll a marathon takes on the body, musculoskeletal therapists Jim and Phil Wharton feel that even 26 days of downtime isn't enough. Instead, they recommend waiting at least 6 weeks to ensure that your body is capable of going the distance again. Also, to avoid making an emotional and hasty decision, Anderson says to wait at least 2 weeks before registering for another marathon. 'Don't act out of frustration,' he says. 'Give yourself time to evaluate if you really are ready.' Those who ran much slower than expected or ended up dropping out of the race may not be as exhausted and ready try again.

If you're not ready, consider a shorter race – your marathon training may serve you well in a 5-K or 10-K. If you do decide to go for another marathon, your runs between races should be moderate, aimed at maintaining – not improving – your condition. Depending on how you feel and how much time there is until your next race, you might work in one or two longer runs between 90 minutes and 2 hours, with a few of those miles at marathon race pace. If you feel any pain or discomfort, back off and reconsider your plans. Know that jumping back into training is asking a lot of your body, so it's important to maintain realistic expectations.

coach Nick Anderson of www.fullpotential.co.uk. 'Remember, you run to add to your quality of life; don't let it negatively affect it, too.'

REWARD YOURSELF. Whether you're absolutely thrilled or less than thrilled with your performance, your effort is an accomplishment in itself and deserves recognition. Treat yourself to dinner out, a pedicure, new running clothes – anything that will help you recognize all your hard work.

MAKE PLANS. The high that comes from a good race can morph into a major downer if you don't have a plan for the aftermath. This is especially common for marathon runners, who devote months to training and suddenly feel aimless once the race is over. You don't need to sign up for another race right away, but having some meaningful goals, such as maintaining a specific weekly mileage or just making sure you run a certain number of days a week, can help you keep your running on track. Of course, it's important to be flexible with your goals to avoid injury. You don't want to do too much too soon. (See Plan B opposite.) Your plans don't have to involve running at all. You could decide to focus your energy on something you didn't have the time to do while preparing for your race. Maybe your next goal is to tackle a hiking trip or to take up swimming. After running a race, you're at a very high fitness level, and with the right focus, you could make the most of it.

ASK RUNNER'S WORLD

Here are our responses to a few race-related questions from readers of the magazine.

Q: Dear Runner's World,

I'm 6'1", 102kg. People tell me I'm too big to run marathons. Is it foolish for me to keep trying to qualify for a good-for-age place at the London Marathon since most good runners have small frames?

A: While sheer physics dictates that an 18-wheeler will never out-accelerate a Ferrari, that shouldn't deter you from barreling down the marathon motorway. Sure, nobody's going to mistake you for a Kenyan. And in the end, you may pay a steeper toll in terms of aching joints and overall wear and tear, but you have as much of a right to the road as anyone else. It'd be easy to say, yeah, Jonny Wilkinson is too slow to play scrum half or Peter Crouch is too tall to play football. But really, when it comes to running, it doesn't matter if your body is built big – as long as your heart is, too.

Q: *Dear Runner's World,*

In a race, when I pass runners who look like they're struggling, I try to say something motivating. My wife tells me I sound condescending. Should I just keep my mouth shut?

A: It depends. A well-intentioned 'doing great' may be a nice push for a first-time marathon runner limping at 22. But say that to an experienced veteran who hit the wall and she may want to make her fist part of your permanent running attire. Not that I want you to judge a runner by the shape of her legs or the brand of his shorts, but I think you can make a safe guess as to who needs two words – and who couldn't care less about your comments. And if your judgment is off? Just keep moving.

Q: *Dear Runner's World,*

Is there a proper way to pin a race number to a top? Mine always looks wrong.

A: Oh, yes – a runner's geometrical conundrum. A horizontal, rectangular race number is diametrically opposed to the vertical, curved torso. Follow these rules of engagement. Location: take your left index finger and place it on your solar plexus. Slide your finger to the left, where your ribs begin to dip. At the moment the bone takes a sharp turn, stop. This is where the top left pin will go. Same thing on the right side (using right finger). Execution: insert and lock all pins in each corner. You'll need both hands free for this. Unlock the top left pin. Slide your non-dominant hand under your shirt. Use this hand to guide the pin and your dominant hand to lock the race number to the top. To avoid unnecessary flapping or wrinkling, attach pins by engaging the opposite corners; the number will stretch taut.

Q: *Dear Runner's World,*

I went towards the front of a large race for a fast start. But a pace group in front of me walked up to the starting line, blocking everyone behind them. Was this acceptable for the group to do?

A: I know it's frustrating when your legs want to get out of the gates like a hare and you're caged in by the pack. But unless you get front-row tickets at the starting line, you're at the mercy of the lead group. If the car in front of you is going 35 in a 55 mph zone with no place to pass, you just have to be patient. In the meantime, take a deep breath and remember that chip timing – the greatest running invention since the waffle sole – will even things out at most large races.

Q: *Dear Runner's World,*

Is there any point doing a pre-marathon sharpener such as a short speed session the day before the race?

A: The final days leading up to a marathon are crucial – you should be tapering to give your body a chance to recover from all your hard training and making sure your energy levels are at their max for the start of the race. It's common to feel a little sluggish, as your body conserves energy for the race to come, but resist the temptation to train. The day before you race, ready your body with a gentle run of 15 to 20 minutes. Throw in some race-pace running for a minute at the end then walk to recover. You should feel light on your feet, relaxed and ready to tackle the marathon.

Q: Dear Runner's World,

Is it rude for fast runners to do their cooldown on the racecourse while mid- and back-of-the-packers are still struggling to finish?

A: I know it may look like backtracking runners are peacocking for the masses, flashing their hamstrings, quads and 'I'm finished' feathers for all the rest of us to see. But I doubt they're trying to rub it in; most are probably just trying to avoid the crush of racers congregating around the finish line and banana stand. Instead of letting it bother you, how about using it as motivation to fly a little faster? And if you're the runner doing the cooldown, don't forget to cheer on the rest of the pack.

Q: Dear Runner's World,

During a race, a runner behind me yelled, 'On your left!' When I ignored her, she nudged me to the side. Who had the right of way?

A: Ideally, she would've veered to the left and you would've veered to the right. But since you both were more inflexible than a torn hamstring, here's my take. Her? She was wrong for acting like a bossy child, and, yes, runners in front have the right of way because they can't see behind them. However, she warned you that she was passing, and since yielding to her would take a millisecond off your time, it would've been the runner-friendly thing to do. By ignoring her, you treated her with as much respect as she did you.

Q: Dear Runner's World,

I have to arrive hours before the start of the London Marathon. What can I do to make the time pass before the gun goes off?

A: Approach it the same way you would any running-related problem: train for it. A couple of times in your programme, simulate the start. Instead of sprinting out the door minutes after your alarm goes off, get up an hour or two beforehand. Or walk around the block a few times before picking up the pace. You can even try standing at your starting point for 30 minutes while visualizing the race, daydreaming or trying to solve a work problem. You may feel like an inmate counting down the days, but that's the idea: get used to what it feels like to be in the holding pen.

Q: Dear Runner's World,

My wife usually walks about 80 per cent of a race and runs only 20 per cent. Should she sign up for the event as a walker or a runner?

A: I don't remember much from my school maths lessons, but this much I know: if a runner decides to walk a fifth of a race, he or she is a runner who does a little walking. That would make your wife a walker who does a little running. As long as she's not competing as a racewalker, where running would be deceiving and unfair, she can safely go with the same mantra that guides politics: majority rules.

Q: Dear Runner's World,

I train with my girlfriend, and we have our first race coming up. Should we stick together or run separately?

A: A few years back, I went out with a woman who could run at least a minute per mile faster than me. We decided to spend time together doing a 10-week training programme for a half-marathon. We did long runs together; we worked out on a track together; we even mixed our sweaty laundry together. It was great (the training, not the laundry). So come race day, we naturally started together. Turns out, she spent the first 2 miles feeling frustrated and I spent the 2 miles feeling guilty, until I finally said, 'Just go.' She had a bad race, I had a bad race, and those 20-some minutes sort of spoiled those 2 previous months. Fine by me if you two talk, run, sweat and plan together. But on race day, unless you have compatible paces and are both really okay with sticking together, you might want to each do your own thing and celebrate together later.

Q: Dear Runner's World,

Is it rude to listen to my MP3 player during a race?

A: Listening to music – if it's safe to do so – can be a great way to enjoy the miles in training, but many race organizers are beginning to realise that having crowds of runners cocooned in their headphones might not be the greatest thing at a race. Concentration and focus are key when you're racing, so being distracted by music may affect your performance. Think about the occasion too: if you're running in a big-city marathon, leaving the MP3 player at home will allow you to interact with other racers and enjoy the supportive atmosphere and screaming crowds.

Q: Dear Runner's World,

Before the start of a race, I like to ask other runners their age so that I know who I'm competing against. Is that rude?

A: We all size up people no matter where we are – at work, in bars, at the gym. No doubt, this kind of visual reconnaissance gives you some clues about what you're up against. But if someone actually asked me what age group I was in, I'd consider the question more freakish than racing in denim shorts. Some runners will feel rightfully skittish about such an up-front question about age. I think this is a case where you ought to go the stealth route – check the race number (age groups are on some bibs), find names from last year's results or simply keep people who look like stiff competition in your sight. If you're going to stalk your fellow racers, do it by trying to catch them on the course – not by interrogating them beforehand.

Q: Dear Runner's World,

What's the best way to wade through a crowd at the start of a race?

A: At one crowded half-marathon, I remember feeling frustrated, mad, anxious and wanting immediately to change to fifth gear, even though I felt stuck in neutral. So I thought, *I'm making a break* – and I darted in and out of everybody until I got clear. The problem was, I cashed in all my adrenaline within the first few minutes. By the end I was sputtering, and I had one of my worst races ever. It taught me something: even if you get boxed in, it's better to wait for an opening. Now I line up in the centre of the road so I don't get cornered by curbs or spectators. That position will allow you to drift and pass in the left or right lane. You'll run slower at first, but gradually building to your cruising speed will benefit you more than trying to Porsche your way to the front. In the end, that's the only way to avoid engine trouble down the road.

Q: Dear Runner's World,

I signed up for a marathon but dropped out 10 weeks before the race. How can I get to the point of no turning back?

A: You need to stop focusing on the final goal. Put it this way: if you run 8 miles by doing laps around the park, you'll stop early because it's easy to quit. But what if your 8-mile run is an out-and-back course? All you have to worry about is getting to the halfway point, and then you *can't* quit. It's the same thing with marathon training. It's easiest to bail when you haven't put in the time and miles. But once you reach a certain point in your training – say, when you're doing 15- and 20-mile runs – you know you can't quit because you've invested too much of yourself. The trick is psychological: get through the first half, and you're almost home.

WHAT'S 6 NEXT?

The euphoria (or maybe it's just a massive sense of relief) you feel after finishing a race is addictive. You want to experience it again and again and again. In the 15 years Steven Seaton has worked as the editor and publisher at *Runner's World*, he has travelled to many of the world's greatest races ('I lost count a few years ago,' he says), including at least one on each continent. So when a *Runner's World* editor is looking for a few race recommendations, guess whose office she visits? Here is a sampling of Seaton-approved races to add to your calendar.

TOP 5-KS

The 5-K is the most popular road racing distance in the UK thanks to the Race for Life Series of women-only events, but it's not a distance that regular racers compete in often. There were about 900 events held in 2007 – and more than a million 5-K finishers. So you're in good company. If you hear about a half-marathon or marathon in your area, check to see if there's also a 5-K. One of the biggest trends in racing today is 'race festivals', which include races of various distances. Some events offer something for everybody – literally – with a marathon, half-marathon, 10-K, 5-K and children's fun runs all in one weekend.

RACE FOR LIFE (SUMMER)

Cancer Research UK's Race for Life series of 5-Ks has grown from a handful of races in 1994 to 280 in 2007. Since its inception, 2.7 million women have taken part in what for many is their first 5-K. The events offer a wonderfully friendly and supportive racing environment and brilliant support from crowds of spectators. More importantly they have raised more than £200 million for Cancer Research's ongoing work in the fight against cancer. To find out more and to register for a race, visit www.raceforlife.org

RUN FOR MOORE (SUMMER)

This series of men-only 5-Ks raises money for the Bobby Moore Fund's research into bowel cancer. Since the series started in 2006 more than 5,000 runners have taken part, raising £450,000 for bowel cancer research. It's nowhere near as big as the women-only Race for Life series but it's catching up, with races taking place up and down the country, from Hull in the north to Bristol in the south. Find out more at www.cancerresearchuk.org

WOMEN'S 5-K CHALLENGE (SEPTEMBER)

The Women's 5-K Challenge races take place on the same day in the three cities: London, Birmingham and Liverpool. A warm welcome, carnival atmosphere and fantastic family day out await you at the UK's biggest women's fun run. More than 30,000 women of all ages and abilities come together for the 5-Ks, so if you're new to racing, these events are a great introduction to road running. Find out more at www.womenschallenge.co.uk

LIVERPOOL SANTA DASH (DECEMBER)

For the past few years over 6,000 runners have turned up in Liverpool dressed in red, in the annual attempt to break the world record for the most number of Santas running a 5-K. The event, held in the heart of Liverpool, enjoys a friendly rivalry with a similar race in Las Vegas, which has vied with it for the record. Other Santa events are springing up round the country, but this race is a true original. The occasional Everton supporter even turns up in a blue Santa costume. Find out more at www.runliverpool.org.uk

SERPENTINE LAST-FRIDAY-OF-THE-MONTH 5-K (EVERY MONTH)

The UK's biggest running club, Serpentine Running Club organizes a monthly 5-K race on the last Friday of every month. It's a chance to enjoy a quick lunchtime blast through London's Hyde Park with some of the UK's top runners. Find out more at www.serpentine.org.uk

TIME TRIALS (ALL YEAR)

If you're keen to track your progress, completing a weekly 5-K time trial is a great way to assess how your training is going. Weekend time trials are springing up all around the country, from Brighton to Middlesbrough, but the Bushy Park Time Trial is one of the original and best. The 5-K time-trial takes place every Saturday morning and is free to enter. Find out more at www.parkrun.com

TOP 10-KS

To say that the 10-K (6.2 miles) is a versatile distance is an understatement. Take a cross-section of any 10-K field and you'll find some people tackling it as their first run beyond a 5-K, others using it as a way to build up to a half-marathon or marathon, and still others making it the focus of their whole training season. There were about 800 events in the UK in 2007 – a close second for the most popular race distance behind the 5-K.

GREAT MANCHESTER RUN (MAY)

Organized by the company that puts on the Great North Run, the Great Manchester Run is a hugely successful city centre 10-K running through the heart of Manchester. The 2008 event was the sixth running of the race that draws a field of 25,000 runners each year to run a course that starts at Portland Street and takes in the sights of Manchester, including Old Trafford football stadium, before finishing in Deansgate. Although it's a mass participation race, it's a fast course that has seen some spectacular times mainly from a elite band of Kenyan and Ethiopian distance runners. For more details go to www. greatrun.org

LONDON 10,000 (MAY)

New for 2008, this event sold out in record time. More than 12,000 runners were attracted to the latest race in the capital that offers a chance to run past many of the city's iconic landmarks. The route tackles an anti-clockwise course around the City of Westminster and the City of London past Westminster Abbey, Houses of Parliament, Big Ben, The London Eye, St Paul's Cathedral, Horseguards, Nelson's Column and Admiralty Arch. Buckingham Palace acts as the backdrop to the start and finish. Find out more at www.london10000.co.uk

CANCER RESEARCH UK 10-K SERIES

Cancer Research's pioneering charity fundraising isn't limited to the 5-K races. Once you've conquered the shorter distance, move up to running a 10-K at one of the stunning locations around the country that host these friendly events. With venues like Leeds Castle in Kent and Ickworth House in Suffolk to choose from, these events offer the opportunity to run in some stunning locations before enjoying a picnic and great day out. Find out more at www.run10-K.org

LEEDS 10-K – 'JANE TOMLINSON'S RUN FOR ALL' (JUNE)

Making its debut in 2007, this race was conceived and organized by inspirational marathon fund-raiser Jane Tomlinson, who tragically died from cancer later that year. It attracted 8,000 people in the first year and raised £500,000 for charity. The second running sold out 11,000 places months in advance. The support along the city centre route compares favourably with a big marathon and the field represents a true cross section of the British running community. If you want your first race to be big on inspiration and support, head for Leeds. Find out more at www.runforall.com

BRITISH 10-K (JULY)

The route of the British 10-K reads like a must-visit list of London's most famous tourist attractions: start in Piccadilly, turn onto Victoria Embankment before heading down towards the City, passing St Paul's Cathedral on the way and continuing to Tower Bridge before turning back to finish on the Mall. More than 20,000 runners – including an impressive array of the world's best athletes – take part in the race every year, making it one of the country's most popular events. To find out more visit www.thebritish10-Klondon.co.uk

TOP 10-MILERS

The 10-miler is the best blend of speed and endurance: short enough to run hard yet long enough to brag about. While there might not be as many 10-milers in the UK (about 150 took place in 2007) as there are half-marathons, there are some classic 10s to choose from.

ROUGH 'N' TUMBLE 10 (JANUARY)

If you're looking to beat your 10-mile personal best, steer clear of this race in Wiltshire. The tough but rewarding event has been described as 'hard enough to make you cry', but the views from the tops of the climbs make the pain worthwhile. Find out more at www.grassrootsevents.co.uk

TERMINATOR 10 (FEBRUARY)

Another crazy race in Wiltshire, the Terminator 10 serves up a testing course that offers myriad opportunities to sample the mud and hills. After leaving Pewsey the route hits the tranquil towpaths of the Kennet & Avon Canal, then crosses usually wet farmland before you reach a sign that says 'The warm-up is over!' Challenges that await you include The Gully, The Coomb, Terminator Hill, The Sting in the Tail and The Shoe Wash. Find out more at www.pewseyvalerunningclub.com

NEW FOREST 10 (JULY)

Beautiful surroundings and a village fete atmosphere make this a race a must if you're in Hampshire in July. There may only be 1,000 runners taking to the tracks of the New Forest for this race, but the organizers provide chip timing if your time is paramount. Every finisher receives a smart commemorative horse brass, and you're encouraged to stay for a picnic and barbeque in idyllic surroundings after the race. Find out more at www.nf10.co.uk

GREAT SOUTH RUN (OCTOBER)

The Bupa Great South Run is Europe's premier 10-mile race, attracting around 16,000 runners each year to the fast, flat course around the coastal town of Portsmouth You'll run past landmarks such as the Spinnaker Tower and Historic Dockyard and finally along the sea front and past the pier for a thrilling finish. Fantastic crowds, bands playing music along the course and super-slick organization make this a race to remember. Find out more at www.greatrun.org

CABBAGE PATCH 10 (OCTOBER)

One of the country's classic 10 milers, the course record for the race was set by Richard Nerurkar at this Thames Valley race in south west London in 2003. Starting and finishing in Twickenham, the course follows a loop, crossing the river in Kingston and Richmond and as always race HQ is the Cabbage Patch pub in Twickenham. If you win, you stand to pocket £600 but don't spend it all in the Cabbage Patch Pub afterwards. Find out more at www.cabbagepatch10.com

BRAMPTON TO CARLISLE 10 (NOVEMBER)

The UK's oldest 10-miler is a fast, flat and mostly rural point-to-point race with start-to-finish kit transport and a generous prize pot, including £100 for breaking the course record. The race celebrates its 57th year in 2008. Find out more at www.borderharriers.co.uk

DROGO 10 (NOVEMBER)

Voted Devon's Race of the Year, this challenging off-roader traverses the beautiful woodland of the Teign Valley. You'll drop down one side of the valley, cross a quaint stone bridge and enjoy riverside trails before a tough hills brings you back to the finish next to impressive Drogo Castle. If you have any energy left, head inside the property for a nose around. Find out more at www.thedrogo.co.uk

TOP HALF-MARATHONS

The half-marathon is growing in popularity. There were about 250 events in the UK in 2007. And it's easy to see why the 13.1-mile distance is so appealing. Runners often say that a half-marathon is half the distance and twice the fun of a marathon. If you're ready to try one, here are a few of the best.

WATFORD HALF-MARATHON (JANUARY)

One of the first big half-marathons of the year, the Watford Half gives you a chance to stick to your well-intentioned New Year's resolutions and start the racing year in style. Expect to join around 2,500 runners on the hilly lapped course that takes in quiet country lanes. Find out more at www.watfordharriers.org.uk

HASTINGS HALF-MARATHON (MARCH)

Looking for a challenging half-marathon? This popular event retraces the route the 1066 invaders took. Celebrating 25 years in 2009, the Hastings Half pioneered everything we take for granted in racing today. Organizer Eric Hardwick encouraged local community involvement from the outset, as well as putting on special trains to bring Londoners down to the coast for the race. The testing hills and unpredictable coastal winds of this seaside town will test even the fittest of runners, but saying you've completed the Hastings Half will earn kudos in running circles. It's also a great charity event, raising more than £3 million since the race started in 1984. Find out more at www.hastings-half.co.uk

BATH HALF-MARATHON (MARCH)

This spring half-marathon offers a fast, flat course around one of the country's most attractive cities. The compact two-lap city centre course guarantees decent crowds as you pass through the Georgian parts of the city. Relax afterwards with a trip to the new Bath Spa complex to treat yourself to the healing waters. Find out more at www.runninghigh.co.uk

READING HALF-MARATHON (MARCH)

A grandstand finish inside Reading FC's Madjeski Stadium is the perfect ending to this perennially popular and well-organized race.

With around 15,000 runners taking part in this sell-out event every year, it's perfect preparation for a big spring marathon. The challenging course, which passes through the attractive Reading University Campus and alongside Green Park, produces surprisingly fast times. Find out more at www.asicsreadinghalfmarathon.co.uk

MIDSUMMER MUNRO HALF-MARATHON (JUNE))

This race is a crazy idea: a trail half-marathon with eight serious climbs up and down Box Hill in Surrey totalling more than 3,000ft of ascent (and descent, thankfully) – the equivalent of a Scottish Munro. Despite the brutally tough course, runners love this race and return year after year, attracted by the faultless organization, great camaraderie and superb scenery. Find out more at www.trionium.com

BRISTOL HALF-MARATHON (SEPTEMBER)

The Bristol Half-Marathon celebrates its 20th anniversary in 2008 and shows no signs of losing its place as one of the largest and most popular half-marathons in the country. The 15,000 places always sell out in a matter of weeks, so if you want to race a fast sea-level course that takes in scenic views of the old city, Avon Gorge and Brunel's famous Suspension Bridge, make sure you sign up early. Find out more at www.bristolhalfmarathon.com

GREAT NORTH RUN (SEPTEMBER/OCTOBER)

You may know Newcastle as a football-mad city, but its inhabitants take running just as seriously, so it's no surprise that the city is home to the world's biggest half-marathon. In 2007, 47,000 runners lined up at the start of the Great North Run in Newcastle before heading out towards the coast for a seafront finish on the promenade at South Shields. Autumn sun, amazing crowds and a Red-Arrows fly-by are the icing on the cake at one of the country's must-do races. Find out more at www.greatrun.org

RUN TO THE BEAT (OCTOBER)

The capital's thirst for great races is being catered to by this new event that starts at the O2 Arena in Greenwich and makes music its theme. The organizers plan to play specially selected music to the 10,000 entrants, to boost their performance. The course will include views of the Thames Barrier before heading back through Greenwich to the finish at the O2 Arena. Find out more at www.runtothebeat.co.uk

ROYAL PARKS FOUNDATION HALF-MARATHON (OCTOBER)

Encompassing the four Royal Parks of central London, this new race starts in Hyde Park before runners wind their way through the stunning autumn landscapes of St James's Park and Green Park, as well as parts of Kensington Gardens which have never officially been raced through before. Expect magnificent views of Buckingham Palace, Wellington Arch, the Albert Memorial and Marble Arch. Find out more at www.royalparkshalf.com

TOP MARATHONS

Whether you're after a fast time or a good time, there's a marathon out there that will suit you. In 2006, 64 certified marathons were held in the United Kingdom. Spring and autumn are the most popular marathon times – cool temperatures usually lead to fast times – but you can find a great 26.2-miler no matter when you prefer to race. Here are a few favourites.

LONDON MARATHON (APRIL)

Since its inception in 1981 with 6,500 runners, the London Marathon has exploded into one of the biggest running events in the world, with more than 34,000 finishers in 2008. Classic London weather (overcast and cool) combined with a flat course, solid organization and masses of lively spectators virtually guarantee a brilliant race. The course runs along history-saturated streets with views of Tower Bridge, Canary Wharf Tower, Big Ben, Westminster Abbey, and the best sight for sore legs – the finish line on the Mall in front of Buckingham Palace. (london-marathon.co.uk)

EDINBURGH MARATHON (MAY)

With an overall drop in height of 230ft, the Edinburgh Marathon is a must if you're looking to score a new marathon personal best. The point-to-point race takes runners through Holyrood Park and past – but thankfully not over – Arthur's Seat before heading along the coast through Portobello for a finish at Musselburgh Race Course. To find out more visit www.edinburgh-marathon.com

ISLE OF WIGHT MARATHON (MAY)

Don't let the flat start around Ryde boating lake fool you into thinking this marathon is a gentle promenade: relentless ups and downs make the UK's longest-running marathon a formidable undertaking for even the most experienced racer. Started in 1957, the event has been run on the island's roads every year since. You'll literally complete a lap of the island, starting from Ryde and heading through Newport and Sandown before the finish in Ryde. Find out more at www.rydeharriers.co.uk

WINDERMERE MARATHON (MAY)

After an absence of 21 years, the Windermere Marathon in Cumbria made a welcome comeback in 2007. Its unbeatable location offers runners the opportunity to race around England's largest and most stunning lake. The course isn't easy, but you'll be rewarded with breathtaking views of the lake, woodland and surrounding hills at every turn. Afterwards enjoy the beer tent and live music at Brathay Hall, where the race starts and finishes. Find out more at www.brathay.org.uk

SOUTH DOWNS MARATHON (JUNE)

One of the most spectacular trail races in the country, the South Downs Marathon starts at Slindon near Chichester and runs a short distance on the Monarch Way before joining the South Downs Way and following the National Trail west to Queen Elizabeth Country Park. A race day bus transfer from the finish to the start is all part of the package, and if you still have some energy afterwards, the country park offers has a visitor centre and plenty of nature walks. Find out more at www.209events.com

ROBIN HOOD MARATHON (SEPTEMBER)

The Robin Hood Marathon was founded in 1981. Back then the race started in the Old Market Square in Nottingham City Centre but as it grew, the start and finish area were moved to the current sit at Victoria Embankment. This race caters for every kind of runner, from the seasoned veteran to the marathon novice. A half-marathon is on offer too. Find out more at www.experianfestivalofrunning.co.uk

A SNOWDONIA MARATHON (OCTOBER)

The 25th anniversary of the Snowdonia Marathon took place in 2007. Voted best British Marathon by Runner's World readers, this event continues to attract runners looking for a challenging race in jaw-droppingly scenic surroundings. The route climbs from Nant Peris 250 metres to the top of the Llanberis Pass then along through Beddgelert before dropping down to the finish in Llanberis. This is a serious race, but the support is brilliant – and a Mars Bar at 12 miles will help to keep you running. Find out more at www.snowdoniamarathon.com

ABINGDON MARATHON (OCTOBER)

After an absence of several years the popular Abingdon Marathon is back with a new sponsor and new route. The two-lap course takes in some of the most scenic villages in Oxfordshire as well as stretches along the bank of the River Thames. The fast, flat course is popular with runners looking to qualify for a Championship place at the London Marathon. Find out more at www.abingdonamblers.co.uk

DESTINATION RACES

Luckily for us, marathons are held in some of the most magnificent locations in the world. Buy a plane ticket, pack your shoes, and you could be off on one on the greatest adventures of a lifetime. What better way is there to experience the sights, sounds and smells of a new country than on your very own two feet?

BOSTON MARATHON (APRIL)

Boston, the oldest marathon in the US, is legendary for its hilly point-to-point course from rural Hopkinton to downtown, as well as its difficult qualifying standards. It's worth the extra training to be part of the tradition. Being invited to the most prestigious race in the world is pretty satisfying, and when you arrive in Boston, you're upgraded to elite status. The entire city focuses on the race. It's held on Patriots' Day, a state holiday, and some of the most raucous spectators in the sport line the streets. The course is virtually unchanged since its 1896 start, so veterans and newbies alike can reminisce about the same highlights along the way. Even climbing the infamous Heartbreak Hill is gratifying. Once you're over it, you're this close to being a member of an elite club: Boston finishers. www.bostonmarathon.org

DUBLIN MARATHON (OCTOBER)

The Dublin Marathon has been treating runners to a great race through the Irish capital's historic Georgian streets for more than 25 years. More than half of the 10,000 runners who enter this friendly race every year come from overseas to sample the legendary hospitality and dynamism of this lively city. With cheap flights from most UK airports, a trip to the Dublin Marathon is a great way to com-

bine a passion for running with a fun city break. Find out more at
www.adidasdublinmarathon.ie

PARIS MARATHON (APRIL)

The cities of Europe offer a tempting array of spectacular marathons,
many just a train or plane ride away. If you fail to win a place at the
sell-out London Marathon, head across the Channel to the French
capital's event, which also takes place in April. You'll join around
30,000 runners along the city's attractive boulevards and around the
idyllic Bois de Boulogne before a finish to remember by the Champs
Elysée. Find out more at www.parismarathon.com

GREAT WALL MARATHON (MAY)

Every year on the third Saturday in May, hundreds of runners from
around the world gather in China's rural Huangyaguan district to
chalk up one of the seven wonders of the world. Whether you run the
marathon or half-marathon, you'll traverse 7 kilometers of 3,700 lac-
tic-acid-inducing stone steps and seven watchtowers (marathon runners do it twice) of a 1,500-year-old section of the wall. Yes, marathon
runners literally hit the wall for the second time at mile 21. When you
pause to catch your breath – and you will – gaze over the wall and
ponder the fate of those silly Mongol invaders who thought they could
breach this ridge-hugging monster. All runners must travel with a tour
group, but it's not just for foreigners. The 2003 and 2004 winner was
the local postman. www.great-wall-marathon.com

INCA TRAIL MARATHON (AUGUST)

The Inca Trail Marathon truly is a once-in-a-lifetime experience. The
27.5-mile race follows the original pilgrimage trail that leads to the
religious capital of the Incas – Machu Picchu. You'll run over mountain terrain that ranges from 2,500 metres to almost 4,000 metres
and pass archaeological sites only seen by people who complete the

whole Inca Trail. Permits sell out fast so plan this one well in advance. Find out more at www.andesadventures.com

MARATHON DU MÉDOC (SEPTEMBER)

Don't be put off by the slogan of the Marathon du Médoc – *le marathon le plus long du monde;* that is, 'the longest marathon in the world'. The French haven't extended the 26.2-mile distance. It's just that the marathon, which runs through the grounds and vineyards of the Bordeaux region of France, includes more than 20 catered wine-tasting stops, serving up such regional specialties as oysters, cheese, pâté and steak, not to mention the most celebrated wine in the world. That's why runners are in no rush to reach the finish. The pre-race pasta party is a swanky affair, held on the grounds of a château featuring pasta, unlimited wine and a live band. Postrace, every finisher receives a bottle of wine, and the revelry continues into the night. www.marathondumedoc.com

NEW YORK CITY MARATHON (NOVEMBER)

There couldn't be a more appropriate locale for one of the biggest, most celebrated athletic events in the world, which attracts 40,000 runners and is so wildly popular, it turns away 45,000 runners each year. The course runs through the city's five boroughs and takes participants on a tour of neighbourhoods as diverse as the runners themselves. Yasso recommends saving your PB aspirations for another race. If your eyes are glued to your watch, you'll miss out on the views of the city, giving high-fives to kids lining the streets, or receiving a reassuring nod from one of the city's finest. www.nycmarathon.org

ATHENS MARATHON (NOVEMBER)

Every marathon geek should trace the steps of the original Greek marathon. In 490 BC, a messenger named Pheidippides ran from Marathon to Athens to announce the town's victory against the invading

Persian army. According to legend, upon delivering the news, the foot soldier collapsed and died. His tragic finish did nothing to discourage future generations of marathon runners, however, including the 4,000 who travel to Athens each year to run the route representing Pheidippides' journey. You might remember the course from when the world's greatest female marathon runner Paula Radcliffe dropped out during the 2004 Athens Olympic Marathon. www.athensmarathon.com

ANTARCTIC ICE MARATHON (DECEMBER)

The world's most southerly marathon is the only race that takes place on mainland Antarctica. The event takes place at 80 degrees south, just a few hundred miles from the South Pole at the foot of the Ellsworth Mountains at 900 metres. An average temperature of -20C (-4F) and strong winds add to the challenge. If you're looking for an exotic ultra, there's a 100-K race on offer too. You won't spot any penguins though – they don't live this far south. Find out more at www.icemarathon.com

RELAY RACES

The premise is simple: get some friends together, organise your transport, devise a cool name, and expect to run one to three legs over the course of a lo-o-ong day. The promise is: fun. You won't sleep much, but you won't mind. Here's info on the country's most popular multilegs, plus one relay that's a little further afield.

GREEN BELT RELAY (MAY)

For a more scenic way to circumnavigate London than the M25, try the Green Belt Relay. This 220-mile clockwise lap of the capital starts at Hampton Court and takes in trails, towpaths and country lanes before heading back to Kingston. Teams of 11 tackle two stages each – one on the first day and one on the second day after an overnight stop – of between 5.6 and 13.8 miles. Find out more at www.greenbeltrelay.org.uk

ROUND NORFOLK RELAY (SEPTEMBER)

Established in 1987, the Round Norfolk Relay starts in Kings Lynn then heads up to the coast for 40 miles, before turning towards Thetford Forest then back towards Kings Lynn. There are 17 unequal stages and 17 runners per team. This is a continuous relay so there's plenty of scope to run at night. Find out more at www. roundnorfolkrelay.com

WELSH CASTLES RELAY (JUNE)

This classic point-to-point relay from Carmarthen in the north of Wales to Cardiff in the south celebrated its 25th running in 2007. The 200-mile race is divided into 20 10-mile stages, with 10 on the first day and 10 on the second after an overnight stop in Newtown. Each stage is a head-to-head race: runners start with the arrival of the first runner from the previous stage. Find out more at www. lescroupiersrunningclub.org.uk/castle

AND A LITTLE FURTHER AFIELD...

HOOD TO COAST RELAY (AUGUST)

The country's most popular relay (1,000 teams compete) sells out early, so if you're interested, get on it in October, when registration opens. The 197-mile distance is split into 36 legs run by 12 team members – each participant runs three times. www.hoodtocoast.com

NOW WHAT?

As I hope this book has demonstrated, the world of road racing is an exciting place full of rich experiences and challenges with an almost unlimited supply of event opportunities around the UK, Europe or the rest of the world. If you've read all the information and absorbed the lessons you can be certain that you have the tools you need to achieve your racing goals, whether that's simply to finish your first 5-K or to crack a particular time barrier in the marathon or beyond.

While it's useful to have a schedule to follow and an understanding of how to maximise your performance through better nutrition or equipment choices, words on a page are worthless if you don't put them into action. Running is increasingly a participatory activity not a spectator sport. The real lessons of the sport come from your personal experience of taking part in the races themselves and the more you race the more you will learn.

The true purpose of this book is to encourage you to participate in more races and to expose yourself to everything they have to offer. The beauty of racing – and indeed running – is its flexibility and universal appeal. It can be whatever you want it to be. You will find that there are no barriers to entry whatever your current standard or aspiration: far from it, most events are desperate to broaden their appeal at the back of the pack as well as the front. There are very few experiences in adult life to match the undiluted satisfaction of finishing your first race or running a personal best time in a marathon.

So you have no excuse. Browse the web or thumb through a copy of *Runner's World* to find your next event, complete the entry form and lace up your shoes because it's time to race. Good luck!

INDEX

Underscored references indicate boxed text or tables.